FANTASTIC DISAPPOINTMENT

The Story of Spurs - 1986-87

STEPHEN PEACE

Copyright © Stephen Peace, 2023

Published: 3rd August 2023 by
FCM Publishing

978-1-914529-72-6 Paperback Edition
978-1-914529-73-3 Ebook

All rights reserved.

The right of Stephen Peace to be identified as the author of this Work has been asserted by him in accordance with sections 77 and 78 of the Copyright, Designs and Patents Act 1988.

No part of this publication may be reproduced, stored in retrieval system, copied in any form or by any means, electronic, mechanical, photocopying, recording or otherwise transmitted without written permission from the publisher. You must not circulate this book in any format.

This book is in part a memoir, reflecting the author's present recollections of experiences over time. Some names and characteristics have been changed and some events have been compressed. Memory can be a fickle thing, so the Author trusts that any minor errors in times, dates and details of particular events will be understood.

Copyright of all illustrations and imagery used within remains solely with their originator. No breach of copyright is implied or intended and all material is believed to be used with permission. Should you feel that your copyright has been impinged, please contact the publisher to ensure appropriate acknowledgment may be made.

Cover Design by Danji's Designs

DEDICATION

For putting up with my nerdy fascination in writing this book, I bestow overwhelming thanks to my brilliant wife Kate and my wonderful daughters Grace, Amelie and Chloe. Your support and belief in me have been astounding.

To my dad, for inspiring me to follow a football club that got underneath my skin from such a young age and that he unknowingly helped me write large sections of this book based around our mutual love for sport, statistics and of course, Spurs.

And finally, thanks to anyone who reads this book. I feel humbled and appreciated in your choice to do so.

ACKNOWLEDGEMENTS

When this process began an 'acknowledgement' section would have been minimal to say the least. But having spent time with the author Simon Hart, he opened my eyes to the possibility and advantage in gaining perspective from other contributors. I'd like to thank Mark Godfrey for putting me in touch with Simon.

I will start by thanking various agents and intermediaries who were instrumental in helping me gain contact with key people. Agents, Dan Gray, Caroline Chignell and Jane Morgan along with former Spur Simon Felstein, Everton's Darren Griffiths, West Brom's Ian Skidmore and Louise Pearson at the PFA. Thanks also go to Robin Tidd and Lynsey Kelly as well as the stoic efforts deployed by John Collier and Radio 5's Gary Flintoff. Distinct thanks go to Nik Hodges, the son of Chas Hodges, who orchestrated contact with the great Dave Peacock.

Thank you to musical legend Dave Peacock and radio royalty Simon Mayo. Special thanks are to the effervescent Norman Jay MBE, time with Norman was simply sublime.

Thanks to former Spurs players Graham Roberts, Gary Mabbutt and Chris Fairclough along with some of most devoted Spurs fans you'll ever meet in Lee Hermitage, Oliver Furnival and Paul Carrington.

Unreserved thanks also go to my publisher Taryn Johnson. In the past we shared a once-in-a-lifetime professional experience, and she was my go-to when I was wondering if it was worth pursuing my idea or not. She had belief in this project at inception and gave me the essential structure I needed to write and produce my first book. Thanks to my designer, Dan Hill, for making the design process so seamlessly enjoyable.

The soul of this book would not have come alive without the wonderful insight of players from that period. I'd like to thank the 'opposition' perspective from Everton's Derek Mountfield and Pat Van Den Hauwe, those conversations were so amusing and fascinating viewpoints from worthy champions.

Coventry City's Keith Houchen broke our hearts, but what a guy. An enthralling chat and I cannot thank you enough. Even time with Arsenal's Ian Allinson and Perry Groves was thoroughly enjoyable despite where they hail from!

Making a dream come true was spending time with some Tottenham greats. Gary Stevens, David Howells and Vinny Samways got the ball rolling and then nostalgic views from Richard Gough, Paul Allen, Danny Thomas, Steve Hodge, Steve Perryman and Clive Allen added further power to my story. The mind of a professional footballer is one thing, delving into the minds of former Spurs greats is a complete pleasure.

The time afforded to me by Stephen Clemence was honourable indeed. Being able to tap into any form of insight from the late, great Ray Clemence was always a bonus and Stephen provided that with ease.

Late in the process I was lucky enough to spend time with John Sheridan. Here is a man who valued his Spurs tenure as much as any player I had spoken to. A wonderful servant to the club and a great man who provided amazing support to players that the public often never really got to witness.

Speaking to John Motson was surreal to say the least. The voice of my footballing youth and of many iconic footballing moments which have been accompanied by his expert commentary. I was lucky enough to speak with him a few months before he died. A legend, a footballing encyclopaedia and an absolute gent.

My final acknowledgement of the contributors must go to David Pleat. I genuinely find it hard to explain my appreciation for the time David gave. He is a fascinating man, a man of integrity and a man who has been dedicated to the world of Association Football nearly all of his life. Our conversations would go off in tangents and down rabbit holes and we had to work hard to keep to our agenda! But that is the measure of man who has a PHD-like knowledge of the sport. One of the best managers Tottenham Hotspur FC have ever had and a creator of one the finest footballing teams in the club's history.

I will leave you with closing thanks to some footballing origins in my life. How I saw football back then, and even how I see it now, is largely down to key people who I played or watched football with.

Thanks to my dad, Tony, and my brother, Jason, who were the brunt of my demands to talk sport nearly all day every day.

To two of my former football coaches, Ron King and Richard Mount, who taught me so many things about the game during my playing days and gave me my early learnings in what coaching is and should be. Thanks also to some of my Spurs supporting friends who, back in the day, would engage in hours of Spurs chat with me - Darren Woodhouse, Allan O'Sullivan and Bill Long.

I hate to say I also gained excellent footballing perspective from some of my Arsenal friends too back then, Oliver James, the late, great Gary Brennan and Neil Grant.

But the guys who were possibly the biggest circle of footballing influence for me were my good friends Kevin Dobson, Kevin Tidd, Lee Morgan and Pat O'Toole. Good times guys, good times.

TABLE OF CONTENTS

Foreword by David Pleat .... *xi*
Saturday 11th April 1987 – Villa Park, Birmingham .... *xiii*

Chapter 1 – Changing Times 1

Chapter 2 – May 1986 17

Chapter 3 – June 1986 41

Chapter 4 – July 1986 67

Chapter 5 – August 1986 85

Chapter 6 – September 1986 139

Chapter 7 – October 1986 169

Chapter 8 – November 1986 193

Chapter 9 – December 1986 243

Chapter 10 – January 1987 285

Chapter 11 – February 1987 323

Chapter 12 – March 1987 347

Chapter 13 – April 1987 379

Chapter 14 – May 1987 419

Chapter 15 – Changing Times II 473

About The Author 499

Source Notes 500

FOREWORD

by David Pleat

There can be few more passionate supporters than Steve Peace. His time and energy that he has put into this book is a true 'labour of love'.

It seems only yesterday that our 4-5-1, 1986-87, formation were winning games with some superb performances. We made friends with football supporters everywhere.

I was manager of Tottenham Hotspur Football Club and privileged to lead a team of exceptionally talented footballers. The 4-2 win away at Oxford United was the catalyst – we found a system of play that suited the players perfectly, with no square pegs in round holes.

With Glenn Hoddle plotting and scheming as a loose forward in his final year at Spurs. With Clive Allen sniffing and scoring chances playing across the width of the 18-yard box and netting a tremendous 49 goals.

With the athletic warrior Richard Gough and the reliable, stout-hearted Gary Mabbutt at the heart of our defence.

With the intelligent indefatigable Paul Allen alongside the classy master footballer Ossie Ardiles in the engine room.

With Steve Hodge, our underrated left midfield engine covering every blade of grass. With Chris Waddle our mesmeric midfielder holding the touchline.

With our array of superb full-backs Chris Hughton, Mitchell Thomas, Gary Stevens and Danny Thomas supporting, defending, covering and all making valuable contributions.

The new signings Richard Gough and Mitchell Thomas found their feet quickly and we loved the pacey contribution of the effervescent Nico Claesen although it was difficult to integrate him into the 'A' team.

Was it really 37 years ago?

Steve Peace has chronicled the story of that season with this brilliantly researched book. He has spent hours gathering reports, news and views from players and media of that year.

I thoroughly enjoyed reading and reminding myself of such a fine season where we, I believe, reached the standards of the Tottenham Hotspur ethos – the game is about glory.

Enjoy the book.

David Pleat
February 2023

Note:
Tottenham Hotspur Football Club;
also known as 'Spurs' and 'Lilywhites'.
'COYS' term; Come on You Spurs

SATURDAY 11TH APRIL 1987 - VILLA PARK, BIRMINGHAM

125 miles northwest of White Hart Lane, an overcast Villa Park housed thousands of football fans. Only half of the 46,000 crowd were buoyant. Time was ticking away and the captain of Tottenham Hotspur (Spurs), Richard Gough, played the ball into the hands of his goalkeeper, Ray Clemence. Clemence calmly gazed up the pitch and then with a subtle nod he launched the ball forward with his distinctive left foot. Then it happened, the final whistle echoed as match day referee Ray Lewis signalled the end of the game.

Noise bellowed from the thousands of Spurs fans who had journeyed up to Birmingham to see their team contest a match that could propel them to Wembley for the 1987 FA Cup Final.

Tottenham had just thumped Watford 4-1 and the final whistle brought immediate elation to the Spurs players on the pitch, staff on the bench and supporters in the stands.

England international, and one of Spurs' midfield wizards, Chris Waddle had fallen to his knees, emotion flowed. Spurs fans flooded on to the pitch to find players celebrating with each other. A beaming Mitchell Thomas ran to Waddle and raised him up for an embrace and to share the experience of them both reaching their first domestic trip to Wembley in English football's finest showpiece.

Tears were still streaming down Waddle's face only to be greeted by his England and musical comrade, Glenn Hoddle. Hoddle was yelling to him alongside another of Spurs' legends, defender Chris Hughton. The players were all coming together, some commiserating with disappointed Watford players, but this was Spurs' time.

This was my first experience of an FA Cup Semi Final which was played at a neutral venue and was the home of Aston Villa FC. Spurs had been in control since early in the first half, which had allowed the fans to possibly enjoy the whole occasion even more. But a trip to Wembley was now on its way and I couldn't have been happier.

This season had brought so many ups and downs. A team of football connoisseurs had been wonderfully assembled by Tottenham manager David Pleat and they were challenging on all fronts. But, at this stage of the season, there were factors as to why Spurs were no longer in the hunt for an unprecedented 'treble'. This book will highlight that journey.

However, the reality was that Spurs had now reached another FA Cup Final and had the opportunity to lift the trophy for a record eighth occasion.

For some players this represented their first and a last opportunity to win something with the club. Following the television highlights of the game that were aired that evening, ITV's Jim Rosenthal had gained access to the Spurs dressing room after the game. He spoke to Glenn Hoddle. Hoddle was revered by Spurs fans and had been so for many years. He was a talent beyond belief and, considering Spurs' traditional style of play, he fitted the mould with consummate ease. Most fans were aware of Glenn's desire to experience football elsewhere having had a long and successful tenure at White Hart Lane. Rosenthal was curious to see if this would be his last ever game for the Lilywhites of North London.

Rosenthal asked Hoddle how he felt 'personally' going back to Wembley. Hoddle replied that he felt the omens were good. Spurs had won the FA Cup in 1961, 1962 and 1967. During this decade, the 1980's, Spurs had won the Cup in 1981, 1982 and was it now Spurs' year again in 1987? He concluded in saying it would be a lovely ending if this was his final year at Spurs. His mind had been made up and he conceded it would be a wonderful story if this did turn out to be his last ever game for Spurs.

Tottenham fans had been through the emotional grinder many times over the season and if this game had ended in a draw, then a replay would have been held a few days later at Stamford Bridge. This would've represented Spurs' 15th cup tie of the season. Fortunately, a replay was not required as Spurs excelled in this convincing 4-1 win over a strong Watford team that possessed the talents of John Barnes, Kevin Richardson, Luther

Blissett and Mark Falco. Falco was another Spurs icon who began this very season at White Hart Lane before moving to Watford in December 1986.

In this game, Clive Allen had scored yet again. What a season he was having. ITV's Rosenthal spoke to Clive and Paul Allen who were clearly elated. In the background Elton John, the Watford chairman, had come in to congratulate the Spurs players along with Tottenham Chairman Irving Scholar, despite the disappointment of his club not reaching Wembley as they had done so three years before in a loss to Everton.

As the champagne flowed, Pleat and his coaching staff knew there was still a long way to go before reaching this Wembley date. There were still nine *TODAY Division 1* league games to go! This was the middle of April 1987 and in around five weeks Spurs would contest the final.

Pleat's charges were sitting third in the league and in four days they would travel to Manchester City. Looking at the League table, Spurs had two games in hand over Liverpool who were six points ahead in second place and one game in hand over league leaders Everton, who were nine points ahead. Spurs still had to visit Goodison Park too. Clearly still lots to play for, but how would Spurs fare? Fatigue was a huge factor around this time of the season and Spurs had already played 46 games before the Watford semi-final. The team had already been involved in some epic Littlewoods League Cup encounters during the season along with displaying some brilliant form in many league games, but consistency was a problem.

There had been substantial changes in personnel from the end of the 1985-86 season to now. A new footballing revolution had begun at White Hart Lane.

That aside; this was a time to celebrate. A cup final appearance in the bag, the stuff of dreams.

The season was 1986-87. It was my first season as a season ticket holder at Tottenham Hotspur. I have such fond memories of the season and I wanted to document it. While researching I have stumbled across some wonderful nuggets of information that directly or indirectly involved Spurs and their players during that season.

English football clubs were currently in the middle of a European ban but visits to Barcelona, Bermuda, Miami and Belfast all featured in Spurs' season. Former European Cup Winners Inter Milan and Hamburg SV also visited White Hart Lane during a period in which Diego Maradona, John Barnes and Kenny Dalglish all appeared for Tottenham Hotspur FC.

There was significant Spurs' player involvement at the 1986 Mexico World Cup along with an interesting link to England's disappointing World Cup Semi Final exit to West Germany in Turin during the 1990 Italian World Cup.

This was also a season to see the emergence in English football of the likes of Paul Ince, David Seaman, Matt Le Tissier, Stuart Pearce along with future Spurs favourites Steve Sedgley and Paul Gascoigne. Another future Spurs favourite, David Ginola, makes his emergence as a talented 19-year-old and Spurs would also line up against a player who would go on to become a Director of Football at White Hart Lane.

Spurs played against some of the brightest talents in Europe too. Young talents Ruud Gullit, Ronald Koeman, Paolo Maldini and Allesandro Costacurta all featured against Spurs along with a 20-year-old midfielder, Mohammed Ali Amar. This name resonates among Spurs fans as he was more commonly known as Nayim, a team he would join a few seasons later.

This book provides a snapshot as we link social, media and political events that took place around this time to the season I have chosen to spotlight. There was not one, but two Spurs connections with BBC's *Top of The Pops* this season and, it is important to point out, there was also a fair amount of football played too!

I have spent six months researching content for this book. As part of my research, I have been unbelievably lucky to speak with ex-players, backroom staff and members of the media. I wanted to gain diverse perspective of this season and for it not to be just one-way traffic from a 'Spurs' point of view only which has allowed me to spend time with players who featured for other clubs that season.

Before digging deeper into the Tottenham's season, 1986-87, a touch of context is needed. Some of the key players that will be impactive during this season had a journey to get to this point, as did the club as a whole.

CHANGING TIMES

I had been seduced by Spurs towards the end of the 1970's and the start of the 1980's. I was introduced to Spurs by my father who moved to London in his late teens and started attending matches at White Hart Lane, luckily enough, during the legendary Double winning team of 1960-61. For years he would regale his memories of that group of players, from Bill Brown's consistent goalkeeping to Danny Blanchflower's superb captaincy. Highlighting the consistency of goals scored by Les Allen and Bobby Smith and marvelling at the wing wizardry of Terry Dyson and Cliff Jones.

But of that team he held a special mention for John White. White was a Scottish international midfielder that had joined the club from Falkirk in 1959. He made a total of 183 appearances for Spurs and scored 40 goals. An outstanding midfielder for club and country. My father would occasionally struggle to put into words how good a player he actually was, but it would always conclude with the sadness of how his life ended at such an early age when he was fatally struck by lightning on the Crews Hill golf course in July 1964.

The only other player he never stopped talking about was Jimmy Greaves.

We all know that football evolves and moves forward; Greaves was someone who could've easily played at high levels in different eras, he was that good. My father would regularly revert to memories of his low centre of gravity, his electrifying pace and quickness of feet. But, more importantly, he was a finisher extraordinaire.

Television coverage of football nowadays is a completely different world to that of the 1980's. Wherever I could get hold of VHS videos that had footage of Greaves, or even just Spurs, I would plead for my parents to buy them, and I would pore over them several times a week.

I can still remember seeing footage of Greaves scoring an unbelievable goal against, the then champions, Manchester United in October 1965. Luckily the BBC cameras were there that day to capture Greaves picking the ball up halfway in the opposition half. With his back to goal, he then turned and raced past the helpless United midfielders and defenders to then slip the ball past Pat Dunne in the United goal. Even watching it now, you really do feel he had the physicality, the pace and indeed the skill to cope in today's game.

So, this was my education.

The first North London derby I ever attended was in 1983 at White Hart Lane. Spurs thumped Arsenal 5-0. Even Spurs' Irish international defender Chris Hughton scored a brace! I can remember saying to my dad that this derby stuff seems pretty easy! He laughed it off and reminded me this was not a regular occurrence and games are usually tighter than that. By the end of this book, you will probably agree with me that he was spot-on with that assessment.

Growing up in the early 80's lots of kids at school followed Liverpool. Bloody glory hunters they were. But suffice to say, they were a superb footballing team and from a young age I genuinely loved watching them. There were the likes of Aston Villa, Ipswich Town, Everton and Manchester United playing some lovely football in the early part of the 80's and that was always my preference instead of the rough and ready physical side of English football that we were so well known for on European and International stages. My VHS collection also included the brilliance of the Brazil team in 1970. They dominated world football with Rivelino, Pele, Jairzinho and Tostao excelling to lift the 1970 World Cup. There was 'Totaal Voetball' delivered by the Dutch masters Cruyff, Neeskens and Johnny Rep in the mid-70s that also piqued my interest in how I liked to see the game played.

But this is where Tottenham Hotspur came in. Keith Burkinshaw took over as manager from Terry Neill in 1976. Burkinshaw, who was nicknamed 'The General' in years to come, joined Spurs as a coach having just been sacked as a coach at Newcastle. Terry Neill had controversially left to manage Arsenal in the summer of 1976 and then Burkinshaw took over. He was soon to embed his style and philosophy that would marry exceptionally well with Spurs' traditional style of play that had been rooted into the club culture during the wonderfully successful Bill Nicholson years. From 1976 to his departure in 1984, Burkinshaw had moulded Spurs into one of the best clubs in English and European football.

The style of football I witnessed growing up following Spurs was, for me, the essence of how football should be played. England had some great midfielders during the early to mid-1980's. I would always have a preference. If I had to choose between Glenn Hoddle and Bryan Robson then it was Hoddle with ease (for the record, Robson was an outstanding player too). I'd rather have a Gordon Cowans over a Steve McMahon or a Jan Molby over a Peter Reid. Clearly, I knew that ball winners and box-to-box players were an essential part of midfield dominance, but I'd rather see my team leading with ball players first.

After Tottenham's disappointing relegation in May 1977, Burkinshaw managed to bring Spurs back into Division 1 at the first time of asking. The 1978-79 season was to explode for Spurs with the sensational double signing of Argentinian footballers Ossie Ardiles and Ricky Villa. A pioneering scoop for the English game but for Spurs it added quality and class to a team that possessed the emerging excellence of Hoddle, Tony Galvin, Paul Miller and Mark Falco alongside the experience of Steve Perryman, John Pratt and John Lacy.

Benefits were reaped in 1981 where Spurs lifted the FA Cup for the sixth time in their history having overcome Manchester City in a replay that was remembered mainly for Ricky Villa's wonderful solo goal. Spurs finished 10th in the league that season with Steve Archibald top scoring with 25 goals.

Burkinshaw made another sensational signing in the summer of 1981 when he snared Ray Clemence from Liverpool. Clemence had won several domestic titles, along with European titles, in his time at Anfield but this was a new chapter at Spurs.

In 1981-82 Spurs finished 4th in the league, were runners up in the league cup, semi-finalists in the European Cup Winners Cup and had made it to the FA Cup final. Having been involved in so much during the season Spurs did manage to go on and win the FA Cup again. Another replay was required and this time against Queens Park Rangers. A game that saw Hoddle's first half penalty strike enough to win the trophy for the seventh time in Spurs' history.

The 1982-83 season saw inconsistency prevail as Spurs finished 4th in the league for the second consecutive season but exited the FA Cup and Cup Winners Cup at relatively early stages. Progression in the league cup was halted in a 4-1 home defeat to Burnley. One of the highlights of that season was the emergence of Gary Mabbutt who had been a summer signing from Bristol Rovers. Mabbutt, who most Spurs fans remember as a heroic centre back, scored 10 goals for Spurs that season having played in the middle of midfield. Mr utility some would say.

What turned out to be Burkinshaw's final season was 1983-84. Summer signings included two 21-year-olds in Danny Thomas and Gary Stevens from Coventry and Brighton respectively. An eighth-placed league finish and early exits from both domestic cups was a disappointing return for such a talented squad. However, that season Spurs were having a memorable UEFA cup run. They had despatched an impressive Feyenoord team in the second round having seen Hoddle produce a midfield masterclass in the well documented match-up against the legendary Johan Cruyff. Spurs then despatched Bayern Munich in the third round, gaining revenge on losing to them in the Cup Winners Cup the year before. A 4-2 aggregate win over Austria Vienna in the quarter final set up a difficult semi-final against Hadjuk Split. Spurs won the tie-on away goals having lost 2-1 away but winning 1-0 at home thanks to a wonderful Micky Hazard Free kick.

For the UEFA Cup Final against a very strong Anderlecht team, led by their brilliant Danish captain Morten Olsen, injuries and suspensions restricted Spurs from fielding some of their most influential players in Clemence, Hoddle and club captain, Steve Perryman. But drama was to be served up over two wonderful legs of Cup Final football. Spurs drew 1-1 in front of 38,000 fans in Brussels thanks to a Paul Miller goal. The home leg was no different. Tight and competitive, the 90 minutes ending in another 1-1 as Graham Roberts bundled the ball over the line for an equaliser seconds after Ardiles had hit the crossbar. Extra time delivered no goals and now it was time for penalties.

Tony Parks had usually been understudying to Ray Clemence in the Spurs goal. Now he was front and centre. Captain on the night, Graham Roberts, scored Spurs' first penalty to then see Parks save Anderlecht's first effort! The White Hart Lane crowd went bonkers! Mark Falco's left foot drive put Spurs 2-0 up only for Anderlecht to score and bring it back to 2-1. Gary Stevens then made it 3-1 which the Belgium side replied by seeing a brilliant, young Enzo Scifo score to make it 3-2 to Spurs.

Archibald made it 4-2 and another Anderlecht success made it 4-3.

Up stepped Danny Thomas. The 21-year-old in his first season at Spurs had the chance to win the UEFA cup for his new club. Thomas struck the ball to the keepers right and it was saved! Thomas put his head in his hands and was immediately greeted and consoled by Steve Archibald. Then it happened, perhaps a moment when the Spurs crowd became that influential 'extra man'. *'One Danny Thomas, there's only one Danny Thomas'*.

Researching this book, my core focus was on content for the 1986-87 season. Danny Thomas is now living and working in Florida, USA. I spent a wonderful couple of hours talking with him about that season, but I couldn't let this opportunity slip by without asking him about that penalty miss.

Thomas recalls, "As soon as the keeper saved it, I was hoping that the ground would open up and swallow me as I don't think I could feel more miserable than I did. Hearing the Spurs fans sing that was so special and I am grateful for my teammates' immediate support. Particularly, I am grateful to Mr Tony Parks. He eased my misery as something like that could've affected me for a very long time".

He was referring to the fact that Tony Parks had dived brilliantly to his right and saved a penalty struck by Anderlecht's Arnór Gudjohnsen, father of the former Chelsea striker Eidur who, incidentally, played 11 games for Spurs while on loan from Monaco in 2010. Parks sprinted away with his arms aloft and White Hart Lane erupted into a state of euphoria as the 46,000 fans celebrated a historic moment for the club.

Spurs were UEFA Cup winners and six days later Keith Burkinshaw resigned. He had become disillusioned in how the club was being run and was allegedly quoted saying, "There used to be a football club over there" when he left.

The General's time was now over. His assistant Peter Shreeves took the reins which provided some much-needed continuity to the squad and club for the start of the 1984-85 season. Shreeves' first summer saw the departure of Steve Archibald and Alan Brazil to Barcelona and Manchester United respectively, but he brought in the striking talent of QPR's Clive Allen and the pacey John Chiedozie from Notts County. At the end of his first season, Spurs had their best league finish since 1971 when they finished third in the league. As holders of the UEFA Cup, they exited the competition in the quarter final losing to Real Madrid 1-0 on aggregate.

The summer of 1985 Shreeves dipped back into the transfer market to scoop the Newcastle winger Chris Waddle along with the industrious midfielder Paul Allen from West Ham United. That summer also saw the departure of Spurs' 1984 UEFA Cup hero Micky Hazard to Chelsea along with the '81 and '82 FA

Cup winning favourite, Garth Crooks, who left the club having struck 48 goals in 125 appearances for the Lilywhites. There was a European ban on English clubs this season but there were still three cup competitions to play for. Exits to Everton in the FA Cup and Portsmouth in the League cup highlighted a poor return for a squad with such talent. The Screen Sport Cup also saw Spurs lose again to Everton and this time at semi-final stage. Both Waddle and Paul Allen struggled to settle in their first season at White Hart Lane with the team's inconsistency evident by finishing tenth in the league.

Another Spurs player I was fortunate to spend some time talking to was Paul Allen. Paul admitted his first season hadn't gone to plan when he recalled: "We started that season well with a great win over Watford. My daughter was born in September 1985 and then her health deteriorated between the September and the December 1985 which didn't help me personally. Settling into a new club is never easy and even though we had a talented squad we didn't have a good run in the cups and slipped away on the league too".

Mark Falco had been top scorer in Shreeves' two seasons in charge and Clive Allen had suffered with injuries. Despite some impressive results in the final few games of the season confidence was not high among the Spurs board.

The Spurs chairman, Irving Scholar, was soon to ring the changes.

* * * *

In the spring of 1986 club captain, and Spurs' appearance record breaker, Steve Perryman had been allowed to speak to other clubs. The White Hart Lane hierarchy had now viewed him as surplus to requirements. A free transfer was on the cards as his contract was about to expire. Perryman amassed 655 league appearances in his 17 years at Spurs but totalled a mammoth number of 866 games including cup appearances. This season had been different though with injuries and squad competition restricting him from playing more.

Perryman's debut season in 1969-70 saw him make 27 appearances. The next 15 seasons saw him average 53 games per season with a peak of 66 games played during the 1981-82 campaign that ended with the FA Cup replay victory over Queens Park Rangers.

This season, 1985-86, had only seen Perryman play a total of 37 times, his lowest since his debut season. In recent seasons, he had spent most of his playing time as a right back but was still captain of the ship with the philosophies of the great Bill Nicholson engrained in him.

Speaking with Perryman I still get a clear indication of his love for the club. It is evident that there have been some people who he did not see eye to eye with and one of them was the club Chairman Irving Scholar.

In the seasons leading up to Steve's eventual departure he was very aware of the competition now building in the squad and he was not getting any younger. He recalls the pre-season when Spurs signed Gary Stevens and Danny Thomas. Photographers were on-site at the club's Cheshunt training ground for profile pictures and action shots. He was sat next to Paul 'Maxi' Miller who said, "They've signed them to replace you and me". "Have they" Steve replied, "Speak for your fucking-self Maxi but I tell you what, they have to be consistent to get in front of me!". Perryman had that steel about him, fully aware of competition but still keen to fight for his place.

In the March of 1986 contract negotiations highlighted that Perryman wanted a two-year contract but the club were only willing to give him one year. Perryman talked candidly on the realisation he was about the leave club when I asked him to recall this time in his career.

"Was I ready to go? Yes, I was" conceded Perryman. "I was ready to go as I was losing faith in the people owning the club, and when your legs are running out as well you need some support, some back up".

The club released a statement that paid tribute to Steve and his service to the club and to this day Perryman would argue that some of the club's ideals and standards were now different to his own, but he still felt that he could've been an asset.

As a club captain you may never find another player to represent Spurs in the way that he did. He completely understood being a leader was not a popularity contest and sometimes, even when he knew he wasn't having the greatest game himself, he would still demand players to do and consider their jobs and/or responsibility. Accountability was key to his drive.

Steve knew I was writing about 1986/87, a season he was not part of, as he eventually left the club to join Oxford United as a player and coach in March of 1986. Perryman still feels that he would have added value to the squad had he stayed on. He's not sure if David Pleat would have been frightened of him and he genuinely felt that Scholar was very wary of him, but he did say "I probably would have not done him any good as a pair of legs! But in terms of experience, knowing how to turn the players on, I would have made them a lot closer to winning the title that year".

Hindsight is a wonderful thing but maybe he had a point. As we unpack the season there will be times when we think that Perryman's drive could've been a positive factor when Spurs came up against those pressure moments in key matches. Especially when mindset, resilience and strength of character plays such a key role.

The club's monthly newspaper, *Spurs News*, ran the headline of 'END OF AN ERA' in the March 1986 edition. Very true indeed as it was also noticeable that he was now the final playing member from the great Bill Nicholson years.

On Bill Nicholson, Perryman could not speak highly enough of his former manager, mentor and leader. A true Spurs legend. "The reason I joined Spurs over Chelsea when I was young was because of Bill Nic. He was so straightforward and honest. No spin, no mind games. I lived in West London, travelling to Chelsea would have been so much easier for me, but travelling across London to work under Bill Nicholson was where I wanted to be".

It was a refreshing statement that even now you can still see the desire and belief in Perryman's eyes when talking about the man who convinced him to join the Lilywhites.

Perryman ended up playing a handful of games at Oxford before moving on to Brentford where he finally finished his playing days in 1990. He returned to White Hart Lane in 1993 as a coach during Ossie Ardiles' managerial tenure and still to this day speaks at Spurs Legends events with many of his teammates from the successful Spurs UEFA, FA and League cup teams of the 70's and 80's. A true club legend.

* * * *

Just before the end of the 1985-86 season there were several Spurs players hoping to be chosen in Bobby Robson's 22-man England squad for the World Cup Finals in Mexico. With three league games to go that season Spurs visited Loftus Road and gave QPR a bit of a footballing lesson. Spurs ran out 5-2 winners. Four players who played that day were keeping their fingers crossed for inclusion to the national squad for Mexico. Glenn Hoddle, Gary Mabbutt, Chris Waddle and Gary Stevens. Another player who would still very much have been part of that England squad was Spurs' goalkeeper and, since the departure of Perryman, now club captain Ray Clemence.

Clemence had, for many years, been in direct competition with Peter Shilton for the coveted No.1 England shirt, but despite making 61 international appearances had not featured for England since 1983.

In February 1985 he was interviewed on *Thames News* giving reasons as to why he did not want to be considered for international selection anymore despite him playing so well for Spurs. Clemence said "I stick by my decision as I feel it was right for me to stand down so a younger keeper can come into the squad to play and work under Peter Shilton as, in my opinion, he will still be number one for the next couple of years at least. I'd like to spend more time with my family and to plan for my future when football eventually finishes".

Suffice to say, it was England's loss. If Shilton was injured Bobby Robson would have had a ready-made, world class keeper to come in his place. That aside, there was still much hope for players looking to join Robson's World Cup party.

On the 28th of April 1986, two days after the rout at Loftus Road, Bobby Robson announced his squad. His 22-man squad featured Glenn Hoddle, Chris Waddle and Gary Stevens. He even announced a 6-man standby group that included the likes of Everton's Paul Bracewell and Arsenal's Stewart Robson but sadly there was no place for midfielder Gary Mabbutt. However, Mabbutt had not featured for England since he started the 3-0 away win against Hungary in Budapest in October 1983 so his inclusion was a long shot.

It is fair to say that Hoddle and Waddle were very good bets to make the squad and Gary Stevens' inclusion was an excellent piece of news for the player and the club. Stevens made his England debut against Finland at Wembley in October 1984. He then played on two more occasions shortly afterwards but then was not included into the squad again until he came on as a sub for Steve Hodge in the 75th minute of the Rous Cup match versus Scotland only a week before this squad announcement.

Speaking with Gary, he recalls the moment of joy when he found out he was included in the squad. "I was at home in Broxbourne, Hertfordshire and was in the garden and my then girlfriend, who became my wife, ran out of the house to tell me that I was included in the squad! It was a very special moment for me". I asked Gary how the news arrived, he chuckled "Well, nowadays players would get a personal call or message from Gareth Southgate or the FA, but my news came via Ceefax!"

Being part of a World Cup was always one of Gary's ambitions and he was gradually ticking them off as he mentioned "It was a dream and ambition of mine as a kid. Playing in a Cup Final, yes. Scoring at Wembley, yes. Playing for England, yes. And now going to a World Cup".

Gary now lives on the other side of the world in Southeast Asia, he still coaches and is a TV pundit. But the memory of that World Cup is something that stays with him. The captain of England was the Manchester United midfield marvel, Bryan Robson. Robson had his fair share of injuries over the years and going into the World Cup there were possibly one or two doubts over his fitness that would become evident in a World Cup warm up match. Stevens remembers "Bryan wasn't fully fit. I am not saying I was Robson's understudy as such but there were links and ties with what I could do in the midfield".

Not only is it curiously amusing to hear players being notified of such a huge announcement via Ceefax, but the level of pride a player must feel representing their country at a major tournament is, I'm sure, forever memorable.

With the squad now announced, Spurs had two final league games that season after the QPR win. Plus, they were about to be involved in a very special occasion for the loyal, gifted and wonderful Ossie Ardiles.

MAY 1986

On Thursday 1st of May 1986, a memorable event was held at White Hart Lane.

Osvaldo 'Ossie' Ardiles had joined Spurs from Huracan FC in the summer of 1978. Despite a short time away from White Hart Lane during the Falklands War in 1982, Ossie had been a wonderful servant to the club and a pivotal player in the club's cup successes since he had arrived eight years before. This match was to celebrate that loyalty to the club he had grown to love.

Opponents for the evening were the mighty Inter Milan. One of the powerhouses of European football. Inter's league season had just finished but they were about to play the first leg of the Coppa Italia quarter final versus Roma in a few days. Finishing sixth in the league and exiting the UEFA Cup a few weeks earlier in a Semi Final loss to Real Madrid highlighted the importance of this Coppa Italia game to salvage their season.

Unsurprisingly, the big names like Karl Heinz-Rumminegge, Allesandro Altobelli, Daniel Passerella, Guisepe Bergomi, Marco Tardelli and Walter Zenga were not included. But the team did include the defensive brilliance of Ricardo Ferri, the attacking prowess of Pietro Fanna and the midfield mastery of Liam Brady. Brady was in his final season at Inter before he moved to Ascoli that summer.

Getting Inter Milan to visit White Hart Lane for a friendly was one thing, but Ardiles had delivered an absolute masterstroke. He had managed to persuade his friend and compatriot Diego Maradona to represent him and Spurs in this benefit match.

Maradona was currently playing in Naples, Southern Italy. He had joined Napoli in the summer of 1984 having spent a couple of years at the Camp Nou where his time at Barcelona had been hampered by injuries and more than a touch of controversy.

If anyone has been lucky enough to see the Asif Kapadia's brilliant 2019 biographical film of Diego Maradona, they would be very well versed in understanding how he had left one of the biggest clubs in the world, Barcelona, to join one of the smallest top-flight clubs in Italy. Naples was considered one of the poorest cities in Europe let alone Italy. The capture of Diego Maradona stunned most people, but to the people of Naples it was like the coming of a messiah. Maradona was looking for a home and a place to be appreciated.

Maradona had joined Barcelona in June 1982 and a few months earlier, before he joined, Spurs had lost a two-legged European Cup Winners Cup semi-final to Barcelona. Barcelona, famed for their attractive footballing style were the complete opposite during this semi-final. One newspaper reported 'ANIMALS! THE BUTCHERS OF BARCELONA SHAKE BATTLING

SPURS'. It was a hatchet job alright that is also sadly remembered for Ray Clemence making an uncharacteristic error allowing Barcelona to score a crucial away goal at White Hart Lane. Clem had been exemplary all season and was devastated by the error that ultimately proved costly.

Only several weeks before Maradona was unveiled at Napoli, he had made his final appearance for Barcelona in the Copa del Rey final defeat to the *Primera Division* league champions Athletic Bilbao.

Everyone loves a story, and this cup final had a prequel several months before to light the fire of this chapter. Maradona had spent several months out with broken ankle from a particularly bad foul. The 'Butcher of Bilbao', Andoni Goikoetxea, was guilty of this offence and Maradona tended not to forget things like that.

Barcelona were 1-0 down quite early on and looking for an equaliser all game which they failed to do. When the final whistle came it meant Bilbao won the Copa Del Rey and therefore claim the Double having already won La Liga.

Cue Carnage. Kung fu kicks flying everywhere! Maradona was taking on all-comers. Punches, kicks and players fighting all over. Maradona was finally led away down the tunnel with his shirt ripped on his way to collect his runners-up medal.

Barcelona had probably had enough; Maradona had not produced the league title win they expected and now this drama had brought a three month ban for the Argentine international. Time for this diminutive talent move on.

In July 1984 he was thrust into the Stadio San Paolo, home of Napoli S.S.C, where he made his way through the back walkways of the stadium waiting to be revealed to the thousands of supporters who had come to welcome him. It felt like a gladiator entering a coliseum as he meandered through the stone and gated areas on his way to the pitch where he would soon perform for his adoring crowd.

Unsurprisingly, whilst Maradona may not be looking for drama, the drama comes to him. Having just been paraded in front of his new fans there was an immediate press conference. Chaos and calamity were clearly heightening the stress levels of the Napoli President Corrado Ferlaino, but it was now time for the first question.

A big sigh of relief and let's get back to football everyone thought. So, what was the first question?

Reporter, "I would like to know if Maradona knows what the Camorra is? And if he knows that the Camorra's money is everywhere here, even in football?"

And we're off! Maradona probably knew what was being asked but he looked a tad bewildered, then President Ferlaino intervened. "This question is highly offensive" he retorted. "I am truly mortified that a journalist would ask such questions. It's so insulting I won't answer it!" There was applause throughout the room and Ferlaino, with his drained facial expression, asked the reporter to leave.

The alleged crime family running Naples at the time were the *Camorra* and these mafia connections, mentioned by the ejected reporter, were something to impact Maradona's time in Naples quite significantly over the next few years.

That aside he was the big fish in a small pond. There were no other huge names at Napoli during his first season where they finished eighth in the league. It was an improvement on the 1983-84 season where they finished in twelfth, two points above the relegation places.

A few days before Ardiles's benefit match, Napoli had beaten Avellino 1-0 to see them finish third in the league behind runners up Roma and champions Juventus. Importantly they finished seven points ahead of tonight's opponents Inter Milan who finished sixth. Improvements had been evidential since his arrival, but now Maradona was at White Hart Lane to pay respect to his compatriot.

Spurs' limp season had seen attendances dwindle with most games, since the turn of the year, attracting crowds of between 10,000 and 20,000. Only the visits of Arsenal and Manchester United had seen crowd numbers rise over 30,000. Even Liverpool's visit at the start of March 1986 was just over 16,000. Not good at all. However, a crowd of 30,536 had ventured to White Hart Lane and watched Maradona don a Spurs shirt. Watching the game, I knew Maradona was a huge player but it's only in hindsight that you realise what an amazing occasion it was for Spurs fans. Attacking football with flair was what us Spurs fans turn up for, Maradona was that in abundance.

Before the game, Danny Thomas recalls being in the presence of such a great player. "He had a Tottenham shirt on, he is in your changing room! He is the world's best player, and he is sat right next to you! I can still remember it so vividly" Thomas beams. But despite this hugely talented footballer being in the changing room Danny remembers how Maradona came across. "He couldn't speak English, but Ossie translated. He came across so humble and he was talking about <u>us</u> being great players!".

Maradona had also turned up without any football boots. Ardiles asked around the dressing room to find someone who shared the same boot size as Maradona. Up step Clive Allen. Clive had a couple of pairs of boots with him and Maradona chose the older pair of the two. The other reason he chose Clive's boots was the fact he was contracted to Puma and would not wear anything else. After the game, Maradona signed the boots Clive had loaned to him. Never to be worn again and the pride of Clive Allen's football memorabilia.

Thomas continued: "We are now all changed, and we are about to warm up. I watched him with a ball at his feet, there was a player walking behind him, I cannot remember who it was, but Diego didn't see him at all, but he put the ball through his legs and nutmegged him. I thought, how on earth is it possible for him to see him?! It was a magnificent little moment".

"He then went out and put on a great show, he was a wonderful character. There he was, a player at the very top of the tree but not just at that particular time, but throughout history". It was clear to see that Danny was thrilled to have this as one of his most memorable football moments of his career.

Another player who recalls that game with fondness is Vinny Samways.

At the time Vinny was 18 years old and part of the South-East Counties squad, the Spurs Youth team. He was flip-flopping between that youth team and the Football Combination team, the Spurs Reserves.

Vinny was another player who was very generous with his time and very open about his early days at Tottenham. He had represented England at various schoolboy levels and was progressing well at Spurs.

He recounts, "During the last few months of the season I remember Peter Shreeves bringing me up to train with the first team. This was amazing. From the very first session I can remember building an immediate rapport with Ossie. In my opinion, one of the best foreign players to ever come into English football. He was an amazing player and I had so much respect for him".

Vinny continues, "I loved the way he played and for some reason he took a liking to me. I'm not sure why, but maybe it was my style of play. I remember being asked to play in the game, it was mind blowing and I still didn't realise how big it was. When

Maradona walked into the changing room my jaw hit the floor. You're thinking, this ain't real! Absolutely amazing".

Maradona was known for wearing the number 10 shirt. In this part of the world that was Glenn Hoddle's shirt. Hoddle gave up the number 10 shirt and wore number 11. We were about to see a midfield four of Hoddle, Waddle, Ardiles and Diego Maradona. There was a wonderful picture taken of Glenn and Diego in the changing rooms. Two very special footballing geniuses.

Inter Milan led out first and lined up vertically to the centre spot in the Paxton Road end of White Hart Lane, then came out the Spurs team. This was led by Ray Clemence as the team lined up symmetrically with Inter.

Over the tannoy, the legendary Spurs voice of Willie Morgan then announced, "But tonight, what it's all about is one very special man we hold very dear, please welcome with Diego Maradona, Ossie Ardiles!"

The crowd erupted as Ossie and Diego walked out holding the hands of Ossie's two sons.

Just before the game began the press are still surrounding Maradona on the pitch as he jogs casually doing his trademark high kicks ups, superb control and pure talent. The crowd were buzzing and all anticipating Maradona's first touch.

Mark Falco kicked off straight to Maradona, two touches and straight into Hoddle's feet, Glenn then gives an early pass to Ossie, the crowd cheer! And we're cooking!

Spurs won the game 2-1. Maradona was excellent throughout, linking well with Hoddle and Ossie. Spurs went 1-0 up after 4 minutes. Created by the White Hart Lane creator-extraordinaire, Glenn Hoddle. Hoddle was quite central in the Inter half, he chipped the ball forward to Falco who took it on his chest and then volleyed home.

There were no more goals in the first half until Inter equalised halfway through the second half when Liam Brady dinked a lovely free kick over the wall for 1-1. Spurs won the game after 89 minutes when Hoddle's free kick was cleared off the line and into the path of Clive Allen who tucked the ball away for the win and a victory for Ossie Ardiles.

Maradona delighted the crowd with touches and through balls. He won the 89th minute free kick for Spurs' winner. The closest Maradona came to scoring was with around 15 minutes left. Young Samways was the architect of the move too. Samways was given the ball in the middle of Inter's half, he threaded a wonderful through ball to Falco who's deft one touch into Maradona saw the Argentine wallop the ball goal bound only for Inter's Lorieri to make a fine save to his left denying the Napoli man.

ITV news covered the game and presented highlights of Maradona's involvement to the backdrop of Queen's June 1986 release of 'It's a Kind of Magic'. After the game, Martin Tyler interviewed Maradona through his interpreter, Ossie Ardiles. Tyler asked if he foresaw any problems at all if England meet Argentina in the latter stages of the upcoming Mexico World Cup, considering the excellent reception he'd had from the Spurs fans?

Diego's reply was short and sweet, "No, not at all". Tyler asked his thoughts on playing in front of an English crowd. Ossie replied for Diego saying, "He felt like he was playing at home, and he was very happy the crowd realised he was trying to win the game".

A wonderful night to see one of the world's greatest players in a Spurs shirt and Maradona's commitment must be applauded. It had been a frenetic few days for Maradona as he had played his final league game of the season for Napoli on the Sunday; on the Wednesday he then flew to Oslo to play against Norway for Argentina and less than 24 hours later he played the full 90 minutes for Ossie at White Hart Lane. Hat off to the man.

Several weeks later there will be a game played in the Azteca Stadium, Mexico City, where Martin Tyler's post-match question may come to fruition.

But for now, Diego had delighted the crowd and seeing Spurs with a midfield of Hoddle, Waddle, Ardiles and Maradona was a once in a lifetime moment for most Spurs fans and an evening of football I will never forget.

* * * *

Two days later, Spurs played their penultimate game of the season. Fresh from the rout at Loftus Road and so soon after having played alongside Diego Maradona, Spurs were back at White Hart Lane to give Aston Villa a 4-2 beating. Then, two days later in the final game of the season Spurs gave their home fans even more delight by thumping Southampton 5-3 and topped off with a Tony Galvin hat-trick! Spurs had scored fourteen goals in the last three league games and a resurgent Clive Allen had scored five of them. He was back from injury, and one would assume he was now looking forward to next season.

The 1985-86 season had finally ended. But there was still more football to play as the club had agreed to play two benefit games.

On the 9th of May 1986 Spurs went to Brentford to play in a Testimonial match for Brentford player Danis Salman. Salman had been at Spurs in the mid-1970s as a youth player but had now completed 11 years at Brentford. Despite fielding a strong side, Spurs lost the game 4-3 with Chiedozie and a Clive Allen brace being Spurs goal scorers. It was an opportunity to see Steve Perryman again though as he turned out for Spurs only weeks before he was recognised in the Queen's Birthday Honours List when he was awarded an MBE for services to football.

Peter Shreeves last game was a friendly against West Ham. He had been part of the successful Burkinshaw years as coach. After Burkinshaw had departed Scholar gave the reins to Shreeves. Shreeves had mixed results over those two seasons but no silverware to show for it. Some good signings had been made with the captures of Chris Waddle, Clive and Paul Allen but none had really materialised as yet.

Plus, he also had some established winners in the squad with the likes of Clemence, Hughton, Hoddle, Roberts, Ardiles, Galvin, Miller and Falco swelling the playing side. When the season finished in a mid-table position with some limp cup exits there was no surprise that change was coming.

Time was now up for Shreeves.

* * * *

On Thursday 15th of May 1986, the *Daily Telegraph* ran a headline, 'NORTH LONDON GIANTS GO HEAD HUNTING'. Telegraph journalist Donald Saunders wrote, "Arsenal and Spurs took significant steps yesterday towards preparing themselves to break Merseyside's domination of English football next season. Londoners were last night digesting the overnight news that Spurs had sacked Peter Shreeves and Arsenal had appointed George Graham from Millwall". Saunders claimed that Terry Venables had been offered the job at Arsenal not long after Don Howe's spring resignation following the news that Arsenal were not renewing his contract. However, the job had now been given to Venables' former teammate at Chelsea, and old Highbury favourite, George Graham.

Despite Spurs not having a great campaign, during the 85-86 season, they did remain unbeaten against their North London rivals with a 0-0 stalemate at Highbury in January 1986. They also won 1-0 at White Hart Lane in March 1986 thanks to a Gary Stevens strike.

However, Shreeves had left Spurs and Arsenal now had Graham at the helm. Kenny Dalglish was still settled as boss of Champions Liverpool, and Everton manager Howard Kendall was also keen on revenge for Liverpool snatching the League and Cup away from his team last season.

Spurs needed to move quickly, they had to appoint someone to challenge these clubs. They did move swiftly, and appointed Luton Town manager David Pleat as the new boss at White Hart Lane.

In the *Sunday Times* that week, Brian Glanville ran the rule over North London's two new managers. Glanville wrote, "On the face of it, Tottenham seem to have won the managerial derby against Arsenal. David Pleat was surely the supreme prize, the outstanding young British manager". He lamented Arsenal for not pushing through in appointing Venables and going for second best in George Graham. Glanville did concede that Graham had some wonderful young talent and then highlighted that Pleat needed to 'manifest holes in the centre of defence' in a little dig towards the Roberts and Miller partnership which had conceded a fair few goals last season.

The May 1986 edition of the *Spurs News* newspaper was released with the front-page headline, 'WELCOME DAVID PLEAT'. Pleat told *Spurs News* that it was an easy decision to join Spurs despite what he had created and built at Luton Town. He claimed that "Spurs and I share the same feeling for football", which suggests he was keen to play the Tottenham way. Oh, how the Spurs fans love to hear those words!

David was a Midlands chap. He was born in Nottingham and began his professional football career at Nottingham Forest during the 1962-63 season. His playing days ended in 1971 having had spells at Luton Town, Shrewsbury Town, Exeter City and Peterborough. His managerial career began at Nuneaton Town in 1971 where he stayed for several years before taking the helm at Luton Town in 1978. He managed to get Luton Town promoted to the First Division in the early 80's and despite narrowly avoiding relegation in 1983 Pleat saw gradual progression in the Bedfordshire based club.

Pleat took Luton to an FA Cup Semi Final in 1985 where they narrowly lost in an extra time thriller at Villa Park to Everton. Everton were heading for the treble that season and were clearly a dominant force, but that was as close as Pleat took his Luton team to a Wembley final.

Pleat was known for developing attacking, young talent. The emergence of Ricky Hill and Brian Stein, who both gained England recognition, was down to Pleat's management, faith and vision. He had an array of talent which made Luton Town one of the most competitive teams in the First Division. Steve Foster, Mal Donaghy, Tim Breacker, Paul Elliott, Mick Harford, Vince Hilaire, Peter Nicholas, Garry Parker and the brilliant goalkeeper Les Sealey among his charges.

But now it was time for Tottenham.

I approached David to talk about this season. He has a wonderful, and very detailed, football brain but his appointment to manage Spurs is a memory that remains vivid for different reasons.

"I had offers from Sunderland, Ipswich and QPR but I had remained very loyal to Luton. When Tottenham came along it was a different story though. I remember going to the City Ground in 1960 to see Spurs visit Nottingham Forest. They won 4-0 and were absolutely fabulous to watch, what a team the Lilywhites were. John White was fantastic but of course Bill Nicholson. He made me think how football should be played. I had made my decision; I had a wonderful time a Luton with some terrific players, but it was time for me to move on and who better than Tottenham".

Not wanting to dampen the spirit of the conversation I was keen to understand how David felt about the words and actions from his departing boss, the Chairman of Luton Town, David Evans. At the time, it did not sound like an amicable departure.

Pleat is happy to discuss and stated, "Evans didn't want me to go. He came to my house with his wife to try and change my mind, I said no, I have made my decision. He gave me champagne and flowers, but I told him I am going to Spurs and I feel I have done many great things at Luton in my eight and a half years".

Pleat's tone slightly dipped a little when he recalled, "His wife started crying as he gave this long spiel about offering the same as what Tottenham had, I would have all the privileges and that I was the best manager in the world!"

Pleat knew the conversation was coming to an end and he led Evans and his wife to the door. Pleat's final words to Evans were, "I'm not going to stay at Luton, I have done my time there and I wish you well". He then said that Evans sternly looked at him and said, "David, you will pay for this".

Those comments stuck with David for some considerable time. He had given so much to Luton, but it was now time to try and new, loftier challenge. After that conversation it seemed that Evans was now a key factor in consolidating Pleat's decision in wanting to leave. Plus, as the weeks went by, some cohorts of the press printed some very nasty comments, and this did upset Pleat.

Pleat had struck an immediate rapport with Irving Scholar. In Scholar's 1992 book '*Behind Closed Doors*' written by journalist Mihir Bose, Scholar mentions his initial approach to Luton Chairman David Evans. He mentions that he called Evans and arranged to meet him in his Cheapside, London office. Scholar stated that Evans seemed surprised that he wanted to talk about approaching Pleat. Evans told him that he would need to contact David, he rang Pleat there and then. Scholar now felt things were staring to happen.

Scholar says, "I spoke to David later that evening and arranged to meet for lunch the following day. I immediately liked his enthusiasm, and he confided in me that he'd always dreamed of managing Spurs as their ideals were the same as his own".

Personal terms were agreed quite quickly, and his only requirement was to bring his coach, Trevor Hartley, and his physiotherapist, John Sheridan, with him. Scholar does highlight that he told Pleat that Mike Varney, Spurs' current physio, was doing a great job and would be an asset. Scholar was disappointed that he wanted to sack him, but he did understand that most managers want to bring in their own back-room staff.

Despite some bitter words in the press from Evans along with his unpleasant visit to Pleat's home, all seemed to be going smoothly. Things were to change though, relationships with Luton Town FC would sour. The first experience of that would be in the home game versus Luton in the October.

That aside, Pleat was now in position.

* * * *

However, much to Scholar's initial disappointment, Pleat was contracted to co-commentate for ITV on various World Cup games in the tournament that was due to kick off in Mexico on the 31st of May 1986.

Pleat said, "I did tell Irving and told him they've asked me to do this. I would like to do it. I'm seeing a lot of football and now I'm going to be managing a top club with Tottenham it will help that I'm seeing a lot of world-class players. I'll be meeting people etc. Irving asked me about when the players come back, they're due to come back for pre-season and you won't be there! First impressions count".

Pleat was clearly aware of the impact first impressions have but he knew he'd be ok developing relationships with the players. Funnily enough, Pleat found Scholar then made it out to Mexico himself!

ITV asked Pleat to interview Glenn Hoddle at the England camp in the Mexican City of Saltillo. It was after that interview that Pleat stayed talking with Glenn about plans for next season. "Glenn wanted to go but then agreed to give me another year" Pleat continued. "Irving had already said to Hoddle that he can leave at the end of the World Cup, but I asked him to please give me one year, we could have a fabulous year together and to be fair to Glenn he did".

Hoddle had committed to one more year at White Hart Lane, which was probably the biggest coup for Spurs' summer so far.

Whilst in Saltillo, David did also introduce himself to Chris Waddle and Gary Stevens. Pleat and his England trio met to have a chat and discuss next season at White Hart Lane.

Stevens recalls that meeting. "I actually have a photo of that" he quipped before saying, "He knew what Hoddle and Waddle were about, but he knew less about me. But it was good to be able to meet the new manager. We asked questions, he told us a few things and then he asked questions. He was highly regarded as a coach; he had some innovative ideas and I think the three of us were looking forward to it".

However, Stevens then went on to say, "About a week after we'd got back from Mexico we were training at Cheshunt and one thing he had previously told me completely changed! From that moment onwards I was uncomfortable with the guy. I just didn't trust him to be honest and that's a potentially damning statement, especially as I haven't elaborated on what was said. I just didn't trust him".

Trust is a key ingredient in any high performing team and high performing arena, in this instance we now had a key member of the Spurs squad that didn't fully trust Pleat from early on. Would Pleat be able to build relationships and rapport with the players?

Stevens had more to say on the relationship with his new manager as the season went by. "I always felt he was watching you with critical eyes. He would even comment on some people's sprinting in the warm-ups, questioning their commitment in the sprint he'd just seen. I sometimes felt he wanted you to know he was watching you".

An example when trust was lacking For Stevens was a time when Pleat phoned him out of the blue during the season. It was a Thursday night. Pleat called and Stevens answered the phone. "Oh, you're at home then he said to me". Stevens slightly bemused replies, "You know, I'm not out on a Thursday night two nights before a game. I won't be out on a Friday night, one night before the game!" Stevens felt if you don't know that about me then you don't know me at all!

Stevens was also very keen to point out, "I have got real respect for him, his football knowledge is very good but personally, I just struggled with him".

* * * *

Just before Pleat's appointment as Spurs' new boss, the England team played their first World Cup warm up match against the Korean Republic in Denver, Colorado on the 14th of May 1986. This is officially denoted as an 'unofficial' international but still acted as a good run-out for Bobby Robson's men.

England won the game 4-1 in front of a small crowd of just over 3,000 people. Hoddle and Waddle both started the game, and it was game to help acclimatise to high altitudes. Denver sits 5,280 feet above sea level, so this was a good test seeing as Mexico would be very similar.

With the Korean Republic game not posing too much of a test, England were then going to face World Cup hosts Mexico in a friendly to be held in the LA Coliseum, Los Angeles.

Mexico were no pushovers though. They did not have their main striker and talisman Hugo Sanchez available as he had just won the UEFA Cup with Real Madrid several days before, but they were technically a very gifted team and more importantly, used to the hot conditions.

Once again, Hoddle and Waddle started for England. England were 3-0 up before half time with a dominant, yet wonderful footballing display that really showcased their tournament credentials.

In front of a 30,000 crowd, Hoddle and AC Milan's Mark Hateley worked well on a few early occasions and Hateley opened the scoring after 22 minutes when he dived in to head Waddle's delectable left wing cross. Hoddle, AC Milan's Ray Wilkins and Newcastle United's Peter Beardsley were really running the show and it was the Newcastle man Beardsley that found Hateley's head for England's second goal. After 37 minutes the game was up. Hoddle took a quick free kick to an open Beardsley who tucked it under the keeper for his first international goal and England's third on the day.

Mexico threw all they had at England in the second half only to come up against an inspired Peter Shilton with the Southampton keeper having an excellent game. After 70 minutes, skipper Bryan Robson had tracked back and thwarted yet another Mexican attack only to crumple on the floor in evidential pain. Minutes later he was trudging off cradling his arm and shoulder injury. Not a great sight for England supporters and this was a picture that would sadly show up again as the tournament begins.

Spurs' Gary Stevens came on as a 71st minute sub to get some more crucial international minutes under his belt. Game won 3-0 and now on to face Canada in 7 days' time for their final warm-up match.

England's final World Cup warm-up match took place on Saturday 24th of May 1986 in the Swanguard Stadium in Metro Vancouver, British Columbia. Now, this arena was only 200 feet above sea level so not necessarily a high-altitude acclimatisation test for Bobby Robson's men, but they were playing Canada who had reached the World Cup for the first time in their history.

The Canadians were in a very strong group that included the current European Champions France and the much-fancied Russians. And to be fair, they gave a very good account of themselves in this game.

It was a heavily overcast afternoon in front of an 8,150 strong crowd. Hoddle and Waddle started yet again, and Aston Villa's Steve Hodge came in to replace Bryan Robson. Striker Gary Lineker had come back into the team up front and alongside Mark Hateley.

An uninteresting game ensued. Mainly focused on getting the win whilst keeping style and shape but crucially, hoping that no one picked up an injury. England won the game 1-0. The goal came from Hoddle's free kick that the keeper parried into the path of Steve Hodge who set up Hateley for the winner.

England heading for the win but not long after the goal, Gary Lineker was involved in an innocuous collision that saw Lineker stay down. England physio, Fred Street, ran on to assess. Lineker was rolling around on the turf clutching his wrist, he looked in considerable pain! The BBC were covering the game and Barry Davies, in his inimitable voice, commented that the England physio looked very concerned.

Lineker's game was over. At this point there was major concern Lineker wouldn't be able to play at all in the World Cup which was to begin for England in 10 days' time. England had won their qualifying group and had scored 21 goals along the way. But, even though Lineker was the number one striker choice for Bobby Robson, he did not score the most goals in qualifying. Bryan Robson topped with five goals with Hateley and Lineker both on three, along with Tony Woodcock who failed to make the squad despite scoring three qualifying goals.

The squad headed to Mexico and Spurs' England contingent had all contributed and played well.

JUNE 1986

Despite Pleat's TV commitments in Mexico, he clearly did not neglect his new role at Tottenham. Before leaving for Mexico there were some key conversations that he needed to have with some players that would be pivotal in the season to come. One such player was Clive Allen.

Clive had joined Spurs for £700,000 from QPR in the summer of 1984. He was now 25-years-old and Spurs were the fifth London club he had played for in his career to date. There was always a connection for Clive at Spurs as his father, Les, was one of the Spurs 1960-61 double winning team.

His first two seasons were frustrating, with a lack of consistency and injury being key factors as to him maybe not living up to his own, and the fans, expectations of him. 1984-85 season Allen struck seven goals in 13 games and in 1985-86 he struck nine goals in 19 games. However, he did hit five goals in his last three games of the 85-86 season so hopefully a sign of things to come.

Speaking with Clive he talks about the moment his relationship began with David Pleat. He refers to a telephone call he received from Pleat asking him how he was going to spend his summer. Clive told Pleat that he was going to train every day. Pleat asked him not to do that, the pre-season was ten weeks long due to the World Cup, so he didn't want Clive to burn out. He wanted Clive to start no more than three weeks before they officially came back.

Clive mentions that Pleat was correct. Despite battling injuries and coming back into some form by the end of the season, he did need a break. He ended up training four weeks before pre-season training officially started.

This small piece of man-management by Pleat had tremendous results as Clive would go on to have the most successful season of his career.

On the back page of the June 1986 edition of the *Spurs News* newspaper, Pleat stated that he and his coach, Trevor Hartley, had spoken to all the players telling them that they did need a break and there would be more than enough time to get ready for the 1986-87 season.

Hartley said, "Our feeling is that the five weeks that we will have together will give us plenty of time". He went on to say, "We want the players to recharge their batteries, so we have told them we'd prefer them to have a rest".

Pre-season would start on Monday 21st of July 1986. If England were successful in reaching the World Cup Final, that game would be held on Sunday 29th June 1986 which was still three weeks before pre-season commenced.

Another player who experienced the 'man-management' side of David Pleat was Graham Roberts. Sadly, this did not seem to have the same positive effect that Pleat had on Clive Allen.

Speaking to the '*Spurs Show LIVE*' podcast in 2018, Roberts recalled the moment he received a phone call from David Pleat. Roberts said his wife told him David Pleat was on the phone. He had never spoken to Pleat before this point. Roberts took the call and stated that Pleat's opening words were, "As soon as I get the right offer, you are being sold". No hello, or any opening pleasantries at all. Roberts' reply was short, sharp and sweet. He replied: "Bollocks" and put the phone down.

Pleat called back immediately and told him to not put the phone down on your new manager and with that, Roberts' reply was, "You won't be for long" and hung up again. Roberts then joked that they did have a good relationship as he did not like me, and I didn't like him!

Concluding that second call, Roberts turned to his wife and told her he felt that Pleat wanted him out and they would not be going on holiday anymore. He was going to work hard during the summer and get as fit as he'd ever been. Roberts stated he trained nearly every single day that summer before pre-season would officially start and even dragged Tony Galvin out on some runs with him too.

Speaking with Pleat his recollection of that call was slightly different. Pleat feels that he would not have used that type of language but essentially, he knew that Roberts was a very strong character in the Spurs dressing room.

Roberts said pre-season went very well and it was Trevor Hartley who wanted to play him in the middle of midfield. Roberts mentioned, as the season went on, he would always room with Chris Waddle and Pleat would ask Waddle to relay messages to Roberts. This clearly annoyed both Waddle and Roberts.

It was now a few weeks into Pleat's tenure and it is fair to say that some players have had a strong opening gambit with Pleat, while others had not. One thing we always need to be clear about is this, certain players suit certain managers. New managers come in and have their own ideas around style, tactics and ultimately personnel. Roberts is perhaps someone who didn't fit the Pleat mould.

Pleat had mentioned an early conversation he had held with the great Bill Nicholson. Pleat is very keen to point out how astute Bill Nicolson was, and this very conversation could've been a catalyst as to why Roberts may not have fitted into Pleat's plans.

Pleat said, "Bill Nicholson was very, very clever. And Bill said to me one day, and very cleverly; 'Do you think the centre backs give away too many free kicks?' In fact, he meant 'foul too much'. Anyway, what he was trying to say to me was he thought that Roberts and Miller had a very good relationship as a centre back pairing. Yes, they were very good together. But times were moving on and Bill was right that they did give away quite a few free kicks. They were both very tough players. And so, I did. I decided then that I needed to bring in a younger quicker one".

Pleat wanted to move Gary Mabbutt back into the centre of defence and to play alongside him Pleat had thought of another defender that would fit the bill perfectly. A couple of options had been discussed with the Irving Scholar but nothing was to materialise until the World Cup had concluded.

* * * *

Most things at White Hart Lane were now on hold as the 1986 World Cup in Mexico had finally begun. The tournament kicked off with a drab 1-1 draw between the holders Italy and Bulgaria. England's first game was on Tuesday 3rd of June 1986. The day before that match, England's other opponents in Group F, Morocco and Poland, kicked off their tournament with a tedious 0-0 draw in the Estadio Universitario, San Nicolas De Los Garza. England were firm favourites to not only get out of the group but to progress to the latter stages of the tournament.

It was now matchday and England took to the field, at the Estadio Tecnológico in Monterrey, to face their European opponents Portugal. Amazingly both Bryan Robson and Gary Lineker were fit and famously Lineker seen wearing an 'approved' cast to protect his damaged wrist. More importantly the Spurs duo of Glenn Hoddle and Chris Waddle were included in the line up too. Hopes were high.

A pretty poor game unfolded with a quiet first half but in the second half, England missed a host of good chances as Lineker, Hateley and Robson saw chances go begging. Then with 15 minutes to go, the ever dependant Arsenal left-back Kenny

Sansom made an uncharacteristic error that allowed a Portuguese cross to be met by Carlos Manuel to tuck home for 1-0 to Portugal.

With 11 minutes to go, Hodge and Beardsley came on for Robson and Waddle, respectively, but to no avail.

England had lost their opener. In a post-match interview Bobby Robson was honest in describing it as a 'shocking start'. A disaster, well that's exactly how the British press saw it with the *Daily Mirror* running the headline, 'WORLD CUP WALLIES'.

With England disappointing in Monterrey, nearly 600 miles south Alex Ferguson was about to lead Scotland into their opening game against Denmark. Ferguson's team included some talented players along with the new Glasgow Rangers player-manager, Graeme Souness. and Dundee United's Richard Gough. Ferguson had a strong outfit but boy was he in a tough group.

One of the tournament favourites West Germany along with two-time winners Uruguay were in Scotland's group along with their first opponents Denmark. Denmark had a wonderful team, and this tournament was about to showcase why.

Scotland lost 1-0 to the Danes. No great shame in that result as Denmark were an excellent side but they faced Germany next, so they now very much needed a result.

Three days after the Portugal debacle, England were back at the Estadio Tecnológico in Monterrey to face Morocco. Surely things will be put right today.

Bobby Robson had named an unchanged team. Everton's Lineker and AC Milan's Hateley led the line again, goals were a must. ITV covered the game. Commentator was Martin Tyler, and his co-commentator was Spurs' new manager, David Pleat.

Another dire game unfolded. The Spurs duo Hoddle and Waddle toiled, but it was another day of limited rewards. The game finished 0-0 but it will be remembered for two key factors that happened within five minutes of each other. In the 38th minute, skipper Bryan Robson had gone down again. His midfield peer, Ray Wilkins, ran over to him as he knew it was not looking good. Within minutes Robson was not only up on his feet but he was trudging off the field of play yet again. Nursing his shoulder in the exact same way he did when he came off against Mexico a few weeks before in Los Angeles.

Steve Hodge came on for Robson. But moments later it was disaster. Wilkins got a yellow card, for tussling with a Moroccan midfielder, and then one minute later was sent off for dissent having thrown the ball at the referee unhappy at the decision just made. Spurs' Gary Stevens came on for Mark Hateley with 15 minutes to go to probably preserve the draw and take a point.

Stevens recalls this moment when he made his World Cup debut. "Robson told me, on you go, you've gotta do a job for the team. You've got good legs and you're a good athlete. Protect the back four and break up play". Stevens knew his task, no goals were conceded so he did do his job, but sadly, England were further in the mire.

The British tabloids went into dramatic overdrive as a return of one point from two games was not good at all. Up next were Poland and they were arguably the sternest opponent in the group for England too, but England now had five days to regroup and try and work on a formula that could see them not only win a game but to progress on to the next phase too.

Two days later, Scotland faced West Germany in Queretaro. Gordon Strachan of Manchester United put the Scots ahead after 18 minutes but the West Germans equalised a few minutes later and then went 2-1 up early in the second half. Two losses and home time beckoned for Ferguson's squad.

However, more importantly, on the same day and in the same group, the world witnessed one of the finest footballing displays at a World Cup Finals. It was the day the 'Dazzling Danes' completely dismantled the South American champions Uruguay. Uruguay had won the Copa America in 1983 and were then to retain that title a year later in 1987. No mean feat when you also have Argentina and Brazil in the same competition. But on this day, they were given a Danish lesson not to forget.

Personally, I was captivated watching this Danish side. I loved their kit too. Not only was their kit made by Hummel, who made Tottenham's kits, but it added aesthetic to their 'Dazzling Danes' tag. A tag that combined their wonderful footballing style with the wonderful red and white kits.

Enzo Francescoli who was Uruguay's main man. He was known as '*El Príncipe*' – The Prince. He had just won the Golden Boot in Argentina and was now leading Uruguay in their World Cup adventure. They had drawn 1-1 with West Germany in their opening game and they seemed ready to face the Europeans.

The next 90 minutes would shatter Francescoli and his team as Denmark ran out 6-1 winners.

Over the years I have taken pleasure in re-watching this game and, at the time, Denmark were my favourites to go on and win the World Cup…after England of course.

On Sunday 8th of June 1986, ITV broadcasted this wonderful game with John Helm commentating. Preben Elkjær opened the scoring for Denmark after 10 minutes. Søren Lerby made it 2-0 before Francescoli scored a penalty for Uruguay to make it 2-1 at half time. Second half the Danes kicked into top gear. Michael Laudrup was Denmark's brilliant number 10 who played for Juventus in Italy. In the 52nd minute he dribbled through the Uruguayan defence with consummate ease to score one of the best world cup goals of all time. Elkjær scored two more to complete his hat-trick and Manchester United's Jesper Olsen finished off the rout late on. What a performance and what a footballing spectacle.

Other than that, there were no huge shock results to the big teams. Apart from England's limp start.

Wednesday 11th of June 1986 was the day of reckoning for Bobby Robson and his team. A positive result was needed. With results in the group landing as they did, England knew a victory would take them through. Simple, eh?

Out went Wilkins (suspended), Robson (injured) and Hateley and Waddle were dropped for Beardsley and Hodge respectively. Two Evertonians came in too, Peter Reid and Trevor Steven.

Waddle had started nearly every game for England during the last year. In Waddle's 1997 biography, written by Mel Stein, Waddle mentions the moment he found out he'd been left out of the team. It states that Bobby Robson did not want Chris to feel he had been dropped and explained it was a tactical decision. Choosing Steven, Hodge and Reid allowed only Hoddle to be the playmaker and Beardsley as the link man. Waddle would've been understanding of this and highlighted Robson's 'kindly' approach. Which essentially highlights one of the reasons that Robson was one of the best 'man-managers' around.

Poland was a dangerous side who possessed one of the best attackers throughout Europe in Zbigniew Boniek. Boniek had played a pivotal part in Juventus' domestic and European successes in the last few seasons, but he was now out of contract and soon to join Roma.

However, in the spring of 1986 Spurs were on the verge of a double signing that would've eclipsed our Argentinian double swoop of Ardiles and Villa in 1978. The March 1986 edition of the *Spurs News* newspaper were able to exclusively reveal that Spurs were so terribly close in bringing Boniek to White Hart

Lane when his contract expired. The other part of the swoop also included Michel Platini. Yes, that's right, Platini. France's skipper and Juventus play maker was planning on moving to Tottenham Hotspur FC. John Fennelly edited Spurs' newspaper and on the back page of that edition he exclusively revealed that the chase for Platini started 18 months before when Irving Scholar jokingly asked Platini, on Italian TV, to move to Spurs.

A move was progressing but when Spurs contacted Platini again in October 1985, he had a change of heart with the player admitting "Brussels was playing on his mind". He was referring to the Heysel Stadium disaster when many fans lost their lives during the European Cup Final between Liverpool and Juventus. Soon afterwards he re-signed for Juventus for another year and an option for one more after that. In the end, Platini stayed at Juve until the summer of 1987 when he retired from football. Scholar believes had the Brussels tragedy not happened then Platini would have joined Spurs after this World Cup.

Scholar was confident that Spurs were at the front of a queue of clubs looking to take Platini as well as his teammate Boniek who he feels would have followed suit. Sadly, things slowed down a little and Italian side AS Roma made an offer that, according to Scholar, no English club could compete with. Both deals were now gone, but we dare to dream don't we.

Even with the brilliant Boniek lining up for Poland, England were out of the blocks early.

Where they had struggled to score in the two previous games, England were 3-0 up within the first 36 minutes. All three goals scored by Gary Lineker. Everton's Gary Stevens and Trevor Steven, along with Villa's Steve Hodge, all assisted Lineker and England deservedly gained all the points and ultimately, progression to the next round.

Spurs' Waddle came on as a 75th minute sub for Beardsley and Gary Stevens was an unused sub. Hoddle was sat in the middle of midfield pulling the strings. Without Robson and Wilkins, Hoddle was allowed that freedom as the industrious Reid, Steven and Hodge worked tirelessly alongside him to consolidate England's midfield dominance.

* * * *

Things were still ticking along back at White Hart Lane during June 1986 too. The club had announced they had sold the Cheshunt training ground in a deal worth £4.9m for residential development. New sites for a training complex were being considered but nothing concrete yet.

The club were also undertaking huge investment on the pitch too, not with the playing staff but with the playing surface. A new undersoil heating system was being installed which would work in conjunction with the existing system. Around 20 miles of 'virtually indestructible' cable was being laid 10 inches below the White Hart Lane turf. It was a system developed in Sweden and recently installed at Everton's Goodison Park and Manchester City's Maine Road stadiums.

There was also a notable departure too. A fee had been agreed with Norwich City for the sale of Ian Crook. He was a cultured midfielder right out of the Spurs mould. He joined in 1979 and turned professional in 1980. He had 20 senior appearances to his name and was part of many successful South-East Counties and Football Combination Spurs teams. He teamed up with former Spurs players Ian Culverhouse and Garry Brooke at Carrow Road. Crook spoke to *Spurs News* and admitted, "The fact I am no longer a Spurs player is taking his time to sink in. I am sorry to leave but I am joining a club that looks to be going places".

It is always sorry for players as talented as Crook move on, but Norwich's new signing would go on to have an excellent season for his new club.

* * * *

It was Wednesday 18th of June 1986. A week had passed since England's fine win over Poland. England had now travelled to the Mexican capital to face Paraguay in the Second Round. They were playing in the Aztec Stadium which can hold around 100,000 people. The stakes were rising and now it was time for knock-out football.

The afternoon sun shone as the players lined up for their respective national anthems. A crowd of 98,728 spectators were ready to witness South Americans take on the Europeans.

Hoddle started once again; Spurs' Stevens was on the bench but no place at all for Chris Waddle.

The game was dominated by England. Lineker put England 1-0 up after 32 minutes when a Hoddle cross was missed by the

Everton frontman, but then hit straight back into Lineker's path by Kenny Sansom who watched Lineker open the scoring. West Ham's Alvin Martin nearly made it 2-0 with a wonderful diving header from a delicious left wing free kick from Hoddle.

Beardsley made it 2-0 after 56 minutes when a Hoddle corner found Terry Butcher whose shot was saved and parried to the welcoming Newcastle striker. Spurs' Gary Stevens came on as a 58th minute substitute for Peter Reid. Reid was looking quite laboured, so Stevens' energy was a superb tonic for England.

Then on 73 minutes England made it 3-0 with the goal of the game, and it was made straight out of Tottenham. Hoddle was in a central position around 20 yards outside of the Paraguay box. With a superb pass using the outside of his left foot he released Spurs' Gary Stevens who had burst forward into the right side of their opponents' penalty area. Steven's swift, right-footed cross found Lineker perfectly to slot home for his second of the game. A glorious goal.

This was a consecutive 3-0 win for England and Hoddle was revelling in this role. England were getting the best out of him.

Also evident after this victory was the blossoming partnership between Beardsley and Lineker. Hodge had been superb on the left side too with the *Mirror's* Harry Miller highlighting that it would be a major mistake to re-shape the midfield in bringing back Wilkins or even a fit Bryan Robson.

Inevitably there would also be talk of the Falklands War that had raged four years before this tournament. Stakes would be high for both teams but, with a slight political agenda bubbling under the surface, it was not at all surprising to see newspapers in both the England and Argentina making connections with that military conflict back and this massive World Cup encounter. In future interviews, various Argentinian players revealed that large levels of motivation for this game was fuelled by seeking revenge for some of those tragic events back in 1982.

Spurs midfielder Gary Stevens clearly sees this moment as the highlight of his international career. Coming on in the knock-out phase and assisting the goal of the game, good times indeed. But I asked him how he felt his chances were being included for the Quarter-Final against Argentina seeing as Peter Reid was looking quite laboured and then replaced by him with over half-an-hour to go.

"Reid was an excellent player, make no mistake about it, he was an excellent player. But Don Howe and Bobby Robson did come and speak to me about man-marking Maradona. They wanted to know had I ever done a man-marking job before? In today's football, the statistics and analytics would have given them that information but, at the time, I do not think there was anyone fitter than me or able to cover more ground to do that job. Maybe my namesake, Gary Stevens at Everton who was a great athlete. But Peter had a slight injury and, in all honesty, I am expecting to play against Argentina because he wasn't fully fit".

But Stevens is not bitter or regretful and concluded, "For whatever reason, Bobby went with the senior players, and to some extent, there was a bit of senior player power there at the time".

With that conversation giving him a touch of hope for a starting place it was not the greatest shock that Bobby Robson did stick with Reid in the middle of midfield alongside Hoddle when the game was played a few days later.

The BBC covered this game and host Des Lynam spoke directly to England and Manchester United legend Bobby Charlton who was speaking from inside the packed Azteca stadium. Charlton felt that this game would genuinely be considered as one of the greatest games in football's sporting history. He was not wrong. This game was to be an epic encounter that is still talked about for so many reasons years and years later.

It was Sunday 22nd of June 1986 and over 114,000 people had crammed into the Estadio Azteca to watch South America's last hope of staying in the tournament. With it being blazingly hot we would not expect and hugely energetic game but more of an encounter of attrition. Argentina were slight favourites going into the game, but England were now starting to put some consistently good performances together.

Spurs' Gary Stevens, Chris Waddle and John Barnes were first to emerge from the tunnel before Robson strode without with his usual beaming smile but more of a pensive focus. The dugout offered little or no shelter at all so the sun was going to be oppressive for all involved.

As the teams came out, BBC commentator Barry Davies quoted Maradona's wish that all supporters would forget politics and support the two fine teams about to contest this match. Davies applied a touch more context when he told viewers Maradona had since mentioned the wonderful support he received at White Hart Lane from over 30,000 fans at Ossie Ardiles' benefit match.

So, would politics really be cast aside in Maradona's mind?

The teams lined up, Maradona and goalkeeper Pumpido ostentatiously eyeing up their European opponents who were to their left as the national anthems belted out.

In Hoddle's 2021 auto-biography '*Playmaker*', he recalls the wonderful night at White Hart Lane during the Ardiles game and tells of how well he and Maradona gelled that evening. He then goes on to say that lining up in this game, he and Maradona shared a nod in the tunnel as a sign of respect before they went out to compete.

But now, all eyes were on the centre circle to begin with, as matchday referee Ali Bennaceur from Tunisia oversaw Peter Shilton and Diego Maradona shaking hands. It was all smiles at this point. It is safe to say, Shilton would never throw a smile in Maradona's direction ever again after today's events unfolded.

During the first half, the game was not a great spectacle of football and it seemed to be more of a cagey affair. However, QPR defender Terry Fenwick's early yellow card after nine minutes would possibly be a pivotal moment as the game wore on.

The second half was a completely different story.

Six minutes after the restart, Maradona picked up the ball in the middle of England's half. He floated past Hoddle with ease, Peter Reid didn't seem to offer a challenge as he wove through, and this pulled both Fenwick and Butcher out of position to put pressure on Maradona. The diminutive Argentinian then played the ball into Jorge Valdano whose inept first touch saw the ball leap up and England's Steve Hodge tried to clear. Hodge's attempted clearance looped up high towards the penalty spot rather than clearing the danger and with Fenwick and Butcher out of the way, Maradona sprints through to challenge the high ball with Peter Shilton.

Pause.

The next passage of play is now arguably one of the most talked about moments in the history of Association Football. By pausing the scene here, most football supporters around the world would give odds in favour of England keeper Peter Shilton. Yes, he may have run out a bit slowly for some people, but he should still have the ability to jump and extend his arm and fist to punch the ball clear.

As we move it frame by frame, we can see Shilton is beaten in the air by a man of five feet five inches in height but with the leap of a salmon. Run the moment at normal speed and to the naked eye it kind of seems that he has headed it just before Shilton could get there, but your mind is also thinking; did he use his hand there? Even BBC commentator Barry Davies' first response was to highlight that there was an offside appeal being made by the England players, rather than hand ball.

In a split second, the balls trickles into the England goal and Maradona lands to the ground and looks around. He then sprints off thinking, I'll have some of that! Only Terry Fenwick and Peter Shilton seem to be remonstrating at what had happened, the Tunisian referee appears to give the goal immediately without looking to his Bulgarian linesman, who did not flag, and watched Maradona run to celebrate his goal with the fans behind where he was standing, flag still down.

Personally, I do not think Maradona planned for this to happen and it was a spur of the moment thing. Poor officiating allowed this injustice.

Linesman Bogdan Dochev died in 2017. *The Sun* newspaper journalist Neil Syson reported that Dochev "did" see it and the Bulgarian mentioned this revelation in a never-published interview. Apparently, Dochev went on to say that the referee did not ask for his opinion. In this alleged interview, Dochev stated that he felt Maradona was, "a great player, but a dishonourable man".

Some England players who experienced this moment on that day have moved on. However, the England keeper and captain that day, Peter Shilton, is still vocal to this day about the injustice.

So, if that goal on 51 minutes was controversial then the next goal of the game was a little bit mind-blowing.

We will start by saying that the England team were probably a little annoyed and a bit shell-shocked at the first goal but four minutes later we were able to witness Maradona's real genius rising to the top.

In the 55th minute it happened.

A touch of controversy again though. While BBC co-commentator, Jimmy Hill, was offering up the point that the England captain was not quick enough off his line for the first goal, the viewers could see that England were moving forward. A swift ball into Beardsley was played back to Hoddle, several yards in the Argentine half, who then attempted a first-time pass to Hodge who was pelting forward on his left. As he made this pass he was clattered into by an Argentinian player. It was right under the referee's nose whose hand signal gestured for Hoddle to get up. Hoddle was now on the ground and a free kick should have been awarded. However, it was not and then followed ten seconds of brilliance.

Of all the different commentary that was broadcasted on this goal, for me, *BBC Radio* commenter Bryon Butler's narration was the best. He describes beautifully how Maradona runs half the length of the pitch, easing past England's midfielders and defenders to slip the ball under Shilton for a 2-0 lead.

Butler's exquisite commentary begins as soon as Maradona gets the ball. "*Maradona turns like a little eel and comes away from trouble, little squat man comes inside Butcher and leaves him for dead, outside Fenwick and leaves him for dead and puts the ball away, and that is why Maradona is the greatest player in the world! He buried the English defence. He picked up that ball 40 yards out, it's a goal of great quality scored by a player of the greatest quality. It's England nil, Argentina two. The first goal should never have been allowed but Maradona has put a seal on his greatness and left his thumbprint on this World Cup"*.

It was a fantastic goal and the Sunday evening viewers in the UK had been stunned whilst watching several minutes of crazy but brilliant football.

Watching it again, we do see an obvious foul on Hoddle just before Maradona gets the ball. However, if we are critical of Shilton being slow for the first goal, then I think it is fair to say Maradona turning away from Peter Reid so easily was just as lamentable. Reid looked knackered as he failed miserably to not just challenge Maradona but to even track back. Butcher had been pulled into central midfield because of Reid's slowness and when Maradona went past him Butcher did ridiculously well to chase back while Maradona skipped past Fenwick. Fenwick was already on a yellow card and, in normal circumstances, you'd expect Fenwick to haul him down. But he probably would have been sent off.

Whilst Butcher gets back, he is the wrong side of Maradona and Shilton offers little protection as Maradona slides the ball underneath him into the empty net that Everton's Gary Stevens so nearly gets back for.

Would Maradona have scored that with Spurs' Gary Stevens negating him and chasing him down? Would Fenwick have received a red card if he pulled him down outside the box? Just like the Hoddle foul, we will never know.

But here we had a guy who had graced White Hart Lane seven weeks earlier and today it was a case of Beauty & The Beast with Maradona's goals.

Robson made two changes not long afterwards bringing on the wide attacking threats of John Barnes and Chris Waddle. With nine minutes left, Barnes skipped down Argentina's right flank and floated in a wonderful cross for Lineker to pull one back. Not long after that goal, Barnes replicated that very move and floated in another cross for Lineker, who looked dead cert to score, only for the ball to be cleared unbelievably well by Argentina. Still to this day that clearance defies logic.

Maradona and Argentina held on to win 2-1. Jubilant scenes in the Aztec Stadium for the winners, but immediately afterwards Bobby Robson aired his dismay at Maradona's first goal when interviewed on BBC he stated, "one is a dubious goal, and one is a miracle".

England were now on their way home. The newspaper headlines were surely to highlight the obvious. In the *Daily Mail*, Jeff Powell's account of the game was headlined with, "HAND IT TO DIEGO! - England KO'd by the punch that mattered". Powell reported that Shilton was terribly upset by Maradona's first goal and that the Argentine boss, Carlos Bilardo, claiming that he did not see the incident on TV and therefore declined to comment further.

That goal was soon labelled, 'The Hand of God' as Maradona had claimed some divine intervention was the reason that happened. Despite Maradona's greatness, that phrase followed him for the rest of his life.

Over the years Maradona has kept politics in when referring to that game. According to notable South American football journalist, Tim Vickery, he sees his first goal as "We're smarter than the English" and his second goal as "We're better than the English". Even over the years, Maradona has been bullish in not apologising claiming that it was "symbolic revenge" for the Falklands War.

Regardless, there were two sides of Diego Maradona. One side was not very nice at all, and the other side was that of a footballing genius.

Maradona went on to demolish Belgium in the World Cup semi-final. Scoring both goals in a 2-0 win setting up final with 1982 finalist's West Germany.

The West Germans shackled Maradona well in that final. Argentina went 2-0 up before the European side levelled it at 2-2. It was Maradona's brilliance that set up the final attack for Argentina's third and winning goal that made us all realise that he truly was world class. He was now a World Cup winning captain. And let's be honest, his team were not that great in comparison to the footballing delights seen in that tournament. Denmark, Brazil, France, Belgium and the West Germans had arguably 'better' teams, but Argentina won it.

Yes, the tournament had seen Maradona provide numerous memorable moments but, despite departing at the Quarter-

Final stage, England were able to boast the most lethal marksman of the tournament. Everton's Gary Lineker finished on six goals ahead of three players who finished with five each, Brazil's Careca, Spain's Butrageuno and of course, Diego Maradona.

As the world left Mexico'86, it was safe to say it was a thoroughly enjoyable tournament. Not long after the tournament concluded I obtained a copy of '*HERO*'. This was FIFA's official world cup film. Watching slow motion footage of Maradona was mesmerising. The film was narrated by Michael Caine and focused on various other World Cup games during that tournament. But, for me, the best game of the tournament, after Uruguay's hiding by Denmark, was the Brazil and France Quarter-Final encounter. 1-1 in normal time then extra-time and penalties. It was an epic game with Brazilians Careca, Zico, Socrates and Frenchmen Platini, Tigana, Giresse all contributing to a dramatic match that was finally won by Luiz Fernandez's penalty shoot-out winner.

* * * *

I have been a fan of Maradona since then. Despite his handball, I thought he was sublime.

My final point on Diego is this. Well, two points. Firstly, he is the Greatest of all Time. The success he had with Argentina and Napoli was unique. He wasn't in a team of *Galactico's*, but he was the driving force in gaining World, European and Domestic successes. The fact that he performed during an era when pitches were generally poor, and he had next to zero protection from the officials, is astounding. Players today get afforded a lot more luxuries, but I do very much understand generational context needs to be considered.

It is hard to separate him from Pele, but maybe I have done so as watching Maradona during that period was quite influential on a teenage boy who was so engrossed in football. Even nowadays, you can find footage of Pele doing things that Cruyff, Zidane, Messi and Cristiano Ronaldo were well known for. Pele was the original King, but I think Maradona tips the balance - for me, anyway.

Like my Jimmy Greaves statement - I believe players like Greaves and Maradona would thrive beyond belief in today's game.

My second point is this: Tottenham Hotspur and Diego Maradona. Maradona had an affinity and a respect for Ossie Ardiles. Like the closeness of a respected older brother and the fact that he was so well received by Spurs fans in early May 1986 also helped. But if it were not for the 'Hand of God' goal and the fact that there was a European ban on English teams during the next few years then I believe Maradona would have found a welcoming home at White Hart Lane. It is also well known that Ardiles tried to sign Maradona when he became Spurs manager in the 1990's, but the deal fizzled out and luckily for Spurs they managed to capture Jurgen Klinsmann instead, who as we remember did not turn out too bad at all.

Spurs have always had a strong connection with Argentinian players, and this would have been no different. Maradona to Spurs would've been a stunning coup and who knows what level of success the club would have had.

But now, with the World Cup over for another four years, it was time for the England squad to return home with the Spurs' contingent taking a well-deserved break in readiness for next season.

June was drawing to its conclusion and, with July on the horizon, preparations would now be underway for the domestic campaign to resume. Pleat's right-hand man, Trevor Hartley, was pivotal in the planning of pre-season training which was due to commence in the third week of July. Hartley told *Spurs News*, "Starting back on the 21st of July is good for us as it gives us five weeks together before the season really starts".

JULY 1986

The Spurs players who had represented England went on holiday soon after the World Cup exit and sometimes players may not get back up to the same fitness levels of their teammates when they eventually join pre-season training.

After the 1982 World Cup, Spurs only had two players in the England Squad, Ray Clemence and Glenn Hoddle. Clem was an unused substitute throughout. Hoddle started in the Group win over Kuwait and came off the bench in the Group win over Czechoslovakia. Not great demands were asked of them, so they returned to the 1982 pre-season relatively fresh.

Spurs started the 1982-83 season in decent form with four wins, one draw and two defeats in the first seven games.

This time around, Hoddle had played in all of England's World Cup games while Waddle and Stevens both had decent involvement too. Again, nothing too strenuous for a squad but still relative fatigue for those involved. No other Spurs player represented any other nation at the Mexico World Cup, but that's not to say any of Pleat's potential new signings would not have been in Mexico.

As Pleat mentioned to Irving Scholar on arrival as new manager, he wanted to use his involvement with ITV in Mexico to run the rule over any potential transfer targets. Pleat wanted to shop in this window as he felt value in recruiting players of certain quality, status and experience.

At the turn of June and into July, most players were off on holiday knowing pre-season training would commence on the 21st of July.

Spurs had announced a string of pre-season friendlies that would be played during the weeks leading up to the opening league fixture on Saturday 23rd August 1986. Spurs' first friendly was the Testimonial match for Paul Miller. Glasgow Rangers would be visiting White Hart Lane on Saturday 2nd August 1986.

* * * *

Part of any successful professional football club is their youth system and framework. There were players in Spurs' current first team that were products of that youth development. Chris Hughton, Paul Miller, Mark Falco and Glenn Hoddle had all been important players during the FA Cup and UEFA Cup successes several years before.

Evidence that there was still talent coming through was showcased in February 1986. Spurs travelled to Hillsborough to take on Sheffield Wednesday. Wednesday were having a good season despite Spurs beating them 5-1 at White Hart Lane in September 1985. Spurs had lost five and drawn one of their last six league games going into this fixture, but alarmingly, they had not scored a solitary goal during the last 450 minutes of League football either.

Youth talent David Howells steps into the fray. Today most Spurs fans will no doubt remember Howellsy being part of the 1991 FA Cup winning team. More specifically, as a midfielder in that successful team. But Howells began his Spurs tenure within the youth/reserve team set-up as a striker.

So much so, he was drafted into the Sheffield Wednesday game as a striker, wearing the number nine shirt and lining up alongside Mark Falco. A cold and snowy Hillsborough was the scene of his senior league debut for the club he joined as an apprentice in the early 1980's. Nothing better than making your professional debut but the fairy-tale continued as he ended up scoring the winning goal in a 2-1 victory. Paul Allen, playing as a right back, produced a buccaneering run and his cross reached the penalty spot to find a perfectly timed Howells run. He did not break stride and struck the ball into the bottom right-hand corner.

Cue the celebrations! Falco, Waddle, Stevens and Chiedozie all racing to embrace him as Howells stood there, arms aloft, taking in the moment. Now I am not sure if this ruins the moment, or perhaps enhances it, but Danny Thomas runs all the way from left-back to plant a smacker on Howells' lips. A moment never to be forgotten for Howells in so many ways.

So, with Howells making a stunning debut as an 18-year-old, another player who had been in the reserve set up for some time was Welshman Mark Bowen. Mark was now 23, he had made his Spurs debut in the 1983-84 season playing seven times. He played six times during the 1984-85 season and during the 1985-86 season he played only a couple of games. However, several weeks after Howells had scored on his debut Bowen grabbed his first ever league goal in the 4-1 home win against Leicester City in April 1986.

Among football fans, Mark Bowen is more well known for being a progressive left-back that had years at Norwich City FC. During his time in Spurs' youth/reserve set up Bowen was an attacking midfielder that would score twenty-plus goals every season. Howells was the same, both scoring for fun.

Spurs' last trophy was the wonderful UEFA Cup win over Anderlecht in 1984. That team included Mark Bowen on the bench for the 2nd leg. Over both legs it included many players who had hailed from Spurs' youth system. Tony Parks, Chris Hughton, Steve Perryman, Paul Miller, Micky Hazard and Mark Falco. In both games Ally Dick, Richard Cooke and Ian Culverhouse all featured on the substitutes bench. That is a total of nine players who had risen from the ranks and contributed to Spurs winning a European trophy. A feat that has still yet to be achieved again 40 years later.

The reserve team this season boasted some brilliant young players. One who had already lined up alongside the great Diego Maradona was of course Vinny Samways.

During the summer of 1986, David Howells and Vinny Samways were part of an England youth Under 18 squad that was to tour China. They were also included with other Spurs starlets, two central defenders, John Polston and Neil Ruddock. Ruddock was a larger-than-life, tough-tackling centre back with a gifted left foot. John Polston played alongside Ruddock and formed a super partnership in the reserve team. Polston was a sleek, pacey and great footballing defender that complimented Ruddock's style. Polston pulled out due to injury.

A great experience for the Spurs youngsters and recognition for being some of the best players within the English youth system.

Speaking to David Howells was a pleasure, and I will be honest in saying he was pivotal in arranging my conversations with many other Spurs players too, when carrying out my research for this book. Still an ambassador at Tottenham he recalls his youth days vividly and, of course, his debut goal at Hillsborough terribly well.

"I was full of excitement for that season (86-87). It was my first year as a professional and a big step up going into 'mens' football. I remember thinking I'd had a great debut and I was sub during the next match as key players were now fit again. That was against Liverpool, who won, but we played really well. The team went on a good run for the rest of that season, and I didn't get another look in, so I wasn't expecting to be part of the first team set-up in 1986-87".

Howells was realistic in his assessment, "The first team group was full of great quality and with a new manager coming in they're always going to sign new players and it felt at the time Spurs were in the market for strikers, which was my position. It was a case of cementing my place further into the reserves, making sure I was first choice in the reserves and if anything happened in the first team I'd be knocking at the door".

Howells obviously buoyed by his debut had a very mature outlook to consider when his time would come. He recalls attending the 'Maradona' game at White Hart Lane before heading off to China with the England under 18's.

Howells spoke of his productive relationship with Mark Bowen, both scoring plenty of goals in a successful reserve team, "He's a great lad Mark, he had an incredible season in the reserves that year and he knew he wasn't really going to break into the first team that much which made him consider his future". Howells jokingly continued, "I still joke that I got him that move to Norwich because of the sheer number of goals we were involved in together".

Bowen stayed at White Hart Lane for the 1986-87 season before moving to Norwich in the summer of 1987. The attacking midfielder is then turned into a left-back at Carrow Road. So, how did Howells make the novation from striker to the defensive midfielder we know from his 335 first team appearances for Spurs?

"I was always an attacking player from the day I joined from my school, district and club teams. But I was always a midfielder as that's where the best players tended to play when they are at that level. But Spurs always regarded me as a striker from when I joined as an Under 12".

"The change happened a couple of seasons later when I was around 20. We had a reserve team game at Arsenal and the reserve manager, Doug Livermore, was short in midfield and asked me if I could play there. I told him that I was actually a midfielder, and I pretty much ran that game and stayed there ever since. Even when playing under Terry Venables, he liked my versatility in being able to play all roles across the midfield when required".

Doug Livermore was the reserve team coach at Tottenham Hotspur. A Liverpudlian who had a superb relationship with the younger players and had a great gift at developing them too.

Livermore had joined the Welsh national team touring party of Canada as coach that summer. That squad also included Spurs' reserve team talent, Mark Bowen - good experience for the young midfielder.

Howells emits a warm tone when speaking of Livermore, "Doug was brilliant. It was a bit of a thankless task being reserve team manager because you have talented young players then you have the likes of Paul 'Maxi' Miller and Chris Hughton who spent time in the reserves that year. Chrissy was brilliant and Maxi was fantastic. You know the first teamers obviously don't want to be there, but they were brilliant with the young players. But Doug, was brilliant at managing those players. He spoke to them in the right way with a massive amount of respect for them and their respective careers".

Howells openly says; "When some players come down to the reserves who would have an attitude and would make it difficult for the rest of the team. Not Maxi though, his attitude was always spot-on and such a will-to-win".

It is safe to say that David Howells knew his chance at Spurs may not be forthcoming in the 1986-87 season, but he was still committed to his role within the reserves and the club. As for Paul Miller, it is no doubt he was always a crowd favourite and to top it all off there was a testimonial match in a few weeks' time to celebrate his tenure at Spurs.

However, another thing to remember is that a new manager was now in post. And we know Pleat was looking to change the centre back pairing of Graham Roberts and Paul Miller after his conversation with Club legend Bill Nicholson.

Along with David Howells, Mark Bowen, John Polston, Neil Ruddock and Vinny Samways there was superb talent oozing from all pores within the youth/reserve teams.

Also making the leap from Youth team to Reserve team this season would be Danny Maddix, John Moncur, Paul Moran, Mark Stimpson and Shaun Close who were all promising youngsters along with even younger talent in Kevin Dearden, Guy Butters, Phil Gray, Billy Manuel and Brian Statham still knocking on the door in the youth ranks. Striker Shaun Close had even joined Swedish Fist Division side Halmstad for the summer to aid his development. The future was bright.

* * * *

As July moved on, the players were now getting closer to the commencement of pre-season training. Players like Graham Roberts and Clive Allen were already putting in the work and first team coach Trevor Hartley was keen to get started.

The players all joined up at Cheshunt on 21st of July 1986, minus the Spurs players involved in the World Cup.

There was already one new player ready to begin the journey and that was Mitchell Thomas. Mitchell had just joined Spurs from Luton Town FC where he'd been managed by David Pleat. Thomas was an attacking left-back who made his debut for Luton in 1982 and had played 107 times for the Bedfordshire based club. He had also gained three England Under 21 caps in 1985 and had now been captured by Spurs for a fee of £275,000.

Since joining Spurs back in May, Pleat had now brought his coach Trevor Hartley, his physiotherapist John Sheridan and now his new left back from his former employers Luton Town. Seeing how things were left with his old Luton Chairman, David Evans, I am not sure Thomas' departure to Spurs went down well. - but more of that later.

With pre-season training underway and friendlies all pencilled in, it was also the month where the Division 1 fixtures were released. For the last three seasons, the English first division had been sponsored by tech giants Canon. A new sponsor was in place for 1986-87.

The new sponsor was relatively new newspaper brand, *TODAY*. The newspaper was launched in March 1986 by owner Eddy Shah. It was considered a middle-market tabloid and it's fair to say sponsoring the English first division was a bit of a coup for Shah and his new venture.

The '*TODAY* League Division 1' fixtures highlighted an interesting set of opening games. Tottenham were to kick off their campaign away at Villa Park against Aston Villa. Spurs had won at Villa Park last season, 2-1, thanks to goals from Gary Mabbutt and Mark Falco. They had also beaten Villa in the penultimate home game of the season, winning 4-2 thanks to a couple of braces by Clive Allen and Mark Falco.

Other notable fixtures were dominated by an interesting game that would see George Graham's Arsenal host Ron Atkinson's Manchester United. League and Cup holders Liverpool were to visit Newcastle at St James Park and expected title challengers Everton were to host Brian Clough's Nottingham Forest.

Eyes were also on the three newly promoted teams too. Division 2 champions Norwich City, runners up Charlton Athletic and finally, the amazing story of lowly Wimbledon FC, who were making their debut in the top-flight football.

Another team looking for a strong start would be John Lyall's West Ham United. West Ham had finished third in Division 1 last season. A brilliant season that saw them finish 4 points off Champions Liverpool and 2 points behind runners-up Everton. Impressively they were also 8 points ahead of Manchester United who were fourth. They had a fearsome goalscoring duo in Frank McAvennie and Tony Cottee. Lead goal scorer McAvennie netted 28 times last season and second in the Division 1 scoring charts to Everton's Gary Lineker who topped the list with 30 goals. Cottee was not far behind either on 26 goals.

Spurs' first four league games seemed very winnable. After the Villa encounter, two home games against Newcastle and Manchester City would be followed by an away game at Southampton. This gave an indication Spurs could make a very strong start. A trip to Highbury was the next game and a potential first real test against a top side. Home to Everton late September and a trip to Anfield to face Liverpool early October.

With the fixtures set in stone it was time to focus on the squad. Fitness, personnel and tactics.

Pre-season was in full flow for all Division 1 teams and there were some high-profile transfers being completed. The most notable move was Mexico World Cup Golden Boot winner Gary Lineker leaving Everton, after only one season, to join Terry Venables' Barcelona for £2.75m. Venables had snared Mark Hughes from Manchester United at the end of 1985-86 season for £2m and they were expected to form a powerful partnership in Spain.

Champions Liverpool bolstered their squad by signing Newcastle United's England U21 international Barry Venison for £2m. Venison was a versatile acquisition and further proof that the Anfield giants were relentless in acquiring yet another League title to their collection.

Another promising talent was on the move too. David Seaman had just been relegated with Birmingham City but performed very well during the '85-86 season, and he joined Queens Park Rangers for £225,000. Seaman was yet another promising England U21 international that was progressing his career in the top-flight.

With Everton looking to gain revenge on their Merseyside rivals, they bolstered their defence by signing Dave Watson from Norwich City for a club record £1m. Howard Kendall already had Derek Mountfield and Kevin Ratcliffe at the club which made his central defensive options very strong indeed.

At Arsenal, George Graham had moved early in the summer when selling Martin Keown to Aston Villa for £125,000. There was evidence to suggest that Graham was about to put faith into one of Arsenal's rising stars, central defender Tony Adams. Adams was only 20 years old and had been a regular for the England U21's in the last year. He made his league debut in the 1983-84 season but was sporadically used in the two seasons leading up to 1986-87. Graham clearly had faith. Graham would also bolster his attacking options when he signed Colchester United's Perry Groves to join the striking competition of Charlie Nicholas, Niall Quinn and Ian Allinson. There was some exciting young talent at Arsenal but how would they fare this season up against some experienced teams.

Coventry City were also looking to reinforce their striking options by signing Keith Houchen from Scunthorpe United for £600,000. He would join Cyrille Regis up front at Highfield Road.

However, the biggest transfer news of the summer lay in Ian Rush's move to Juventus. Rush had been smashing goalscoring records season after season. Then a day after Lineker's transfer record move to Barcelona, it was announced that Italian giants Juventus had purchased Rush for a mammoth £3.2m. Another new British record transfer fee.

All would not be lost for Liverpool fans though. They had agreed to leave Rush at Anfield, on loan, for the 1986-87 season. He would join the Turin club in the summer of 1987. Rush and Liverpool would be hoping for a happy ending.

An important point to consider is the loss of such players from English football. This would be the second season of the European ban on English clubs and now high-profile players like Gary Lineker, Glenn Hoddle, Ian Rush and Mark Hughes were all heading off to ply their trade on the continent. Crowds had been dipping over the last 12-18 months in England, this would be a contributing factor too perhaps.

* * * *

One of Arsenal's young talents was England U21 international midfielder David Rocastle. When George Graham took over at Arsenal in May 1986 there were several players out of contract. In Irving Scholar's *Behind Closed Doors* he muses over various transfers that could have happened but didn't. David Rocastle was one of them.

Scholar mentions that he was contacted to be told Rocastle was out of contract and would quite like to go to Spurs. Scholar approaches Pleat with this news and tells his new manager that Spurs could sign him tomorrow. Scholar left Rocastle's contact details with Pleat. A couple of days passed by, and nothing had happened. Scholar called Pleat and asked why. Apparently, Pleat was not too keen in talking about it, but Scholar wanted an answer. "I couldn't do that to George" was Pleat's gentlemanly response. This was a measure of a principled man, but arguably a wasted opportunity.

Scholar reveals that a few years later he posed that very scenario to Terry Venables, who was a good friend to George Graham as well. Venables, ever the businessman, replied that he would have had no problem at all in taking Rocastle with his view that, "That is football!".

Scholar talks of two other signings that he wanted Pleat to pursue that amounted to nothing. Firstly, it was Bradley Allen.

Bradley was another professional footballer straight out of the 'Allen' family stable. Cousins Clive and Paul were at Spurs already, Les Allen was a former Spur and club legend and

Scholar wanted young Bradley too. Scholar claims that he and Pleat were convinced he would join Spurs but frustratingly he ended up signing for Queens Park Rangers where he made his league debut in 1988. Scholar writes that Clive Allen got some stick by some of the Spurs players as they felt he was the one who convinced Bradley to go to QPR but with Clive alleging that his father, Les, was the reason why and not him.

Another deal was that of Ian Wright. So, Mr Ian Wright was close to joining Spurs? Scholar claims that Pleat rejected the opportunity to make a double swoop from Crystal Palace to sign both Ian Wright and Andy Gray. Palace were a Second Division side then and were happy to accept £150,000 each for them. Wright went on to join Arsenal a couple of seasons later for £2.5m and had an awfully good scoring record against Tottenham. Andy Gray ended up joining Spurs in 1992 as well.

Finally, Scholar also cited that Spurs were quite close in bringing Nigel Winterburn to White Hart Lane too. When Pleat joined, he was told that Peter Shreeves had been speaking to Wimbledon for some time about their promising left-back, Winterburn. Pleat was told Spurs had first refusal but, alas, he was not interested. Pleat was keen to bring in Mitchell Thomas at left-back instead.

Pleat told me that the Winterburn transfer was never on his table, Thomas had been acquired and that was possibly a player Shreeves had been looking at.

We could just file these away with the near misses of Platini, Maradona, Boniek and, apparently, even Rivaldo was close to joining Spurs during Hoddle's tenure as manager in the early 2000's!

Discussing some of the potential transfers with Pleat, I was surprised to find out he had never read Scholar's book which was published back in 1992. Pleat disputes that the potential Rocastle capture was a conversation that ever happened, even more so as he says any manager would have easily taken Rocastle, Pleat refutes that was ever an option for him and underpins this by stating that he doubted George Graham would have even considered getting rid of him to anyone, let alone Spurs.

Also, with the Wright-Gray double swoop. Pleat disputes this and stated Scholar did not speak to him about those players. Again, Pleat doubted that the Palace manager, Steve Coppell, would have even let them go at that point in their pursuit to get into Division 1 during that time.

On the Bradley Allen move, Pleat mentioned that Les Allen was always key to that deal, and even though Bradley was a Spurs schoolboy, the move to QPR was more lucrative which saw him depart to West London.

I am sure most clubs have many stories about players who nearly joined, but the fact was Spurs had a very strong squad. Mitchell Thomas had joined Spurs' pre-season training with only Chris Hughton as the most recognised left-back at the club.

There were still a couple of areas Pleat was considering changing but it seemed that there may need to be one or two more departures before other players came in. It is fair to say that Pleat probably wanted to see what players he had at his disposal first and this made the pre-season friendly matches even more important.

Another player leaving the club was Ally Dick. Ally was released by Spurs having made only a small number of appearances during his five years at the club. He ended up joining Ajax of all places, but sadly he rarely featured for them.

Also spending time with their international sides were Tony Galvin and Chris Hughton. They joined up with Jack Charlton's Republic of Ireland squad in Iceland to win a small international tournament that saw them beat Czechoslovakia and Iceland. Hughton's trip was cut short when he aggravated an ankle injury during the first tour match. At this point it was not known how long he would be out of action for.

As July closed out, the training at Cheshunt intensified, levels of optimism were high and were boosted further when Chris Waddle and Gary Stevens both returned to training a week earlier from their extended leave, post-World Cup involvement.

Even Graham Roberts cited the training demands when he spoke to *Spurs News*. "Tough but enjoyable" was his headline comment. Roberts continued, "Our training is very different, and I would describe it as the hardest I have known at Tottenham. It has been hard work but, because of the variety, it has been enjoyable, and I feel 100% better than I did at the same point last year".

Waddle's early return from extended leave saw him plunge into the new training schedule and he echoed Robbo's comments; "This is the hardest pre-season I have ever known. Still, we know it will all pay off when the season starts".

All new managers bring their own methods and plans in training and preparation. But one area that Waddles struggled with was Pleat's new 'code' words.

In Waddle's 1997 auto-biography, *Chris Waddle* written by Mel Stein, Waddle recalls his confusion as he mentions Pleat introducing a series of code-words for various moves. 'Jack' meant let it go, 'Sid' meant take over and 'Fred' meant a back-heel. Waddle sometimes struggled to remember what meant what and even more confusion reigned when they played Luton Town later in the season where both sets of players would sometimes use the same terms!

But, with the players getting stronger it was time to get some match practice in. Six friendly matches were scheduled in the first three weeks of August. All in readiness to face Villa in the season opener on the 23rd of August 1986.

AUGUST 1986

Glenn Hoddle had returned to pre-season training after taking a well-deserved break following his World Cup exploits with England and fresh from agreeing to give Pleat one more season at White Hart Lane.

Pleat had six games to assess his new squad. Assessment in match conditions is a wholly different world to the training ground. Pleat was looking at pairings in different areas of the pitch and how certain dynamics work, or even better, if they don't work. The centre back pairing was still one of his main priorities and there were a couple of transfer targets being discussed by Pleat and Scholar.

One of the current centre backs was Paul Millar. Paul was now in his tenth year at the club, and he had his testimonial coming up which would be Spurs' first friendly game of their pre-season preparations.

The pre-season games commenced on the 2nd of August 1986. The friendly matches would include a few testimonial games but also a European tournament to experience too. Spurs had been invited to the Camp Nou in Barcelona for the *Joan Gamper Tournament* involving three other giants of European football.

The final game against AC Milan would be played three days before the season opener at Villa Park.

Pleat had also announced his intention to keep goalkeeper Ray Clemence in the position of club captain. Clem had taken over the role in March 1986 after Steve Perryman had departed for Oxford United. This seemed an obvious appointment, Clem was the most successful player in the squad having won numerous domestic and European titles at Liverpool and his early FA Cup success with Spurs. He was also one of the most vocal in the squad. Players were happy to point out that his communication skills were one of Clem's dominant strengths.

Speaking in the August edition of *Spurs News*, Mitchell Thomas provides his perspective on pre-season training, his transition to Spurs and working previously with Pleat, Hartley and new physio John Sheridan.

"I haven't had to move from my Luton home, so it's all been very easy. I have worked with David, Trevor and John over the last five years and the lads have been great with a very good team spirit. The quality at this club increases competition for places which I believe is a benefit to everybody". On 'player competition' Thomas continued, "It certainly keeps the man in position on his toes and that has got to be good".

Thomas did represent England at Under 21 level on three occasions but did harbour further international recognition. He believed joining Spurs would increase those chances. He was out of contract and expressed his desire to join Spurs, shortly after a tribunal set the transfer fee at £275,000.

Spurs also announced that one of the Youth team coaches, Keith Waldon, had joined the coaching staff having been a part-time coach for the previous few seasons.

With Pleat and Hartley embedding their requirements, plans, ideas and philosophies into their new squad it would be fair to say that new physiotherapist would be working with all the players as the season wore on.

John Sheridan had replaced the previous physio, Mike Varney, who was a favourite among the Spurs players so Sheridan would have big boots to fill.

He joined Luton several years before. Pleat approached the FA looking for a physiotherapist recommendation and Sheridan's name came up. When asked by *Spurs News* how he felt joining the Spurs back-room staff he said, "When you get an opportunity to join a great club like Tottenham you have to take it. This is one of the biggest clubs in the world and it's every physio's dream to work in a place like this. The facilities are magnificent, and people are very easy to get on with".

* * * *

The first friendly game against Rangers was to celebrate Paul Miller's time at Spurs.

Paul Miller joined Spurs in 1976 as an apprentice before being rewarded with a professional contract a year later in 1977. He was part of a group of youngsters who were propelled into first team football by Keith Burkinshaw. In 1978 he went to Norway and joined Oslo based side Skeid FC on loan.

He made his Spurs debut against Arsenal in a 1-0 loss at Highbury in April 1979 and had gone on to make 285 league and cup appearances during his Spurs tenure. He was not known for his goals, but he had netted on 10 occasions for the lilywhites.

More importantly, 'Maxi' Miller was known for being a no-nonsense defender, terribly vocal and a 3-time cup winner being a key member of the 1981, 1982 FA Cup winning teams and the UEFA cup success in 1984. Known for his relentless commitment in training, Miller was a huge 'career pathway' success for Spurs to boast. It was testament to what happens when you give youth a chance. This man played for the badge, the club, his teammates and the supporters.

Over 16,000 fans attended White Hart Lane on a beautiful and sunny summer day. Glasgow Rangers were today's opponents, and they were being led by Graeme Souness, the former Liverpool legend and now the Player-Manager at Ibrox.

Plus, we must not forget, Souness was a former Spurs player too. Can we please add his name to the 'ones-who-got-away' list. Souness had managed only one senior game for Spurs before he was sold. His one appearance was as a substitute in a UEFA cup match before he was shipped off the Canadian side Montreal Olympique on loan.

He did have some success at Spurs though. On the 1st of May 1970 he scored the winner in a 1-0 FA Youth Cup Final win over Coventry City. Souness was the difference that day in a Spurs side that included Steve Perryman and Barry Daines.

In 1972 Spurs sold him to Middlesborough. As time went by, Souness turned into one of the best British central midfielders of all time. Arguably the best Scottish central midfielder of all time too. Souness was a stunning player, a force of nature and he was starting a huge wave of change at Ibrox that would impact Scottish football for a generation to come.

But today Souness would pit himself against one of England's best football teams. What team would Pleat play? Would this line-up give us an indication how he saw his team would look come the season opener at Villa?

Probably not as he kept his England contingent of Hoddle, Waddle and Stevens on the bench for the start of this game.

Ray Clemence started in goal in this 4-4-2 formation. Both Thomas's were at full backs, Danny on the right and Mitchell on the left. Mitchell making his first ever Spurs start too. Pleat stuck with tried and tested in the middle with Miller and Roberts.

The midfield four were Ossie Ardiles, Gary Mabbutt, Tony Galvin and reserve midfielder Richard Cooke. Clive Allen and Mark Falco started up front.

Chris Hughton had recovered from his ankle knock to join the England trio on the bench alongside Spurs' promising young centre back, Neil Ruddock.

A great day for Maxi that finished in a 1-1 draw. Rangers' Cammy Fraser opened the scoring after 9 minutes and Clive Allen equalised just after half-time. Miller was replaced by Neil Ruddock and received a rousing, respectful response from the Spurs fans. Chris Hughton had come on as a second half sub for Mitchell Thomas and the England trio all came on in the second half.

No injuries were sustained, and this was a strong test for Pleat's new squad, only two days until the next pre-season run out against Aldershot.

The only noticeable absentee from the squad was Paul Allen. Paul recalls his pre-season frustration and his desire to impress the new regime: "Any new manager appointment favours some players and some players it doesn't. There could be opportunities for players out-of-favour with the previous manager but sure, everyone wants to impress the new manager. I had injured my knee during pre-season which contributed to a bit of a stop-start opening to the season for me".

Allen then revealed how optimistic the squad felt leading into this set of pre-season games, "We were all quietly optimistic and very positive. You looked around the squad and saw the players we had, so that was impressive enough".

Allen would miss the next few games but would return for the Barcelona trip and he knew competition for places would be strong.

"You know, Spurs is a very competitive club. The expectations were high, and you'd look around the dressing room and see such a good squad, but good experience as well. We had some talented youngsters coming through too. Maybe there were not quite ready for first team football at that time but players like David Howells, Vinny Samways, John Moncur and John Polston were a good group of players that made the whole squad even more competitive".

Knowing the playing style of Paul Allen, you know it is littered with grit, determination and a will to win. If you lose your midfield berth to him then you may struggle to get it back, but at the time there was not really a position that you would fix to his name. Maybe he was too versatile. He could play central midfield; he had been playing right midfield and sometimes right back too.

I reminded Paul that most of us knew him as a central midfielder from his West Ham days before joining Spurs, Allen agreed, "That's where I originally started then, due to injuries, I ended up playing on the right-hand side. I was not a natural winger, and I am no Chrissy Waddle, but I preferred playing in the middle anyway. As the weeks went by, David Pleat helped me get that back".

As the season would head into the autumn months Paul Allen becomes such a pivotal player in Pleat's plans, but for now, he was trying to get back to full fitness.

Pleat fondly recalls his first game at White Hart Lane in charge of Spurs, "It was a lovely sunny day and the crowd was bigger than I expected. This was exciting for me and I was looking forward to the new challenge".

* * * *

A few days after the home draw with Glasgow Rangers, Spurs took a strong 20-man squad to Aldershot's Recreation Ground. Another occasion for Pleat to see his players in action.

It was near enough the same group of players that played during the Rangers match who featured against Aldershot. The only main change was Tony Parks in goal replacing Ray Clemence.

There was no matchday programme, more of a matchday A4 sheet of typed paper. It detailed a summary of Aldershot's last friendly against Gillingham and the evening's hosts and Spurs team/squad lists.

In this unglossy A4 communique, the Spurs manager was denoted as 'Dave Pleat'. Not that I asked David Pleat the question of how he likes to be referred to, but I'm sure he was not amused at being called 'Dave'. He doesn't look like a Dave, but then again, Rodney Trotter didn't did he? Rest in Peace Roger Lloyd-Pack, Trigger's one-liners are a piece of timeless comedy, and we know he was Spurs through and through.

Aldershot did have a few familiar players lining up against Spurs that night. Starting for home side was central defender Giorgio Mazzon. Not a household name to most but a former Spur nonetheless playing in the Youth Team with Mark Falco.

Pleat was essentially looking for a result and a performance, but Spurs could only manage a 3-2 win. Clive Allen scored a brace and Tony Galvin grabbed the other.

Mazzon played only one senior game for Spurs, but he must've taken pride in not allowing his former teammate Mark Falco to score on this occasion.

Still, a win is a win. Yet another 90 minutes for the players who were building their pre-season stamina and endurance that 'Dave' and Hartley were so keen to develop. Plus, the small crowd of just under 3,000 spectators where spoilt to have the likes of Hoddle, Ardiles, Waddle and Clive Allen on show.

Regardless of the quality of opposition during the pre-season games so far, Clive Allen had three goals in two games. He was hitting the back of the net nicely and, even though he had a strong finish to last season, these were good signs for Clive considering the injury nightmares he had come back from.

The squad was still looking strong, but Pleat was still musing over his centre back partnership. Pleat was keen to get Mabbutt into a centre back role and there had been talk of putting Graham Roberts into a central 'holding' midfielder role. Mabbutt would take on the right-side of the centre back pairing when lining up alongside Paul Miller.

Pleat was looking for a left-footed centre back. Someone with experience, someone who had a proven track record and someone who had also just come back from Mexico. Pleat was keen on capturing the Ipswich Town and England central defender, Terry Butcher. Pleat had already spoken with Butcher and there was a desire to join Spurs. It was time to discuss this with Irving Scholar and put some action to the words.

Heading back to London after the game, Pleat was still considering the Butcher transfer. He had spoken to Scholar but there was another player who seemed to be involved in this scenario - Dundee United's Scottish international defender, Richard Gough.

Pleat recalled, "Well, I wanted Terry Butcher. I'll be honest, I did want Butcher. Terry had the experience. I actually got a call from Ipswich manager Bobby Ferguson who told me Butcher was going for around £750,000 and I said to Irving, Butcher's the man. On the other hand, we had looked at Richard Gough. We fancied Gough strongly, but no-one could get him away from Jim McLean, the Dundee Utd manager".

Pleat re-reiterated that he left this deal with Irving Scholar, but it appears Scholar gave Pleat the same treatment he had received from Pleat in the alleged Rocastle transfer attempt.

Pleat continues, "Irving made no attempt. Although I wanted Butcher, and had spoken to him, this was dragging on and I then realised that Irving had let me down. He never made contact with Ipswich and then I got a call from Butcher who was actually at Heathrow airport. He said that he could not wait any longer and had an offer from Glasgow Rangers and was going to take it. Mr Pleat, I have no option and I am going to Scotland, and I cannot hold on any longer. I asked him to wait but he said no as he needed to sort his life out".

Two days later Butcher made his debut for Rangers at Hibernian. They lost the game 2-1 and, shock-horror, Souness got sent off too.

* * * *

With the potential Gough transfer still bubbling behind the scenes, Pleat took his side down to the South Coast to play Brighton at the Goldstone in a testimonial for Gerry Ryan.

Gerry Ryan's career was ended in 1985 when he broke his leg in a game against Crystal Palace. Ryan had spent time at Bohemians, Derby County and Crystal Palace during a career that included 18 international caps for the Republic of Ireland. During his international career, the Irish striker had lined up for his country alongside Spurs' Irish internationals, Tony Galvin and Chris Hughton.

Ryan's career was ended through injury. Bizarrely, in a connection with Chris Hughton too. Brighton were playing Crystal Palace and a challenge from Palace defender Henry Hughton, the younger brother of Chris Hughton, was the moment that ended his career.

Just under 11,000 fans turned up on a warm Friday evening to watch Spurs face Brighton. A wonderful night of football that saw Spurs prevail as 4-0 victors.

Mark Falco scored two, as did Chris Waddle with one of Waddle's goals being a converted penalty. Yes, a Waddle penalty, but more of Waddle taking penalties later.

During the game, the Mabbutt/Miller partnership was on show again in central defence with Roberts sitting just in front of them occupying the central midfield 'anchor' role. It seemed to work well.

* * * *

Another relatively quick turnaround saw Spurs travel to Gillingham. Gillingham skipper Mark Weatherley had been at the club since 1975 so a very well-deserved testimonial for The Gills long serving defender to be played against the North London giants from White Hart Lane.

Gillingham's main threat was 24-year-old striker Tony Cascarino. Cascarino had scored 21 times last season and expectations were high again this season. The young striker had also made his debut for the Republic of Ireland in September 1985 and was known for his aerial presence just as much as his ability in finding the back of the net.

This was to be Spurs' final domestic pre-season match before heading off to Barcelona. Pleat didn't need injuries and started the game with the same eleven players who began the recent match at Brighton.

Not a riveting game for the spectators one may assume, as it finished 1-1 with Mark Falco getting Spurs' goal.

Another game notched off in readiness for a sterner test that would face them in the Camp Nou in seven days' time.

Before Spurs departed for Spain there was one player, who hadn't featured since the first friendly game against Glasgow Rangers. Ossie Ardiles.

Ossie was now 34 years old and into his eighth season at the club, he had been out after knee surgery but had started training again. Questions had come up about Ardiles when Scholar was discussing the squad with David Pleat. Did Pleat see Ossie as a key player in his plans moving forward?

I asked Pleat if he was happy with his squad going into those final pre-season games, Pleat revealed "I will tell you about one incident, Irving and I were talking about Ossie Ardiles. It was a general conversation, and quite relaxed, where I mentioned it might be time for us to move Ossie on".

Gasps all round I would expect!

Pleat candidly continued, "To be fair to Scholar, he said to me, don't make any rash decisions. Although aware that he was now into his thirties but to give it time and you might find a role for Ossie. And you know what, it proved to be true".

As the season would move on there would be some players moving on from the club and some formational changes too.

Ossie would prove to be an essential player in that scenario. Good work Mr Chairman.

Spurs were due to fly out to Barcelona, but Ossie did manage to get some match minutes under his belt just before the trip. The Spurs reserve team had a friendly match at Barnet that finished 2-2. Paul Allen also played, to aid his return from injury. Both he and Ardiles played the full 90minutes.

* * * *

A few days had passed since the Terry Butcher disappointment but, more importantly, the Gough transfer was progressing. Pleat was adamant to get across that he still very much wanted Richard Gough and simply felt Butcher had different attributes to Gough.

"To be fair to Irving", continued Pleat, "he said, let's get the younger player. Irving wanted Richard Gough. I wanted Richard, don't get me wrong, of course I would take Richard. But I am going to tell you, Butcher was the first choice as I thought of his experience. In fact, he was the left-footed centre back I wanted to play alongside Gary Mabbutt as a right-sided centre back, but it didn't happen".

But Scholar and Pleat had managed to strike a deal with McLean and Dundee United that did see Richard venture south.

"I met Gough on a Sunday morning at the West Lodge Park Hotel in Hadley Wood. And I do remember Ken Bates trying to hijack that deal. They had the usual story, a phone call from a certain Mr. Bates saying whatever Tottenham offer you don't do anything, come and see us first. It happens in football. It's an illegal approach. But Richard Gough is an absolute gentleman. We knew Chelsea were trying to get him, but he said, I am coming to Tottenham, I want to come to Tottenham".

In the Premier League era, Spurs have been gazumped many a time by Chelsea as money has been no object for the West London club. It is genuinely nice to hear the opposite story for once.

Gough had represented Scotland in Mexico having played in all three of Scotland's group games. Known to Spurs fans as a centre back but deployed at right back for his club and country, he was very quick, good in the air and a wonderful reader of the game.

Gough was open to discuss this season. He was very generous with his time, and it is fair to say, season 1986-87 had left a lasting impression on him.

Richard remembered his World Cup experience fondly, despite losing each game. I asked him how he felt being included in Alex Ferguson's squad for Mexico, "It was a great feeling, I mean, I had played for Scotland a fair few times before but this was my first World Cup. Fantastic".

Another member of the Scotland squad was Glasgow Rangers' player-manager Graeme Souness. Richard openly says, "Around that time there was a lot of talk about me and there were a lot of

English teams coming in for me, as well Rangers. Funny enough, Souness was the captain of Scotland too!"

There had been speculation over the years that Dundee United and Manager Jim McLean had a reluctance to sell their players to Rangers. Speculation also circulated that Gough would need to go to another club first before Rangers could get their mitts on him. All speculation of course.

Gough continues, "In May 1986, Souness appointed Walter Smith as his assistant. Walter was the Assistant Manager at Dundee United so there were lots of rumours that I was going to be the first signing. I think they put in a few bids but nothing went through. Sorry, should I say, Dundee United and Jim McLean wouldn't accept from Rangers".

As the World Cup went on Gough was aware the rumours were still continuing about Rangers, but Gough stated, "Dundee United were not going to accept an offer from another Scottish club and when I came back from the World Cup and into pre-season training there were not other offers at all".

Gough had prepared himself that he may be at Dundee United for another season. "I played the first three league games of that season". The season opener on 9th August 1986 was at home to Aberdeen. Dundee United won 2-1 with Gough scoring the opening goal.

The following weekend Dundee United headed to Ibrox to face Rangers. He was facing the team that so desperately wanted him and, in fact, this turned out to be Gough's last game for Dundee United too.

Souness was fielding one his new signings and the man who Pleat nearly snared, Terry Butcher. Prolific striker Ally McCoist had put Rangers 2-0 at half time with an impressive brace. The second half was a different story though. Dundee United striker, Kevin Gallacher, replied with a brace of his own. His equaliser coming with seven minutes to go.

Amazingly Dundee United claimed the win when they grabbed he winner in the 88th minute. A loss for the mighty Rangers and Dundee United were flying high.

Gough knew a few things were going on before the season began. McLean wanted him to play in the first three games as the English season was to commence two weeks later.

The move happened swiftly after the Rangers game. The next day Gough was heading to London as he'd been told that his club had accepted offers from both Chelsea and Tottenham.

"But no one knew that I was going to leave, it only got announced after the we beat Rangers at Ibrox 3-2. After the game, Jim McLean hadn't even spoken to me. I went home and I got a call from one of the Directors who told me he was picking me up in the morning and we are going to speak to Tottenham. However, he did mention that they had agreed a fee with Chelsea as well, so I needed to go and see them too".

Gough travelled to London and met Spurs first. "I spoke to Irving Scholar and quickly I was convinced I wanted to join Spurs. Scholar knew I was meeting Chelsea but joked how he didn't want to let me leave the room! I told him I was happy with that because I want to sign for Tottenham!".

At that point Gough told Scholar that he needed to call Ken Bates, the Chelsea chairman, to tell him he had agreed to join Spurs. "Irving said that he would call Bates for me, but I said no, I want to call him and tell him". A very mature response from a 23-year-old man.

Gough continued saying, "I called Ken and said look, I have agreed to sign for Tottenham, so I don't want to waste your time and not coming over to the other side of London to talk. At that point Bates went ballistic. He was effing this and effing that and all I could see was Irving Scholar laughing his head off in the background".

Tottenham had bought one of the most promising defenders in European football for £750,000. Soon after, Gough was made aware that he would be partnering Gary Mabbutt in the centre of Spurs' defence.

But Pleat was still a bit of an unknown entity to Gough. "I was glad to be at Tottenham. I knew Pleat did well at Luton Town but didn't know that much about him. I was aware there had been a play with myself and Terry Butcher going up to Rangers, plus I knew that both Spurs and Manchester United had seemingly come in for Butcher too".

Spurs were about to fly out to Spain and Gough was now on board. Spirits were high as the squad departed.

* * * *

This tournament was an opportunity to see Spurs flex their muscles among Europe's elite clubs.

This game was the first of two games played on consecutive evenings. PSV Eindhoven were the current champions of Dutch football. They had won the 1985-86 Eredivisie by eight points ahead of runners-up, and rivals, Ajax Amsterdam.

This four-team tournament would boast some of the world's best players. There were some talented youngsters too that would go on and set European and World football alight over the next several years and into the 1990's.

This was the bigger stage that Pleat was hoping for. He was now managing one of England's elite football clubs and was now pitting his managerial skill and wit against some of the best managers in European football.

The Dutch champions PSV were managed by Jan Reker. It was Reker's first title during the 1985-86 season and he was helped by some talented coaches in Hans Kraay and Guus Hiddink. Hiddink would go on to manage PSV the following season and then win 3 consecutive league title until he departed in 1990 when Bobby Robson left his role as England manager to take over PSV.

Spurs' second opponents were AC Milan. Milan were led by the Swede, Nils Liedholm. Liedholm had won Serie A managing both AC Milan and AS Roma. He also took Roma to the European Cup Final in 1984, eventually losing out to Liverpool.

The hosts, Barcelona, were managed by Englishman Terry Venables since 1984. Venables was well known to Pleat and the Spurs squad. Not only was he a former Spur, being part of the 1967 FA Cup winning side, but he also managed QPR in their 1982 FA Cup Final loss to Tottenham. A cup final replay that was settled by a Glenn Hoddle penalty. Venables had relative success with Crystal Palace and QPR before his move to Barcelona and was considered one of the best coaches in European football.

One of Venables' first signings when he took over at Barcelona, was his capture of Spurs striker Steve Archibald. Archibald had joined Barca not long after Maradona departed for Napoli. Archibald wanted to wear his favourite number eight shirt, but midfielder Bernd Schuster would not give it up. This meant that Archibald had to wear the number ten shirt, recently free after Maradona's exit. Big boots to fill indeed.

Venables' first team coach was Englishman Alan Harris.

But Venables, Harris and Archibald all had success in their first season by winning La Liga. Something Maradona failed to do. In his second season, 1985-86, Venables won the Spanish League Cup but were runners up in their title defence, losing out to Real Madrid.

However, a few months earlier, Venables had steered Barcelona to the European Cup Final against Steaua Bucharest. Barca were favourites. It was a turgid game that finished 0-0 and saw the Romanian side win on penalties. Bizarrely, Barcelona missed every single one of their penalties and lost 2-0 to a Steaua side experiencing their first ever European Cup Final.

Within 18 months, Venables and Harris would have an even closer connection to Spurs when they would be given the responsibility of replacing Pleat and Hartley. However, there is a lot to cover before that scenario happened.

It was safe to say that some of the best managerial talent was seen in Barcelona over the next two days.

This would be a chance for Pleat to show his hand with a line-up that could face Aston Villa in four days' time.

The players emerged from the tunnel to be greeted by an 80,000-strong crowd. Pleat had gone with a 4-4-2 formation and no real surprises in the line-up. New signing, Richard Gough, started on the bench. Considering he had joined Spurs less than 48 hours before that was not too surprising.

Line up v PSV Eindhoven: Clemence; Stevens, Miller, Mabbutt, M Thomas; Waddle, Roberts, Hoddle, Galvin; Falco, Allen C.

Spurs captain, Ray Clemence, met the PSV captain in the middle. The PSV skipper was Ruud Gullit. At this point in time, Gullit was one of the most dominant and brilliant talents in world football. A league title winner with Feyenoord in 1984,

Gullit moved to PSV in the summer 1985 where he won Eredivisie in his first season. Now club captain, the dreadlocked attacking midfielder was part of a promising group of Dutch talent that was progressing the national side too.

Today he wore no.10. He would be going up against Spurs' no.10, Glenn Hoddle.

The PSV side included some familiar faces and some more emerging talent too. Hans Van Breukelen was in goal, the former Nottingham Forest goalkeeper was also the Dutch national keeper and still a well-known face to the Spurs players. Another familiar face was that of Eric Gerets.

Gerets was a brilliant full-back and part of the Belgium national side that had reached the World Cup Semi-Final against Argentina a few weeks before. To England fans, Gerets is most remembered for the free-kick he conceded during the England-Belgium 2nd round game of the 1990 World Cup in Italy. The game was poised at 0-0 and edging towards the end of extra time and inevitable penalties it seemed. With less than a minute remaining, England's Paul Gascoigne surged forward in a limp attempt to launch a final attack before the final whistle. Gerets nudges him a tiny bit, but a tired Gascoinge goes down. England have a free-kick 25 yards outside the Belgium penalty box. Gascoinge lofts the ball into the box, hoping to bypass the line of Belgian defenders, and there he finds his fellow midfielder, David Platt. Platt had spun around to hook a volley over his shoulder and pass the floundering Belgium goalkeeper! The England players were delirious, the England fans in complete heaven. England were through to the Quarterfinals. Ahem, thanks Eric.

The game was aired on French and Spanish TV. Just before the game, two PSV players were interviewed. They spoke to Gerets, then the interviewer spoke to one of the PSV substitutes. This substitute was Frank Arnesen.

Spurs fans will remember Arnesen for two reasons. Firstly, he was part of the Anderlecht side that were beaten by Spurs in the 1984 UEFA Cup Final. He came on as an 82nd minute substitute in the first leg and started the second leg at White Hart Lane.

Secondly, and more recently, he was brought in as Director of Football at Tottenham during the 2004-05 season. He worked alongside Jacques Santini, during his very brief Spurs tenure, before bringing in Martin Jol. Let's face it, Jol was a wonderful acquisition and the most progressive manager Spurs had had for years!

The Dutch champions also lined up with Ronald Koeman. The 23-year-old defender was one of the brightest talents in Dutch football and was already starting to establish himself as a regular in the National team. But today, and especially during the first half, Spurs' Mark Falco gave him a bit of trouble.

Spurs started the game positively and Roberts was, once again, deployed in the holding midfield role just behind Hoddle. Roberts' game was short lived as he hobbled off after half an hour following a three-player clash with Paul Miller and a PSV midfielder. It seemed that Miller's challenge had impacted

Roberts and he was soon replaced by Ardiles. Falco had an early penalty save and several minutes later, as Ardiles thrust forward, he released Mitchell Thomas. Thomas flighted a lovely left-wing cross to Falco who nodded in at the back post. A well-deserved lead.

Two minutes before half time PSV equalised. Well, in fact it was Paul Miller own goal. PSV had broken down the Spurs left hand side and had put in an innocuous cross where Miller was completely alone. Miller's attempt to clear his lines turned into a thumping volley into the top corner of the Spurs goal shooting past a confused Ray Clemence. At first look, it seemed as though Miller was nonchalantly attempting a 'no-look' clearance, but you cannot fail to laugh as you see Miller trudge away and Clemence watching him, hand on hips, trying to process what had just happened.

To give you a bit of context to what an amazing goal it was, Ray Clemence referenced it two months later. In the October matchday programme, versus Sheffield Wednesday, questions were posed to Clem. Questions like; What is your greatest footballing memory? Clem answers the first time he won the European Cup in 1977. What is the best save you have ever seen? Clem answers with his memory of Gordon Banks wonder save from Pele during the 1970 World Cup.

He was then asked; What is the Greatest Goal seen scored? Clem's answer was "Paul Miller's own goal in Barcelona this pre-season!" So, I think it's fair to say that Clem has seen and experienced some top-level football.

The game trickled on and there was no further scoring. This tournament required a winning result in each game so a penalty shoot-out would now take place.

During the second half, Richard Gough had come on to replace Paul Miller to make his Spurs debut. Early on you could see his pace was evident and there was an element of dynamism to his game.

Chris Waddle, Richard Gough and Gary Stevens all scored their penalties. Arnesen was among the PSV scorers too. Paul Allen saw his effort saved but two other penalties were saved too and arguably they were the best players on the pitch. Both Ruud Gullit and Glenn Hoddle were the unsuccessful penalty takers. You would never have expected that. Nor would they have, just like they may not have foreseen Hoddle recruit Gullit when he was manager of Chelsea in the mid-1990s.

PSV won the penalty shoot-out but, for me, there was one hugely noticeable event in this game. During the penalty shoot-out Spurs' first penalty was converted by, Chris Waddle.

Why is this so noticeable then? In the time Waddle played for Spurs he was never the designated penalty taker. Those responsibilities lay with Clive Allen and then, in Waddle's last season, with future Spur, Terry Fenwick.

Through the records, I can only find Waddle scoring three other penalties for Spurs, one recently in a friendly and then one in a friendly win against Barnet in 1988 and the other would be towards the end of this year, 1986, in an overseas friendly.

When the word penalty and Chris Waddle are mentioned in the same sentence it is impossible to forget that famous night in Turin, Italy on the 4th of July 1990. There are a few occasions in football that I, and probably many others, still think about with emotional recollection. This match was one of them. England were facing West Germany in the semi-finals of the 1990 World Cup. West Germany were clearly the team of the tournament and England had, through skill and luck, managed to get themselves into their first World Cup semi-final since the victorious 1966 campaign.

During the game, England were outstanding. By far their best performance of their entire tournament. Waddle was superb during that game and, for me, he was England's best player that evening.

The game finished 1-1 and went to a penalty shoot-out. Chris Waddle was one of England's nominated penalty takers. He was not known for his penalty taking successes, but he did step up.

This now brings us back to this evening in Barcelona. Watching this game back and seeing Waddle step up to take Spurs' first penalty it immediately reminds of you of that 1990 semi-final event. But I genuinely gasped watching Waddle take his penalty. His penalty against PSV is an exact replica of his 1990 effort in Turin. Where in 1990 his penalty kick goes over the bar and into heart-breaking oblivion, on this evening, four years earlier, Waddle put's his PSV effort in the top left-hand corner for a stunningly successful strike. I replayed it a couple of times and mused over 'what could have been' if Waddle had scored and kept England in the penalty shoot-out against the Germans.

Suffice to say, fast-forward to 1990, it would still have required Peter Shilton to actually keep out a West German effort for England to have succeeded, but I am sure many fans still believe that if England had won that shoot-out then we would have seen off Argentina in the final. Argentina blagged their way to that final using 'shithousery' rather than skill en-route to their second consecutive World Cup final.

Another sliding door moment passes us by. That seems to be the life of an England and Spurs fan.

Despite losing to PSV on penalties, this was another useful match for Pleat to hone his players into their season opener. Paul Allen and Ossie Ardiles had both spent time on the field after their recent injuries. Mabbutt was looking very assured and settled at the back and the Graham Roberts injury seemed the only blot on another successful exercise.

* * * *

The following day Spurs now faced Italian giants AC Milan in front of 100,000 spectators. Despite this being a friendly, Spurs had not faced AC Milan competitively since the UEFA Cup Final success over the Rossoneri in 1972. The two-legged match is fondly remembered for Steve Perryman's brace in the first leg at White Hart Lane before Alan Mullery's goal helped Spurs to a 1-1 draw, and 3-1 aggregate win, in the San Siro, Milan.

Milan had been beaten 3-1 by Barcelona the day before. Terry Venables new stellar signing, Gary Lineker, was not thrust into this tournament but Mark Hughes had scored during this victory and Hateley scored the Italians solitary goal.

Another notable event during Barca's win over Milan was Terry Venables' introduction of a young 20-year-old midfielder as a second half substitute who making his first team debut for Barcelona. Mohammed Ali Amar was more commonly known as Nayim. He had been a regular in Barcelona B & C teams since 1984. Venables felt it right to propel him into the first team during this tournament.

It is fair to say that Nayim struggled to make an impact during his time at Barcelona. Later that season he made his senior competitive debut in the Copa Del Rey but only managed to make several first team appearances over the next two seasons. Nayim's time at Barcelona was to come to an end when he joined Tottenham Hotspur on loan in November 1988. A wonderfully talented footballer and made 112 appearances during his five years at White Hart Lane. A player never to be forgotten as he played a critical role in Spurs' midfield that went on to win the 1991 FA Cup.

Paul Allen was also part of the 1991 FA Cup winning team that played alongside Nayim. I mentioned to Paul that Nayim had played his first game for the Barcelona senior team in that tournament.

Paul was surprised, "He played in that tournament, did he? I did not know that." Allen continued, "Nayim was a very, very talented footballer and he adapted so well to the English game. He had a great combination of skill and technique, but he was also so very determined, and he liked to express himself too. In some ways like Glenn did."

Spurs did not get to play against Hughes, Nayim and Barcelona, but today there were up against a Milan team that had finished in a disappointing seventh position in Serie A last season.

Italian international defenders Franco Baresi and Dario Bonnetti were on show alongside two of England's recent World Cup squad members, Ray Wilkins and Mark Hateley. But this team also boasted the amazing young talent of Paolo Maldini, Alessandro Costacurta, Mauro Tassotti and Roberto Donadoni. The following season, the summer of 1987, Nils Liedholm would be replaced by Arrigo Sacchi and they would bring in Ajax's Marco Van Basten, Roma's Carlo Ancelotti and PSV star Ruud Gullit. This team would go on to have such significant domestic and European success in the late 1980's and early 1990's, that these players will be remembered as world class legends in the annals of footballing history.

But for now, this was a transition period for them and this evening it was Tottenham Hotspur up against them.

Pleat made a few changes from the previous night as Roberts was injured but it was to see the comeback from injury of the pacey right winger John Chiedozie. Richard Gough made his first start in a Spurs shirt and a rare start for reserve teamer, Richard Cooke. There was not a recognised striker in the starting line up and it appeared that Hoddle and Cooke were pushed slightly further forward.

Line up v AC Milan: Clemence; D Thomas, Gough, Miller, Hughton; Chiedozie, Ardiles, P Allen, Waddle; Hoddle, Cooke.

This evening there were 100,000 spectators in the Camp Nou as the crowd would be staying on to watch the Barcelona/PSV Eindhoven match that would follow the Spurs/Milan game.

Tottenham claimed a well-deserved victory over Milan, despite the Rossoneri being reduced to ten men towards the end of the first half.

Spurs went behind just before the half-hour mark when Dario Bonnetti rose high to head home a Milan corner. Arguably, Ray Clemence might have saved the Italians effort but he collided with Ardiles who was defending on the goal line.

AC Milan were reduced to ten men on the 37th minute when the talented young centre-back, Alessandro Costacurta, was sent off after two bookable offences. The following day, the Daily Telegraph reported that Costacurta had committed 'two blatant and stupid offences, one pulling a spurs shirt and the other catching the ball'.

Pleat changed things in the second half by bringing on Mark Falco for Chris Waddle. Falco was now a focal point up front and on the hour, he rose to head his second goal of the tournament following a left wing cross from Chris Hughton. Bit of a carbon copy of his goal against PSV provided by Mitchell Thomas's left wing cross. It was now 1-1.

Gary Mabbutt came on to replace Hoddle and that was a crucial change. With the game seemingly petering out to another draw, Richard Cooke provided a wonderful cross for Gary Mabbutt to head home with a minute to go. 2-1 to Spurs.

Mr Versatile had won the game for Spurs. He had started the tournament at centre-back, he was now playing in a midfield berth and he wins the game doing a striker's job! What an asset he is to Pleat.

Despite Roberts''s injury it had been a good tournament for Pleat's men and Pleat himself.

In a *Daily Telegraph* article the following day, the reporter was very keen to point out that Chiedozie was Spurs' best player on the night by highlighting that he 'never stopped running and was a constant threat to the Milan defenders'. It was safe to say that Pleat had a strong squad of players to choose from and if he wanted to attempt the three trophies on offer this season then this squad was strong enough to compete.

Pleat recalls, "I do remember that tournament and Chiedozie and Falco both playing well. I also remember going out for a meal with Irving Scholar and Terry Venables. Irving was gushing over Terry, like a little boy in many ways. It was like hero-worship. He said how wonderful it was sitting in between two brainy football people. It was hard to explain but it was quite schmaltzy".

Little did we all know that in around 18 months things would change so dramatically at Spurs with Pleat, Scholar and Venables being at the epicentre of Tottenham's evolution in the late 1980's.

It was now time to make the 700-mile journey home to London and prepare for Aston Villa on Saturday.

* * * *

The following day, Brian Scovell in the Daily Mail reported on Spurs' victory in the Camp Nou, and despite Milan playing with ten men for the entire second half, he felt Spurs merited the victory. His headline read, "SUB MABBUTT IS A LAST GASP HERO".

Just below Scovell's piece, there was a quote from Gordon Taylor, the Professional Footballers' Association (PFA) Secretary, where he was highlighting the need for English clubs to evolve.

Taylor was urging English clubs to adopt the methods employed by overseas teams to not just ensure survival, but to keep up with the footballing elite. Taylor felt our clubs were being too insular and said, "We must be prepared to learn more in how the game is conducted overseas. Look at the business Barcelona have attracted through their multi-purpose complex for a start".

In the last few years, the world of football had been changing. Clubs in Spain and Italy were leading the change. Professional Football Clubs were starting to evolve and over the next few years there would be a huge shift in commercial ventures involving football clubs. Keith Burkinshaw had seen the signs a few years before, when he left Spurs, as he felt these changes might be detrimental. But the fact remained that things were changing, and Irving Scholar was progressive in his desire to keep up.

From a commercial standpoint, television rights were gradually gaining more and more traction every season. The recent World Cup had been a televisual success and in four years' time the bar would be raised even more when Italy hosted and broadcasted the biggest football tournament on earth.

The upcoming 1986-87 season would see the arrival of even more live matches on British TV screens. Without European competition, and the continued disease of football hooliganism, it was quite noticeable that attendances had been dwindling across English football clubs. It was hoped that the TV audiences, along with the recent interest in the Mexico World Cup, would help inspire interest again.

For years, *Match of the Day* on BBC TV was staple television viewing for football supporters, but the demands were changing. Less than a year before, in October 1985, ITV aired the *Saint & Greavsie* football show.

What a success it was, and the show continued to run until 1992. The comedy and footballing insight of Liverpool legend Ian St John and Spurs hero, Jimmy Greaves, was a delight for football supporters. With BBC's *Football Focus* delighting football fans since 1974, ITV's Saturday lunchtime alternative was a comedic masterclass as viewers would probably spend the whole episode laughing continually alongside presenter Ian St John who could never fail to chuckle away at the constant comedy and hilarious anecdotes that would spew from Jimmy Greaves' lips.

Infectiously, the *Saint & Greavsie* show also adopted the ITV Mexico World Cup theme when the opening and closing credits rolled. The theme tune was 'Aztec Gold' by Silsoe and was also embraced by ITV's *Big Match* TV programme. This was a refreshing brand of footballing broadcasting. The programme would cover the lighter side of all aspects of domestic, European and World football during its seven-year stretch.

Undoubtedly the most bizarre moment was when *Saint & Greavsie* travelled to New York and visited Donald Trump who assisted them in the League Cup 5th Round draw. The future President of the United States of America welcomed them to Trump Tower. Greavsie immediately retorted by saying, "This is beautiful. I've not seen a boardroom like this since I was in Doug Ellis' office at Aston Villa". Ian St John chuckled away, as per, but so did Trump. I doubt Trump knew who Doug Ellis was but he simply felt like laughing along.

Scholar and Spurs had just been to Barcelona and experienced this environment first hand. In an interview a year later, on the

11th of August 1987, Irving Scholar spoke to the BBC's *London Plus* where he discusses the need for Tottenham Hotspur FC to diversify to compete with top clubs like Juventus, Real Madrid, AC Milan, Roma and Barcelona. He mentions that Barcelona and Madrid can take in revenue of around £1m per game.

English clubs were way off that level of revenue generation. Just over two years later, Tottenham redeveloped their East Stand and soon after it opened they played Arsenal at home in the League. The attendance was just under 34,000 and gate receipts were £300,000. At the time, this set a record for a League match in England.

Scholar's thinking was to be less reliant on football income alone and to consider different areas that would provide alternative revenue streams. Commercial thinking was now creeping into board rooms across world football.

It was well known that Scholar was a key member of a group of Chairman that explored the feasibility of creating a different world that would ultimately begin in 1992 with Sky TV and the creation of the Premier League.

In some ways it was not hard to see the potential and scope of what could be done. Major sports in the United States had been there, done that and bought the t-shirt. Even College sport in the States was big business. However, at this point the United States' involvement in world football was miniscule. Despite an attempt to arouse interest with the emergence of the North American Soccer League during the 1970's, the desire was not evident among the big-spending American market. Things would gradually change for America in 1988 when FIFA awarded them host nation of the 1994 World Cup Finals.

In fact, not long after the 1986 World Cup Final, a charity game was played in the United States to help raise the profile of the game in the USA. The UNICEF-FIFA Charity match was played at the Pasadena Rose Bowl, Los Angeles in front of 57,000 spectators. The match was *the Americas versus Rest of the World (ROW)*. England's Terry Butcher played for the *ROW* and opened the scoring with a header in the first half. The *Americas* won the game on penalties with, the irrepressible, Diego Maradona scoring the winning penalty. The game was broadcast live on ITV with Brian Moore commentating.

So, with an event like this in mind, do we seem surprised that two years later FIFA award the '94 World Cup to the United States? FIFA, for some years, had been reaping the benefits of their 'commercial' arrangements and you could say they were ahead of the game. Albeit controversially as we were to find out in *Netflix's* 2022 documentary on corruption within the world's largest sporting organisation.

Nevertheless, commercial lessons could be learnt from FIFA and American sport. However, stringent financial control would need to be an essential ingredient, as various footballing bodies were to detrimentally find out in years to come.

* * * *

With only a day to go until Spurs' opening fixture up at Villa Park there were revelations of player conduct being raised.

PFA Secretary Gordon Taylor was again in the news. He had been urging all players to consider their on-field conduct as the season was about to begin. This came hot off an FA disciplinary hearing involving Tottenham's Mark Falco.

Falco's recent case had been the heaviest ever punishment for an offence of that kind.

In the penultimate game of last season, Spurs beat Aston Villa 4-2. Falco scored two goals in that victory but he was seen, by a Police Chief Inspector, holding up three fingers to the Villa fans after Spurs had gone 3-0 up. He then went on to hold up four fingers to the Villa fans when the fourth goal went in.

Falco was apparently close to receiving a criminal charge for those actions until the police decided to hand it over to the FA to deal with the matter.

It does seem bizarre that a player, gesturing that his team were 3-0 up, would be on a criminal charge for doing so, but context is needed here. Football hooliganism was so rife at the time, and considered to being out of control, that this incendiary gesture by Falco was a very bad decision by the Spurs striker. English teams were now serving a second season of a European ban that was introduced because of hooliganism.

Even more so as only two weeks before, on the 8th of August 1986, trouble flared on a ferry crossing from England to

Holland. Manchester United and West Ham United fans were travelling to see their teams play respective pre-season friendly matches. Sure enough, as the alcohol flowed then so did the verbal insults. Fighting broke out involving around 150 people that included knives and broken bottles. The ferry had to turn back and was greeted in Harwich by police. Another stain on English football and further evidence that insults can incite violence.

Back to Falco then. Not that I am saying it was Falco's intention to incite such violence but, in the interest of balance, you may assume that Falco resorted to that gesture due to insults he may have received from the crowd.

Watching football during that time period was a very dark time. The language, the racism and the sexism was extreme near enough every match. Going to football as a kid it was quite shocking to experience this, but it happened week in, week out. The amount of violence most fans witnessed was so commonplace that it kept lots of people from going to games. Would you see many women and children at footballs matches? Not likely.

Falco received a two-match ban and a £1,500 fine, which was huge at the time.

The FA had recently fined QPR Terry Fenwick for doing something similar up at Newcastle. However, the Scottish FA had just hit Glasgow Rangers' manager Greame Souness with a whopping £5,000 fine and three match ban. That would not be the last time Souness was up in front of a disciplinary committee.

Coincidently, Falco's offence had been committed against Aston Villa. The next day, Spurs were playing Aston Villa. Luckily for Falco, his ban would not start until Spurs played Manchester City at home and then Southampton away in two weeks' time.

With violence a concern, both inside and outside of the stadiums, Clubs were regularly issuing please for fans to behave. Spurs and Pleat were no different when the new Spurs boss appealed to fans to consider their behaviour, "Anybody who has ever thought of supporting Tottenham Hotspur Football Club isn't a supporter if he, at any time, gets involved in trouble". His words were relayed in the *Spurs News* newspaper and he continued by saying, "Winning means almost everything, but not quite everything". He was urging sportsmanlike behaviour both on and off the pitch.

* * * *

Saturday 23rd August 1986 – Villa Park, Birmingham
(Att: 24,712)
Aston Villa v Tottenham Hotspur
(TODAY League Division 1)

The opening league game had finally arrived. Now this is a special moment in any football supporter's season.

It's a clean slate, we all start from scratch. Levels of hope and optimism remain high as fans look to see if their team can get off to a winning start. Spurs had not lost in the league at Villa Park since 1982 so it was a relatively strong hunting ground for the Lilywhites.

Villa finished 16th in Division 1 last season and only three points above relegation, but despite their league finish they did have some strong players. Paul Elliott was a rock at the back, and well known to David Pleat as Elliott joined Villa from Luton Town in 1985. Tony Dorigo was impressive, attacking full back but Villa's strength lay in their midfield. Tony Daley was a speedy right-winger and they had the guile and thrust of England's Steve Hodge. Up front they had the clever Simon Stainrod and the strong Garry Thompson. Spurs' new centre back pairing would be up against it today.

Despite Villa's poor season in the 1985-86 season, Graham Turner remained in charge. He would need to get some momentum going early that would see Villa loiter in the top half of the table rather than perilously close to relegation again.

Still, Spurs were in a good place, and they had a full squad to choose from. Graham Roberts had recovered from his clash with paul Miller in the Camp Nou four days earlier and was to take his place in the middle of Spurs' midfield.

Line up v Aston Villa: Clemence; Stevens, Gough, Mabbutt, M Thomas; Waddle, Roberts, Hoddle, Galvin; Falco, C Allen. Sub: P Allen

Pleat had opted for a 4-4-2 formation with Waddle and Galvin providing natural width. Roberts tucked in behind Hoddle and

Pleat had decided with Gary Stevens over Danny Thomas and new signing Mitchell Thomas over Chris Hughton.

Spurs took to a sunny Villa Park wearing white shirts, navy shorts and navy socks. These were the days when only one substitute was permitted in the league but two were now allowed in cup games. Today's choice was versatile midfielder, Paul Allen.

With Mitchell Thomas making his debut, it was the same for Richard Gough. Mitchell had been playing in Division 1 for the last few seasons, but this was a baptism for Gough. Being up against Garry Thompson would test his physicality as well as his footballing prowess.

Richard Gough recalls his league debut at Villa Park with fond memories. He had only been at Spurs for less than a week, he had an interesting conversation with Hoddle in the Camp Nou. Gough said, "I remember Hoddle coming to speak to me in Barcelona, He said "I've played against you a few times in the England/Scotland games, I see you can pass the ball, when you get it just make me your first pass." Richard then asked Hoddle why, and Hoddle told him that he'd always be free for him. "Because you never run back?" Gough joked, and Hoddle confirmed that wasn't his game.

Four minutes into Gough's debut he did just that. "I remember nicking the ball off big Garry Thompson and then played it straight to Hoddle who volleyed it first time into Roberts, on to Tony Galvin who's cross found Clive Allen for 1-0".

What a start!

Gough confirmed, "From then on that's all I looked to do". Thompson and Stainrod gave Gough a tough debut, but he stayed cool and kept to his game.

Spurs had started strong. Dominant in midfield as resolute at the back. It was to get even better after 26 minutes when Spurs went 2-0 up through Clive Allen again. Hoddle was once again the architect. Hoddle's free kick was expertly headed down by Mark Flaco into the path of Clive who volleyed home for his second of the game.

That seemed to kill the game off as Spurs had silenced the crowd and were playing some delightful football. Paul Allen came on to replace Hoddle who had picked up a slight knock. Waddle moved into a central role and came close to scoring Spurs' third of the game.

Villa were not completely out of the game as they struck the woodwork on a couple of occasions, but Spurs had Clemence on hand for everything else.

But it was Clive Allen's day. With 13 minutes left, Spurs sped from one end of the pitch to the other with a swift Roberts and Falco combination that released Paul Allen to fly forward and fool the Villa keeper before slipping it back to Clive for his opening day hat-trick.

The final whistle sounded which saw elation from the travelling Spurs fans but a disappointing familiarity from the Villa fans.

This result was an indication how the season would go for both teams.

The Birmingham Evening Mail reported a positive stance from the Villa manager Graham Turner, he admitted, "3-0 at home looks a disaster and it was certainly disappointing. But it was not one to panic about". Maybe not time to panic, but in a few weeks' time it would turn into disaster for Turner when he lost his job after a continuation of poor results.

Result: Aston Villa 0-3 Tottenham Hotspur (C Allen 3)

Apart from Hoddle limping off in the second half it was close to a perfect day. Pleat summed up the performance as being 'efficient'. Not huge praise but Pleat was possibly not wanting to get too excited too early into his tenure.

Substitute Paul Allen was disappointed not to start but pleased with his assist for Spurs' and Clive's third goal. But ever the team man, Allen recalls, "I think to get a win, particularly away, from our first game of the season gives everyone a lift. The guys were really encouraged by that result, and we couldn't have got off to a better start. That instils a lot of confidence within the players, the club, the fans, and as I say, we couldn't have got off to a better start, a more positive start".

Winning the opening game in such impressive fashion was a superb start for the club. Clive Allen's hat-trick was electric but the final thought on the game is that of Graham Roberts.

Effective in his defensive duties and also from an attacking aspect. A few days earlier he hobbled off in Barcelona but this game he was back to his battling best.

Three points were in the bag, but Spurs were not the biggest scorers of the day. Clive Allen was also not the only player to snare a hat-trick either. Southampton were top of the league having beat QPR 5-1 at The Dell. Colin Clarke joined Southampton that summer from Bournemouth and had a dream debut with his three goals.

Pleat and Spurs were up and running.

* * * *

Monday 25th August 1986 – White Hart Lane, London
(Att: 25,381)
Tottenham Hotspur v Newcastle United
(TODAY League Division 1)

Two days after the win at Villa Park Spurs were hosting Newcastle United at White Hart Lane for their first League game of the season.

Newcastle's visit last season produced a footballing masterclass from Spurs. They thumped Newcastle 5-1 and that was to be a theme of many results in Shreeve's last season.

Newcastle manager, Willie McFaul, had recently brought in West Ham striker, Paul Goodard and Bradford's solid centre back, Peter Jackson was on the verge of joining to pair up with captain Glenn Roeder. Big Billy Whitehurst would lead the line with one of England's Mexico heroes, Peter Beardsley playing just behind him.

The matchday programme also denoted one of Newcastle's young talents, Paul Gascoinge, as starting. Gascoinge did not feature in the game and was out injured for some time in the early months of the season, but hopes were high for this precocious 19-year-old who had risen up the ranks from apprentice to first team and was second top league scorer for Newcastle last season with nine goals behind Beardsley's 18 goals.

The matchday programme had new manager David Pleat pictured on the front, at a cost of 80 pence. David Pleat wrote all of his matchday programme notes and with an obvious welcome to today's opponents he was keen to outline that he, and his support staff, were focused on moving forward together as players, staff and fans over this coming season.

Line up v Newcastle: Clemence; Stevens, Gough, Mabbutt, M Thomas; Waddle, Roberts, Hoddle, Galvin; Falco, C Allen. Sub: P Allen

Hoddle had recovered from his knock at Villa Park and Pleat was able to name an unchanged team from the positive result gained a few days before.

It was the August Bank Holiday and 25,000 spectators turned up on a very dreary, grey and overcast Monday afternoon. Spirits and hopes were high and there was probably an expectation that Spurs would brush Newcastle aside following Saturday's win.

Spurs took to the field in an all-white kit and began strongly putting pressure on Martin Thomas in the Newcastle goal. Spurs were to find out that Thomas was about to have an inspired game.

The first half it was all Spurs, Falco and Clive Allen squandered a couple of chances but a minute before half time Spurs did manage to go into the lead. Ardiles burst forward on the counterattack to release Waddle on the left wing. Waddle's swift cross into the area saw the ball reach Clive Allen who tumbled the ball home. 1-0 Spurs.

The second half was no different. Spurs controlling the game but nothing materialising up front, Hoddle and Waddle looking dominant and even Roberts bursting forward with one of his trademark runs was again thwarted by Thomas.

Spurs were to rue their wasted possession and chances when England international Peter Beardsley danced through the Spurs midfield, played a one-two with Whitehurst and tucked in between Gary Stevens and debutant Gough to slip the ball past Clemence and equalise with three minutes to go.

A grey day and although it wasn't a grey performance it was a lack of clinical finishing that saw Spurs throw away two points.

Result: Tottenham Hotspur 1-1 Newcastle United (C Allen)

Newcastle were considered one of several teams that could be relegated this season so this result very much suited them rather than Spurs.

After the game, Pleat's assessment was accurate when identifying that Spurs had the chances but simply failed to kill them off. The following day, *The Guardian* newspaper reported on the game and made another perceptive evaluation when saying Spurs should rightly be furious with themselves having overwhelmed Newcastle with their 'surging possession play'.

Alas, two points may have been lost but at least a point gained.

The players had played four games in the last seven days since the Barcelona trip, then up to Villa Park and onto today's game. There would be a bit more time to re-group as there were now four days between now and when Manchester City would visit for the next league game.

* * * *

Saturday 30th August 1986 – White Hart Lane, London (Att: 23,764) Tottenham Hotspur v Manchester City *(TODAY League Division 1)*

The next match at White Hart Lane saw the arrival of Manchester City. Although only two league games had been played, Spurs were second in the table and City not far behind in fourth position. Attention would be paid to the table a little, but more when around a dozen league games had been played.

City were managed by Billy McNeil and coming into today's game they had beaten league newcomers, Wimbledon, on the opening day and then gained an impressive goalless draw at Anfield.

City were a good unit but lacked any 'star-quality' type player. Irish international defender Mick McCarthy was a no-nonsense centre back and they had solid attacking talent in Gordon Davies, Trevor Christie and the young winger Paul Simpson. Central to their midfield plans was the former Spur, Neil McNab. McNab played over 70 times for Spurs during the mid-1970's and apart from spending time at Bolton and Brighton, he seemed to find a home at City where he played until 1990.

Not a team Spurs should be worried about, but then again, the same could've been said for Newcastle a few days earlier.

In the matchday programme Pleat's programme notes paid tribute to the work Billy McNeil and his assistant, Jimmy Frizzell, had been conducting at Maine Road and he highlighted these impressive areas of 'business development' around the club and cited the revenue success that club had by selling over £1m of season tickets.

At the time, revenue numbers like that were quite significant. I was a 'Junior' season ticket holder that season and my ticket, which I still have to this day, cost £120. Oh, if only things were that cheap nowadays! The season ticket booklet was light green in colour and allowed me admission to League, Littlewoods Cup, FA Cup and Football Combination matches.

I was seated in the Paxton Road upper stand, Seat 68, Block R, Row K. And this was to be my seat for a few years to come.

'WE'RE THE PAXTON, WE'RE THE PAXTON, WE'RE THE PAXTON WHITE HART LANE'. There was nothing better than a full house at White Hart Lane when it bellowed out support and songs. We all knew that many of the West Stand Upper fans were a different breed, arguably not as vocal as Paxton, Park Lane and The Shelf, but the collective camaraderie you experience in crowds like that is such a huge pull for any football supporter.

Away games are also a completely different beast. You have the obvious excitement of seeing Spurs play, but you were also riddled with apprehension dependent on what ground you were visiting. But if you were lucky to avoid trouble, then the solidarity among the away support was intoxicating.

However, Spurs were at home. It was time to make White Hart Lane into a fortress. This would be an essential ingredient if Pleat was to mount a title challenge. There were to be a handful of matches played at White Hart Lane this season, that still stick in the memory nowadays, for being an unbelievably good atmosphere. The fans had a responsibility, but then again, the players did too.

The programme also showcased the new team bus that would be ferrying the team to and from away matches. The bus highlighted the continuing association with main club sponsor, Holsten Pils.

The bus, provided by Holsten, was a luxurious upgrade on previous modes of transport. Alan Bridgett, Holsten Managing Director, said, "This is the first time a football club and it's sponsor have co-operated in this way, and it underlines the close relationship we have with Tottenham".

In several months' time, Spurs would put their relationship with Holsten to the test on a couple of occasions.

This was another commercial initiative deployed by Irving Scholar. The initiatives were not going to stop there either.

The club were about to launch their own 'Clubcall' telephone line. The club would allow fans to dial up the number and listen to the latest news and goings-on at White Hart Lane. Spurs fans lapped it up, especially the younger fans, and it all came at a price. Calling 0898 100 500 would give you access to this news. Mike Rollo, the Spurs Commercial Manager, voiced the news heard down the line at a cost-per-minute fee to the listener. I am sure that there were many parents of Spurs supporting children who had some shockingly high phone bills come through during that time.

The phone line was to be launched at the start of December 1986 and at its peak, Spurs estimated receiving 20,000 calls per week. This was yet another revenue stream for Spurs and Scholar.

Away from the matchday programme there was a game to focus on.

Pleat had named the same team for the opening two league games and this time he was making a change. This was enforced by Falco's suspension and Pleat made only one change, bringing in John Chiedozie to replace the suspended striker.

Line up v Manchester City: Clemence; Stevens, Gough, Mabbutt, M Thomas; Waddle, Roberts, Hoddle, Galvin; Chiedozie, C Allen. Sub; D Thomas

Chiedozie would not play in Falco's role but just forward slightly more than his usual midfield berth to support Clive Allen.

Once again Spurs were wearing all an all-white kit. Just under 24,000 fans were hoping to see an improvement on the disappointing draw with Newcastle but early signs were ominous.

Last time out the Newcastle keeper, Martin Thomas, had a superb game and today Perry Suckling in the City goal was to do the same.

The first half was full of possession for Spurs but with no end product. Clive Allen, Tony Galvin and Richard Gough all going close. The best chance in the first half was a superb volley from Hoddle, twenty yards out, that was tipped over the bar by Suckling.

Goalless at half-time. I doubt there was much Pleat could say but to go out and keep doing the same and hopefully breakdown the City defensive wall.

City were wearing an away strip of black and red squares. The shirts looked like a chessboard, and they were certainly playing to a strategic gameplan.

Suckling was playing well but his defiance was to slip in the 65th minute.

Graham Roberts expertly broke up play and went on another one of his buccaneering runs where he finished by hitting a right-foot thunderbolt into the top right-hand corner past the flailing hands of Suckling. 1-0 Spurs.

A wonderful strike and no more than Spurs deserved. Spurs held their 1-0 lead, and the game was won.

Result: Tottenham Hotspur 1-0 Manchester City (Roberts)

In the Sunday Telegraph, journalist Ivo Morton headlined with, 'ROBERTS LIFTS SPURS TOP' and accurately summarised, "Tottenham were worth the victory, having considerably more possession, and they did not give City space for a single chance".

Despite both teams being in the top half of the table, it was clear to see two teams at opposite ends of the scale. McNeil's pedigree was evident, but his style and tactics were contrary to Pleat's attacking machine. The *Sunday Times* reported, "This was always likely to be a match between Millionaires and Misers". It was a slight dig at City's miserly defensive strategy and the well-paid attacking flair of Tottenham.

The Daily Telegraph's Donald Saunders saw things slightly differently. His headline read, 'TOTTENHAM FLATTER, BUT OFTEN DECEIVE'. Saunders saw a more positive approach to McNeil's five-man defensive wall and felt McNeil should take satisfaction from it nearly working. He clearly forgot that City offered nothing at all going forward. However, Spurs did flatter with their league position. Even though they were unbeaten in their opening three games, Saunders planted early seeds of doubt in how consistent Tottenham would be moving forward. When it comes to Spurs, it is a very apt point, but we shall wait and see.

After the game, Pleat did concede that Ray Clemence sprained his ankle early in the first half but played on. Luckily the Spurs back four protected him and he had little to do.

Pleat would be pleased with the back four. Mitchell Thomas and Gough had settled in quickly, Gary Mabbutt was excelling in his left-sided centre back role and Gary Stevens brought intelligent and industrious footballing output behind Chris Waddle.

Spurs were top of the table and let's provide a special mention to the matchwinner during the City game, Graham Roberts.

Roberts had a difficult start to his relationship with Pleat but, in fairness to his new manager, he was now enjoying this new midfield-anchor role and playing really well too. He looked fit and lean which was testament to the pre-season work he worked on in readiness for pre-season.

SEPTEMBER 1986

Tuesday 2nd September 1986 – The Dell, Southampton
(Att: 17,911)
Southampton v Tottenham Hotspur
(TODAY League Division 1)

Three days after the home win over Manchester City, Spurs travelled to the South Coast to face Southampton at The Dell.

Spurs had not won at Southampton in the league since a 2-1 win in May 1983 and in the three seasons after that victory, Spurs had lost 5-0, 1-0 and 1-0. The Dell was not a happy place for Spurs, but they headed into this game top of the table and unbeaten.

Southampton were managed by former player and Northern Ireland international Chris Nicholl, and he did have a fair bit of talent at his disposal too.

The England captain and goalkeeper Peter Shilton was his key man. A League and European Cup champion, Shilton was aging but still revered as one of the best goalkeepers in Europe. Just beneath Shilton was a young Tim Flowers. He was an England Under 21 international goalkeeper who had just joined from Wolverhampton Wanderers, and he would make his debut a few weeks later against Manchester United at Old Trafford and, within a decade, Flowers would himself be a league title winner with Blackburn Rovers.

Further youth talent at The Dell was young midfielder Andy Townsend. A left-footed midfielder who liked getting forward and had a thrust to his game. Wingers Danny Wallace and David Armstrong completed a strong midfield with Colin Clarke up front. Clarke who bagged a hat-trick on his league debut just over a week ago.

However, this was a game that would see the first league start for a young attacking midfielder called Matt Le Tissier. At the time, Le Tissier was still on the Youth Training Scheme and would sign professional in October 1986. He had made his league debut in the loss to Norwich at Carrow Road a few days earlier and now he was starting against Spurs.

Le Tissier would end up playing nearly 450 times for Southampton during a career where he was known for scoring wonder goals. In 1995 he won the BBC Goal of the Season for his mazy run and 35-yard strike against Blackburn Rovers. In goal for Blackburn that day, was none other than his current teammate, Tim Flowers.

Tottenham arrived at The Dell in their new luxurious coach.

As they players exited their new transport, it was evident to see that the Spurs players were now complying to a dress code. Navy jackets, grey trousers, pale blue shirts and a club tie was the chosen attire for the players. Pleat clearly focusing on all areas of the players responsibility to heighten levels of professionalism within the club.

BBC Sports' Tony Gubba spoke to some Spurs fans, who had made the 95-mile journey south, how they felt Spurs being top of the league coming into this game. It was nice to see that the fans were not getting too excited and they remained cautious, but they did address a feeling of inspiration that David Pleat was now at the helm considering the good job he did at Luton Town.

Ray Clemence had sprained his ankle a few days before but was fit to face Southampton and his former England goalkeeping nemesis, Peter Shilton.

Line up v Southampton: Clemence; Stevens, Gough, Mabbutt, M Thomas; Waddle, Roberts, Hoddle, Galvin; Falco, C Allen. Sub: D Thomas

Mark Falco only ended up serving a reduced one match ban and that saw him return at the expense of John Chiedozie.

It turns out, the game against Manchester City would be John Chiedozie's last match in a Tottenham shirt. He was to experience a series of injuries which hampered his availability then he simply fell out of favour. He would eventually move to Derby County in August 1988, but even though his Spurs career fizzled out he is still fondly remembered among Spurs fans.

Spurs lined up to face Southampton wearing their away strip of all pale blue and it all started so badly. When after only two minutes Colin Clarke sped into the box to smash the ball past Clemence to give Southampton the lead.

Despite going 1-0 down Spurs dominated possession and searched for openings. Just like against Newcastle and Manchester City, the approach play was excellent but no end product. On the odd occasions Spurs did break through they would find an inspired Shilton keeping them at bay.

Shilton made superb saves from Falco and Galvin while Southampton had a couple of chances too with Danny Wallace looking menacing every time he went forward. In the 25th minute, a long clearance up field saw Le Tissier brilliantly bring the ball down. He threw a few shimmies to Mitchell Thomas before sliding a lovely through ball to Wallace who spurned the chance.

The second half saw Shilton make more great saves from Hoddle and Falco, but it looked like an equaliser was coming when Clive Allen raced on to a through ball when he was clipped from behind by defender, Kevin Bond. In a split-second Clive stayed up and the referee played the advantage before Clive eventually weakly hit the ball into Shilton. The chance of the half came to Waddle. Hoddle took a left-wing corner and swung it into the penalty spot where Gough towered over Bond to head down where Waddle then headed the ball over the bar from two yards out.

Danny Thomas came on to replace Roberts, who needed stiches in a nose injury, which saw Gary Stevens move into central midfield.

Despite the chances and the possession, it felt Spurs had not recovered from the shock early Clarke goal, and with ten minutes left the game was lost. The impressive Danny Wallace made it 2-0 when he rifled his shot past Clemence. Oddly, the passage of play was the same as Southampton's first goal yet this time it was a different goal scorer. 2-0 to Southampton.

It was game over. Despite Spurs playing well it was a miserable night as none of their attacking play seemed to pay off.

Result: Southampton 2-0 Tottenham Hotspur

A few days earlier the Daily Telegraph's Donald Saunders wrote that Spurs flattered their league position and as the season went on consistency would be their biggest threat.

He was spot on. A game that Spurs should've won but not even a point was gained. Saunders' article in the Telegraph the following morning headlined, 'DEFIANT SAINTS END SPURS' BRIEF REIGN'. Not only did he call this scenario in his last article, but it was a lack of consistency that ruined Spurs' last season. Fingers crossed it was not coming back again.

Praise was rightly given to the 17-year-old Le Tissier who impressed on his first senior start, but wasteful Tottenham was the lingering memory that consumed Spurs fans who made their journey home that evening.

Saturday 6th September 1986 – Highbury, London
(Att: 44,707)
Arsenal v Tottenham Hotspur
(TODAY League Division 1)

After the disappointing trip to The Dell, it was now time for a trip across North London to face Arsenal. Going into the game, George Graham's team had won two and lost two. An opening day win over Manchester United was followed by narrow defeats away at Coventry City and Liverpool. When Spurs were losing at The Dell, Arsenal won at home to Sheffield Wednesday when two of Graham's youngsters, Tony Adams and Niall Quinn grabbed the goals in a 2-0 win.

Arsenal had just dipped into the transfer market too when Graham snared a young winger from Colchester United called Perry Groves.

Spurs had drawn and won on their last two visits to Highbury, so it wasn't necessarily a bleak hunting ground, but this was Arsenal.

Both teams were going through a transition period with new managers, but derby day would always raise the bar. Well, usually it would.

The game would turn into a bit of a drab affair. No doubt, both sides would have been confident in taking all three points and most fans would have expected a goal or two.

Spurs and Arsenal had significant attacking talent on show as well as a healthy mix of youth and experience. Arsenal's defence was testament to that fact as England international's Viv Anderson and Kenny Sansom were at full back while David O'Leary partnered the youthful Adams.

Graham Rix was the star name in Arsenal's midfield that flanked the midfield alongside young David Rocastle on Arsenal's right.

Scotland international Charlie Nicholas partnered the young Irish striker Niall Quinn.

Pleat had kept faith with the team that faced Southampton a few days before with only Ardiles replacing Danny Thomas on the Spurs bench.

Line up v Arsenal: Clemence; Stevens, Gough, Mabbutt, M Thomas; Waddle, Roberts, Hoddle, Galvin; Falco, C Allen. Sub: Ardiles.

Last season's trip to Highbury ended in a 0-0 stalemate. Groundhog Day prevailed as this game finished 0-0 too. Roberts maintained his excellent form in his midfield role, plus you could never expect him to let you down in a North London derby.

England manager, Bobby Robson, was also in attendance and keen to see so many of his international players on show. Sadly, not many impressed. The only player who seemed to impress was Ossie Ardiles when he came on in the second half to replace Mark Falco.

Result: Arsenal 0-0 Tottenham Hotspur

The following day, Deryk Brown wrote in his *Sunday Times* article that Ardiles was the only shining light in an otherwise dull game. He headlined 'ARDILES SHINES IN LONDON GLOOM' and let the readers know that the Merseyside teams could sleep well if they felt they could challenge the might of Liverpool and Everton. He concluded the game was littered with errors and the second half was awful.

Ardiles orchestrated three moves that saw Spurs move with purpose but with no goals to show for his effort and drive.

After the game, Pleat praised his players effort but agreed the game could've turned out differently if he had started Ardiles, while George Graham feared that future London derbies could be like this. If London derbies turned into this, then the paying public would diminish even further! Spurs had generated nearly £3m in replica shirt sales that summer – surely we can expect better.

On the Wednesday several of the Spurs squad were included in the England squad for England's first game since the Mexico World Cup. Mitchell Thomas had received his first international call up and was joined by Hoddle, Stevens and Waddle.

England were away in Sweden and the game was a tad disastrous as England lost 1-0 in Solna to a second half goal by Johnny Ekstrom. Hoddle played the full 90 minutes and Waddles came on as a second half sub for Everton's Trevor Steven.

Richard Gough had been called up for Scotland's home friendly versus Bulgaria. Gough played the whole game in what was an uninspiring 0-0 draw.

Tony Galvin and Chris Hughton were both called up for the Republic of Ireland and started the friendly in Brussels against World Cup semi-finalists Belgium. This turned out to be one of the best games of that international week. Belgium's Nico Claesen had put the home side 1-0 early on only to see Frank Stapleton equalise a few minutes later from a wonderful Tony Galvin cross. The goal of the game was scored midway through the second half by the wonderfully talented Enzo Scifo who headed the ball home from the edge of the penalty area.

Ireland equalised with a minute to go through Liam Brady to finish the game at 2-2. A great game and a pretty impressive performance too from the Belgium striker Nico Claesen. Rumours had been flying around that David Pleat had his eye on the pacey attacker, maybe a player of interest but we will wait and see.

* * * *

Saturday 13th September 1986 – White Hart Lane, London (Att: 28,202)
Tottenham Hotspur v Chelsea *(TODAY League Division 1)*

Going into the Chelsea game Spurs sat sixth in the league table. Bizarrely, the league leaders were the Division 1 new boys Wimbledon. The Dons had accumulated twelve points from their opening five games and at the other end of the scale were

Manchester United who were propping up the table with one point from their opening four games. United boss Ron Atkinson was under increasing pressure and probably the most scrutiny he was starting to experience during his tenure at Old Trafford.

Chelsea only had three points from their opening five games and sat one point above the relegation zone. Rightly, Spurs were very much favourites to win this game.

Lining up for Chelsea were two familiar faces to Tottenham. Chelsea striker Kerry Dixon was part of England's recent World Cup squad in Mexico and had netted 38 times for Chelsea during the past two seasons in Division 1. Dixon was part of a successful Spurs youth team in the late 1970's but was deemed surplus to requirements when Spurs released him. He was eventually picked up by non-league Chesham United and then Dunstable before Reading soon acquired his services where he scored 51 goals in 116 games before moving to Stamford Bridge. Dixon had also featured for England in the midweek loss to Sweden. He failed to score in a makeshift England front-line where he played alongside Watford's John Barnes.

But a face the was significantly more familiar to Spurs fans than Dixon was that of Micky Hazard. Hazard had been at Spurs for seven years before he was sold to Chelsea in the autumn of 1985. Coming back to Spurs must have been a bittersweet moment for Hazard. This was a ground where his free-kick goal in the UEFA semi-final of 1984 remains a strong memory for any Tottenham fan alongside his success in the 1982 FA Cup Final and of course the UEFA Final in 1984.

Always nice to see old faces.

Back in their all-white kit, Pleat named the same team that faced Arsenal the weekend before. Paul Allen replaced Ardiles on the bench and Spurs were hoping to bounce back after their last two league games that had produced only one point from a possible six.

Line up v Chelsea: Clemence; Stevens, Gough, Mabbutt, M Thomas; Waddle, Roberts, Hoddle, Galvin; Falco, C Allen. Sub: P Allen.

In summary, the less said about this game the better. As a Tottenham fan we have our natural rivalry with Arsenal, but for some reason I have always held a healthier disdain for Chelsea. Losing to Arsenal is always difficult but losing to Chelsea always seems to cut me deeper.

Spurs were poor from start to finish. It was yet another glum and gloomy day and losing to Chelsea made it even gloomier. To make matters even worse, the main protagonists were two of our former players.

Mitchell Thomas's clumsy tackle on Pat Nevin saw Chelsea being awarded a 23rd minute penalty. Who steps up to take it? Micky Hazard. Hazard sent Clemence the wrong way and ran off punching the air. Very much a moment to savour for Hazard.

Spurs went in at half time 1-0 down. Spurs had been rocked by an eighth minute injury to Richard Gough, but they hadn't done much to claw their way back into the game either. Hazard was again at the centre of things in the 58th minute where he was played the ball on the edge of Spurs' box and his first time shot rifled into the bottom right corner to see Chelsea's lead doubled. Groans around White Hart Lane. A brilliant goal, in fairness.

Spurs fought back ten minutes later when Mark Falco was fouled in the Chelsea penalty area and Spurs were awarded a penalty. A dubious decision as Falco went down terribly easily but Clive Allen stepped up to convert his penalty and made it 1-2.

The game was settled with fifteen minutes to go when, yes, you guessed it, another former Spur Kerry Dixon made it 3-1 to the Blues. Chasing onto a through ball, Dixon muscled his way past Mabbutt, Roberts tried to catch up as Dixon fired the ball past Clemence for the victory. This time Dixon ran off with his arms aloft in celebration.

The final whistle blew and all that could be heard were the jubilant Chelsea fans. Eurgh, an awful day.

Result: Tottenham Hotspur 1-3 Chelsea (C Allen)

I can remember asking my dad why Spurs were so inconsistent. He would always apply a thought-based approach rather than focus on any one or two key individuals that were underperforming. I knew that individual player errors were damning factors, but dad would always talk about the collective responsibility. This is probably around the time when I started to understand that teams are not necessarily about individual brilliance, but you are more likely to get consistent results when teams start to gel as a group. The odd outstanding performance from a few key contributors was not enough and to gain consistency as the group needed to perform on that regular basis to see results flow.

Dad would talk about allowing time for a new manager to get his ideas across and to create a team he felt fitted his ideas and plans. The honeymoon period for Pleat was dwindling and continuity was gradual. This was around the time when I started to understand how important attitude and conduct was in team environments. If players were unhappy, would they want to perform at an optimum level? If they had felt that Pleat, their own role in the team or the club's direction was not for them how could they fully commit to putting in elite performances every week. The role of a professional sports people is that you are expected to perform at the highest-level week in and week out, however, they are human. They have good days and bad days, they have personal issues and professional issues and life is not that simple.

Take golf for example. Anyone of us who plays golf, are often frustrated by the lack of consistency. One day they are driving well but putting is wayward. The next day they are putting well but the approach play is not as strong. Next time it could all be the reverse again. Front nine is good, but back nine is poor. The higher up the ladder you go in professional sport you tend to see it's the people that can perform consistently become the ones that people remember and have success.

Pleat needed to get that consistency right and you could see a nucleus of eight or nine players that you felt were starters, a few tweaks were required. My dad was right, but I was starting to look at football differently now I was watching it live nearly every week.

Watching players off the ball is just as fascinating as watching them with the ball. Ardiles was a master at that, his positional play was exemplary.

A few years later, when Gary Lineker joined Spurs, he would give defenders the run-around. Off the ball, he would not stop running. For every ten runs he made, only one or two might amount to something, but he never stopped. It was a nightmare for a back four as he would not sit still and wait for his teammates to serve everything on a plate for him. That was part of Lineker's world class talent.

But for now, Spurs had now slipped to eleventh in the league table. Their promising start was unravelling but what was more alarming was the lack of bite up front. Falco and Allen had a great pre-season, but they were not firing as effectively now.

Colin Gibson wrote in his *Daily Telegraph* column, 'HAZARD RELISHES SPURS RETURN'. This seems a painfully obvious headline but painfully true too.

Hazard was replaced by John Hollins just before Chelsea's third goal as he got hit with cramp, but he told Gibson, "I didn't want to come off, but the cramp was getting worse. Maybe the cramp was down to the tension of my homecoming. I still have a lot of friends at this club". Hazard had an emotional connection with Tottenham, and it is always understandable when a former, discarded player returns to show what they can do.

Tottenham had lacked a bit of bite in the midfield during the Chelsea loss. Gough's loss during the game meant Roberts went back into the back four alongside Gary Mabbutt. Roberts had been superb in his anchor midfield role, and it was noticeable that bite was missing when he slipped into the centre back role.

In September's issue of *Spurs News*, Roberts was interviewed where he highlighted how he had been raring to go and enjoying his new role. He had put large portions of his effectiveness down to his fitness levels. Roberts said. "I am a lot fitter than at the same stage last season and playing in a role that is actually helping me. I can get forward, defend when needed and basically express myself a bit more. I feel that I have got more than just defending in me and I'm so happy to leave that to Richard Gough who is a world class player". Roberts continued to praise his new teammate, "He's strong in the air, good on the ground and is quick. He gives the team more assurance and I like to think I am helping him and Mabbsy in my role just in front of them".

It seemed that Roberts had put his early frustrations with Pleat behind him and it appeared that Pleat was valuing Roberts in his new role too.

A trip to Filbert Street was up next against a mid-table Leicester City. How would Pleat play this one out.

* * * *

Saturday 20th September 1986 – Filbert Street, Leicester
(Att: 13,141)
Leicester City v Tottenham Hotspur
(TODAY League Division 1)

Tottenham travelled 100 miles northwest of White Hart Lane to face Bryan Hamilton's Leicester.

Hamilton, the former Northern Ireland international midfielder, had only one league victory to his name during the opening six league games. This was, impressively, over the league champions Liverpool, but results against more comparable teams were not that impressive.

He had a decent team with some strong experience and talented youth too. Former Ipswich and England international Russel Osman was his defensive lynchpin alongside the younger talent of centre backs Steve Walsh and Mark Venus.

Scotland U21 midfielder Gary McAllister was the playmaker and young striker Alan Smith was the club top scorer and apparently being eyed up for a move with one of Division 1's bigger teams.

Pleat knew something had to change and he tweaked a couple of areas which would be beneficial. Two changes were applied. Danny Thomas came in for Falco, he would slot in as right back. Gough had recovered from his injury and was to line up alongside Gary Stevens in the middle of Spurs' defence. This meant Gary Mabbutt would join Graham Roberts in the middle of midfield. Paul Allen came in to replace Tony Galvin. Paul Allen and Waddle would play wide and Hoddle a little further forward alongside Clive Allen.

This was not your classic 4-4-2 formation. Was Hoddle a second striker or was he a fifth midfielder? This was one of a few away leagues games I went to this season, and I can recall my dad telling me he didn't think it was a conventional 4-4-2 as Hoddle was much more advanced than normal. We used to talk tactics and formations for hours, so this was a huge talking point for us both.

Line up v Leicester: Clemence; D Thomas, Stevens, Gough, M Thomas; Waddle, Roberts, Mabbutt, Hoddle, P Allen; C Allen. Sub: Ardiles.

On a gloriously sunny day, Spurs lined up in white shirts and a change of navy shorts and navy socks.

The home team nearly took an early lead when Clemence was penalised for 'time wasting' (so early in the game!) and Leicester were awarded an in-direct free kick on the six-yard line. The whole Spurs team lined up on the goal line and Clemence flung himself in front of the balls to save his blushes.

Spurs dominated most of the first half but failed the cutting edge to find an opener. Gary Stevens was playing superbly well alongside Gough with Alan Smith and Steve Moran getting little or nothing to show for their exertions in trying to get the better of Spur's defending. It was evident to see Hoddle looking different in this hybrid-type role. He was not up front, nor was he in the heart of the midfield, but he was floating about and looking purposeful every time he was given the ball.

Hoddle cranked things up a notch in the first minute of the second half. He lofted an inch perfect free kick into Clive Allen's feet whilst he had his back to goal in the middle of the box. Allen then turned sharply and shot past Ian Andrews with a sweet left foot strike. A wonderful goal, 1-0 to Spurs.

Six minutes later Spurs were 2-0 up. Hoddle took a right-wing corner and swung the ball out near the penalty spot where Richard Gough leapt higher than anyone to head down for Clive Allen to half-volley the ball in from six yards out.

Spurs were well worth their 2-0 lead. Things got a little ropey when Gary Stevens hobbled off with a knee injury -an injury that would keep him out for serval matches it turned out. Ardiles came on and Mabbutt shifted into the back four. Spurs then got a little nervy.

Leicester were starting to press more now and they pulled one back through Simon Morgan with ten minutes to play.

In the last few minutes Spurs were looking pretty chaotic at the back and the home side nearly salvaged a point with a minute to go as some pinball defending saw the ball land at the feet of Leicester midfielder Andy Feeley who shot wide of Clemence's right hand post.

When the final whistle blew it was Spurs who took all three points. They deserved the win over the ninety minutes, but the last ten minutes were not overly inspiring.

Result: Leicester City 2-1 Tottenham Hotspur (C Allen 2)

This was the first time Spurs had scored more than one goal since the opening day 3-0 win over Aston Villa. Once again it was Clive Allen with an impressive brace, but Hoddle and Gough were just as impressive with their superb assists.

Gary Stevens remembers the win at Filbert Street. He recalls the injury he sustained that day with nine minutes to go in the match, "I went in for a 50/50 challenge with a Leicester midfielder, it was a bit of a swashbuckling challenge, but I went into it fairly. However, I went into it with my side foot, and it forced my knee back and it opened up the knee joint on the inside and it strained my medial ligament. It's worse than a muscle strain as ligaments take so long to heal. I knew if I had gone more straight footed in might've been ok".

This would keep Stevens out for a month. He had been playing so well at right back and even better during this game alongside Gough in the middle. He knew competition was strong as Danny Thomas would be more than ready to fill in at right back.

Stevens and Danny Thomas both joined Spurs at the same time in the summer of 1983. They had built a strong friendship and still, to this day, they remain very good friends. Stevens continued, "David Pleat saw Danny and myself as right back rivals, but Burkinshaw had signed me as a centre half to provide competition to Paul Miller. David Pleat did prefer me at right back to Danny Thomas and I think Danny would initially agree with me. He liked big defenders and said he preferred a good 'big' one over a good 'small' one".

Stevens was possibly correct as Pleat also preferred Mitchell Thomas over Chris Hughton at left back. Spurs were very lucky to have Danny Thomas and Chris Hughton as back-ups to Stevens and Mitchell Thomas.

The *Sunday Times*' Martin Bashir headlined Spurs' victory with, 'ALLEN DOUBLE SINKS LEICESTER'. Bashir astutely reported that Leicester had deployed an unconventional sweeper system but that allowed Hoddle, Roberts and Mabbutt to dominate the middle of midfield.

But Spurs were back to its winning ways and winning breeds confidence. Up next were Everton. Everton would visit White Hart Lane the following Saturday having been runners up to Liverpool in last year's championship race. Liverpool and Everton were favourites for the title this year and Spurs were trying to bridge the gap.

But the league campaign would go on pause for the time being as Spurs were about to start their League Cup campaign. The Littlewoods Cup 3rd round draw had seen Spurs plucked to play Barnsley who were languishing at the lower end of Division 2. Spurs would travel to South Yorkshire on Tuesday for the first leg.

FANTASTIC DISAPPOINTMENT

Tuesday 23rd September 1986 – Oakwell, Barnsley
(Att: 9,979)
Barnsley v Tottenham Hotspur
(Littlewoods League Cup 2nd Round, 1st Leg)

Spurs ventured 175 miles north up the M1 motorway to face Barnsley on a cool Tuesday autumn evening. Early cup rounds are sometimes tricky but most topflight teams should tend to walk away with a victory. It wouldn't be easy, that's for sure.

Pleat took a strong team to Oakwell and started ten players that took to the field at Leicester three days before. Paul Miller had come in for the injured Gary Stevens to make his first start of the season and Mark Falco returned to the bench at Ardiles' expense.

Line up v Barnsley: Clemence; D Thomas, Gough, Miller, M Thomas; Waddle, Roberts, Mabbutt, Hoddle, P Allen; C Allen. Sub: Falco, Ardiles.

Spurs began strong and were aggressive in the tackle. Not often you'd describe Hoddle as the ball-winner, but he dispossessed a Barnsley midfielder and played a lovely ball into Waddle who struck the ball first time with his right foot and under the advancing keeper for Spurs' first on the night and his first goal of the season. A smiling Waddle looked relived as Clive Allen pounced on him to celebrate Spurs' opener.

Things went a little wrong after that. The strong start evolved into a weak show that would see Barnsley take a 2-1 lead into half time. A right-wing free kick was swung into the far post and

Stuart Gray beat Mabbutt to powerfully head home the equaliser. Surprisingly Mabbutt was very slow to react.

Into the second half, Barnsley were awarded a penalty when after another spell of pinball defending in the Spurs penalty area, a fallen Graham Roberts was adjudged to have handled the ball among the chaos of players and feet flying everywhere. Stuart Gray stepped up to convert the penalty and it was his second of the game.

Spurs were now 2-1 down against a team who were three points above the Division 2 relegation zone and had only scored one goal in their last nine hours of football. Come on Spurs.

Tottenham did increase the tempo with 14 minutes to go. A right-wing Hoddle corner found its way to Waddle outside the area who played a simple pass to Graham Roberts who hammered the ball into the top right-hand corner from 25 yards out. 2-2 and Spurs were on the look for a winner.,

Pleat brought on Falco to add extra fire power and surprisingly took Hoddle off. But the game was won with six minutes to go when Clive Allen curled a lovely free kick in from just outside the box. 3-2 and a hard-earned victory.

Result: Barnsley 2-3 Tottenham Hotspur
(Waddle, Roberts, C Allen)

The following day, Stuart Jones wrote in *The Times*, 'ALLEN AND ROBERTS JUST IN TIME'. He highlighted that despite some of Spurs' dazzling play there was a littering of errors and mistakes.

Spurs' defensive record last season was poor. Pleat had assembled a good back line, but errors, slowness and mistakes needed to be eradicated if Spurs wanted to challenge for honours. An away win nonetheless and onwards to a mouth-watering league encounter with Everton on Saturday.

* * * *

In September the Official Club Handbook was published. The front cover saw Clive Allen and Ray Clemence wrestling each other on the shoulders of Mark Falco and Graham Roberts, while under the watchful eye of David Pleat who was kitted out in Hummel training attire. The image on the back was Glenn Hoddle battling with Diego Maradona in June's epic World Cup quarter final encounter in Mexico City.

The Handbook provided profiles of Pleat's new management team that included Trevor Hartley as his new first team coach and Doug Livermore had stayed on to lead the Reserve team. Keith Blunt and Keith Waldon were leading the Youth team and physiotherapists John Sheridan and Cliff Speight completed his backroom team.

There was also a profile on the 'kit' men, Johnny Wallis and Roy Reyland. Most seasons this area of expertise may not figure too much, but there will be a couple of events where the 'kit' men would negatively come into the spotlight and sadly one event that was particularly high profile.

Finally, the playing staff were profiled. From Ray Clemence to Clive Allen, and from Ossie Ardiles to Mark Bowen. The only 'unknown' player included in the profiling was Youth goalkeeper, Kingsley Banks. A player that I did not know of or even remember at the time. That season Banks would go on to make only a single appearance for the Spurs South-East Counties Division 2 team. He never did play professionally for Tottenham and ended his career with non-league Essex side Heybridge Swifts.

Another publication that was considered 'staple' for Spurs' younger fans was the 1987 Panini Football album. The front cover was an action shot taken from an Everton and Aston Villa league encounter. The two players showcased on that front cover were Villa striker Andy Gray and the Everton player who was always hard to guess. I always thought it was Everton captain Kevin Ratcliffe but still, to this day, I am not 100% sure.

The Panini Sticker album was essential for young football fans. That season, 12 pence would've been the cost of a packet of six stickers. Thirteen Spurs player stickers were required, along with David Pleat and a team sticker too.

Those Panini sticker albums were an absolute-must at school. I'd often fall short of completing an album and have scores and scores of doubles that I would struggle to get rid of. Completing Spurs was always a priority. I cared little for collecting all of the Arsenal and Chelsea stickers but everyday I'd head off to school with my wad of stickers ready to trade for a sticker that I 'needed'.

Still to this day, I remember Aston Villa's Martin Keown's sticker. He, and his hair, looked more like Frankie Carbone from *Goodfellas* than the Keown we probably all know. I read some time ago that the actor who played Carbone, Frank Sivero, tried to sue The Simpsons for using a gangster character for over a decade that had a very similar likeness to him. Maybe Keown had a case too!

On the back page of the 1987 Panini sticker album was an advert for the Bobby Charlton Soccer School and had images of kids with Manchester United's Bryan Robson, Liverpool's Craig Johnston and Everton boss Howard Kendall.

I was lucky enough to attend the Bobby Charlton Soccer School in the summer of 1988. It was a great experience. During my stay we visited Old Trafford and, with it being my first time there, I was in a bit of awe at the size of the stadium in comparison to White Hart Lane.

Sadly, the same calibre of footballer as Robson and Johnston was on show during my visit.

Former Manchester City goalkeeper, Alex Williams, was the only professional who came to share some tips and give some insight into the world of professional football. He was a genuinely lovely guy and had a great rapport with the coaches and kids. There were scores of lads in attendance during that trip but the highlight for me was to be chosen in the Bobby Charlton Soccer School select XI to face a youth team from Glasgow Rangers. I do recall we lost the game, but it was a superb experience and I am glad to say that I performed pretty well on the right side of midfield.

During this time the Panini sticker album, the club handbook and the matchday programmes were essential reading for younger fans. Still to this day I have all home matchday programmes from 1986-87 and they have been a superb resource when researching and writing this book.

Alongside them were the glossy football publications *Shoot* and *Match*. Before the rise of the internet these were our sources of information alongside BBC's *Ceefax* and ITV's *Teletext* services. Now these were the original go-to sources of up-to-date information for football fans.

Ceefax, page 302, enough said.

* * * *

Saturday 27th September 1986 – White Hart Lane, London (Att: 28,007)
Tottenham Hotspur v Everton
(TODAY League Division 1)

Many of the September games had been played under grey and overcast skies. For the visit of Everton, the sun was shining over White Hart Lane.

Spurs were buoyed from the midweek win at Barnsley and two players were about to reach significant milestones. Glenn Hoddle was making his 350th league appearance for the club and his midfield teammate, Graham Roberts, was making his 200th league appearance.

Goal scoring had been a problem of late though. Clive Allen was scoring so that was a good sign. However, his seven league goals so far did not see him top the Division 1 goalscoring charts. If not Allen, then it must be either Liverpool's Ian Rush or West Ham's Tony Cottee. Wrong. Nottingham Forest were top of Division 1 and England U21 midfielder, Neil Webb, had scored ten goals already!

Everton were second in the league and were the only unbeaten team in Division 1. Today was going to be a tough task for Spurs.

Pleat had brought Tony Galvin back into the team at the expense of Paul Miller. Gary Mabbutt reverted into his central defensive partnership with Richard Gough and Hoddle was once again playing in the same role assisting Clive Allen.

Chris Waddle had taken a slightly more central role inside Paul Allen on the right-hand side and it was to prove to be a lucrative partnership.

Line up v Everton: Clemence; D Thomas, Gough, Mabbutt, M Thomas; P Allen, Waddle, Roberts, Hoddle, Galvin; C Allen. Sub: Falco.

Everton were packed with winners. Defenders Kevin Ratcliffe and Derek Mountfield, midfielders Trevor Steven and Kevin Sheedy and strikers Graeme Sharp and Adrian Heath had all been part of successful League, FA Cup and European Cup

Winners Cup teams. There were a few notable absentees that day, including England right back, Gary Stevens and Welsh goalkeeper Neville Southall. Southall had arguably been the best British goalkeeper for the last 3-4 years but today Bobby Mimms was deputising. In a couple of years' time, Mimms would end up at White Hart Lane and today he gave an excellent account of himself as he foiled several Spurs attacks. Everton would also miss the midfield bite of Peter Reid and the aggressive attacking full back, Pat Van Den Hauwe but surely, they still had enough quality to forge a result.

Spurs went 1-0 up after 26 minutes. Some superb interplay between Paul Allen and Chris Waddle saw Allen flight in a wonderful right-wing cross for his cousin, Clive, to get ahead of Kevin Ratcliffe and head home. A brilliant goal and a brilliant header from a player who was not renowned for his headed goals.

Spurs dominated possession for most of the first half and gave Everton little chance to pile forward for an equaliser.

With 20 minutes to go in the second half Spurs did double their lead. Once again it was Clive Allen. This time the source of Allen's set-up was not from Hoddle, Waddle or Paul Allen, but Ray Clemence was to pick up his first and only assist of the season. A left footed clearance by Clemence saw the ball bounce around 20 yards outside the Everton area. Clive Allen expertly eased aside Paul Power to volley first-time past a despairing Bobby Mimms. Another superb goal.

Clive Allen nearly got his second hat-trick of the season when he shot just wide from a lovely chip into the box from Hoddle. Allen lost Derek Mountfield only to see his limp volley sail wide as he collided with an on-coming Mitchell Thomas.

Result: Tottenham Hotspur 2-0 Everton (C Allen 2)

One of Everton's defenders that day was Derek Mountfield. I spoke to him as the season would turn out to be very memorable for him and his club.

He recalls playing at White Hart Lane and his encounters with Chris Waddle. Waddle was on fire that afternoon and sadly for Everton, their usual right back Gary Stevens was injured so Mountfield filled that role. "Chris gave me a roasting that day and usually we would let Gary Stevens look after him as he had the pace to keep up! We knew it was always tough at Tottenham. Glenn Hoddle would always put the ball on a sixpence and obviously they had the great Ray Clemence in goal. Generally, we did not pay too much attention to other teams and their key players when preparing. We focused on our own team and our own performance. That day it was Tottenham's and what a season Clive Allen would end up having. Despite that, we still felt confident in what we needed to do that season".

Mountfield and his Everton teammates had lost out on the league and FA Cup to Liverpool the year before, so they were determined to make amends.

Mountfield was also aware of Spurs' new defensive signing that season, Richard Gough. "He was such an elegant and comfortable footballer. That era was so strong and aggressive, but he seemed to read the game so well. He was a fantastic footballer. You could see him, and Gary Mabbutt had a good relationship and complimented each other well. Just like myself and Kevin Ratcliffe over the years".

Everton would look for revenge in the corresponding fixture later in the season. Derek Mountfield will be a key contributor to the result of that game too.

The following day, The *Sunday Times* praised Spurs' result with a subtle, yet accurate headline. 'EVERTON UNDONE BY ALLEN'. Brian Glanville highlighted the dynamism of Paul Allen and the sheer quality of Chris Waddle, but special mention for the man of the moment, Clive Allen. Glanville incorrectly pointed out that Allen had now scored 10 of the team's 11 goals in the league, when in fact he'd scored nine out of 10. It was simple, goals needed to come from other sources too.

As September ended, Tottenham were sixth in the league with 14 points from their opening eight league games.

Nine league and cup games had been played in total so far. Won five, drawn two and lost two. 13 goals had been scored and nine conceded. Clive Allen had netted on ten occasions, a couple for Graham Roberts and one for Chris Waddle.

Not too bad, but improvement was required without doubt.

OCTOBER 1986

Saturday 4th October 1986 – White Hart Lane, London
(Att: 22,738)
Tottenham Hotspur v Luton Town
(TODAY League Division 1)

Spurs welcomed Luton Town to White Hart Lane in the first October fixture. Aside of the result on the pitch, this game would be remembered for a few other reasons.

There had been some bad blood and crossed words in the media, but Pleat was focused on his new challenge at Spurs rather than getting involved but further tension was also heightened due to a 'typo' in Pleat's notes within the matchday programme.

Pleat always wrote his own notes and club Editor, John Fennelly, was tasked in proofreading and putting all content together. As we know, there was huge tension between the Luton chairman David Evans and Spurs boss David Pleat. Pleat's notes concluded with, "Enjoy the game. May the headlines not be about hooligan chairman, manager gossip and slander but entertaining football". Oh dear.

It was meant to read, "…not about hooligans, chairman…". It was a simple 'typo' but now Evans would've read Pleat referring to him as a hooligan chairman! We can laugh now, but at the time it did not help the strained relations.

Excitingly though, Spurs were unveiling a new player. Just before kick-off, Belgium international striker, Nico Claesen, was introduced to the White Hart Lane crowd having just joined the club for £600,000 from Standard Liege. Claesen was a slick attacking player who had superb pace and an eye for goal. He was part of the Belgium team that navigated themselves to the World Cup semi-final in Mexico a few months before.

Sadly, Claesen was unavailable today and his signing had also meant the end of another player's time at Tottenham. Striker Mark Falco had left the day before to join Watford. Pleat had deemed him surplus to requirements as he was bringing Claesen into the club. Falco had been fantastic in his time at Spurs. A surprise departure yes, especially as he had a good pre-season. However, his opening to this season hadn't gone to plan and Pleat had other ideas.

In '*Behind Closed Doors*', Irving Scholar gives an account of how Pleat's wily transfer brain had orchestrated Falco's move to Watford. Scholar mentions that Falco was not fitting into Pleat's plans and wondered how he could 'drum up interest' as there were no offers coming in for Falco. Pleat decided to call his friend and manager of Watford, Graham Taylor. He told Taylor that Falco was doing well in the reserves and deserved a first team spot, but the Tottenham board were keen to sell him. He told Taylor that several teams were interested, and his call was to seek Taylor's advice in what to do in this situation. The call had aroused Graham Taylor's interest, Taylor asked Pleat if he was serious in letting Falco leave as he felt Watford would be very interested in securing the services of Falco.

With the seed planted, the transfer grew legs and within days an offer had come in. Spurs accepted £300,000 for Falco and with that, he was off across London to ply his trade at Vicarage Road.

Pleat was quoted in *Spurs News*, "I am delighted that Mark has gone to such a progressive club with a good manager. They are probably one of the few clubs who would have attracted Mark because of their geographical location". This move paved the way for Claesen to come in.

Falco netted 68 times in his 174 Spurs appearances. Such a pivotal player in the UEFA Cup winning team and rose the ranks from apprentice to first team during his eight year tenure. Once again, another Spurs legend had departed. Amusingly, Falco kept in-line with his Tottenham roots by scoring on his debut for Watford, against Arsenal of course.

With Falco gone and Claesen unavailable to play it was quite alarming to then find out that Clive Allen was struggling with a hamstring injury on the morning of the Luton game. A fitness test then proved that he was unable to play. Would Pleat deploy Waddle or Hoddle up front or would he perhaps dip into the reserve team squad who had playing scoring for fun and had netted 23 goals in 7 reserve league games.

Shaun Close and David Howells were top scorers and Pleat decided to go with the player who had already made his debut and scored on his debut too. Howells was chosen to play his first senior game of the season.

Howells was playing in Clive Allen's role with Hoddle, Waddle and Galvin just behind him.

Line up v Luton Town: Clemence; D Thomas, Gough, Mabbutt, M Thomas; P Allen, Waddle, Roberts, Hoddle, Galvin; Howells. Sub: Ardiles.

Hopes were high after the Everton win, but Spurs produced a drab and relatively lifeless performance. Young Howells was struggling, he was up against two huge and experienced centre backs in Steve Foster and Mal Donaghy.

Howells recalls, "I knew Clive was struggling and, on the Friday, there was a possibility I might play. I had not played up front on my own before. Clive was an 18-yard box striker whereas I used to drop in short to receive the ball. In the reserves, Shaun Close played up front ahead of me and Mark Bowen running off us too. Disappointingly, I didn't get any advice or pointers from Pleat. I barely got a touch all game and when I attempted to come short, the midfield was packed with Glenn, Ossie, Chrissy Waddle and Paul Allen. This was my home debut, and I was really disappointed. It was a boring 0-0 draw, and I don't remember being involved in the game too much." Howell's time would surely come, and he happily returned to the reserve team to continue his development.

Luton had beaten Spurs 3-1 in the corresponding fixture last season and looked the more likely team to gain 3 points at White Hart Lane again.

Ray Clemence was inspired though. Another bright and sunny Saturday saw the Spurs skipper don a baseball cap during the game. He made flying saves from Mark Stein, Steve Foster and Mike Newell to claim a man of the match performance for the home team. His Luton counterpart, Les Sealey, had little to do all game, apart from tipping over one long range effort from Hoddle.

Result: Tottenham Hotspur 0-0 Luton Town

Pleat told me that he recalls the 0-0 draw at White Hart Lane, but his mind was preoccupied with some nasty comments made by David Evans in the press that week.

Luton Town were in the press regularly during that part of the season as they had banned all away supporters from attending games at Luton's Kenilworth Road ground. Previous events of shameless hooliganism had forced the Luton chairman to take this unprecedented measure. Not everyone in football agreed with this stance though.

A few days earlier Irving Scholar had spoken to the Daily *Telegraph* to emphasise Tottenham's stance in trying to beat the hooligans. Spurs had created a special 'Junior Spurs' enclosure for younger fans to enjoy the game away from any potential thuggery. *Telegraph* journalist, Colin Gibson, wrote how Scholar had offered 677 'Junior Hatters', and their families entrance into the Junior Spurs enclosure. Gibson reported that Spurs were pioneers in attempting to influence the Football League in making family enclosures 'compulsory' across the game. Scholar was quoted saying, "The game's motto should always be the Family Affair and that is what we are trying to create at White Hart Lane". An excellent idea and an excellent public relations exercise too.

More alarming was the hypocrisy of behaviour amongst the visiting Luton fans. David Pleat had spoken to *The Sunday Times*' Mihir Bose. He mentioned that he was glad to see the back of this game and hoped that people could now 'move on'. Bose also reported on the away supporter's behaviour.

He wrote, "Mitchell Thomas was booed and hissed with a racial animosity that would have done credit to the National Front. Even poor Ossie Ardiles, coming on as a sub, was taunted with Falklands war chants. Luton's away fans deserve to be banned from every away ground in the country".

Bose's observations were shocking to hear but this was the state of many pockets of support in English football during those times. Bose was keen to point out that this did not apply to the Luton team who played with a mixture of 'inventiveness and dash' that Pleat did so much himself to foster.

Tottenham were not due to visit Kenilworth Road to play Luton again until the Spring of 1987, hopefully things would die down a little by then.

* * * *

FANTASTIC DISAPPOINTMENT

Wednesday 8th October 1986 – White Hart Lane, London
(Att: 12,299)
Tottenham Hotspur v Barnsley
(Littlewoods League Cup 2nd Round, 2nd leg)

After the complexity surrounding the Luton game, Spurs were able to take their mind off their inconsistent league form and refocus on the League Cup with a visit from Barnsley.

Spurs were 3-2 up from the first leg and despite some of the worrying moments in the first leg, Spurs were sure to progress now they were at home.

The matchday programme featured Richard Gough making his first appearance on the front cover. David Pleat provided his usual programme notes welcoming the visitors and there was also a 'Celebrity View' page featuring the one and only Peter Cook.

Cook was an elite comedian and a high-profile Spurs fan too. Cook spoke of how he started following the club in the late 1950's and even though his career had taken him all around the world he still seeks out the Spurs results every single match. However, Cook did make a slight dig at some of the fickle Tottenham fan-base and mentioned that most seasons the fans usually found someone to pick on. "Yes, we are a funny lot at Tottenham. Some of us never think we are as good as we used to be and some more of us love to have someone to hate".

Known for his comedy and amusingly cunning use of the English language, this was a more serious interview than most would expect as Cook concluded, "I've got two hopes for this season: that the supporters get behind the club again and we get back to where we should be, among the honours on a regular basis". A sentiment held dear to most fans we would suspect.

But, back under the midweek lights, Pleat had made changes. Ardiles came in to replace Paul Allen, who had dropped to the bench, and Shaun Close came in to make his senior debut at the expense of David Howells. Clive Allen had also returned but was on the bench alongside Paul. The final change was Paul Miller coming on for Gary Mabbutt to make his second appearance of the season.

Line up v Barnsley: Clemence; D Thomas, Gough, Miller, M Thomas; Waddle, Roberts, Ardiles, Hoddle, Galvin; Close. Sub: P Allen, C Allen.

Tottenham had a couple of early chances Shaun Close scored his debut Spurs goal from a corner that Gough had knocked down to him.

Hoddle got his first goal of the season when he slotted home from several yards out before Beresford scored for Barnsley and clawed one back to go into half-time 2-1 behind.

Not long into the second half Hoddle then scored a 25-yard belter. Ardiles and Waddle took a short corner before the latter passed to Hoddle for a first time right footed shot into Barnsley's top right corner. 3-1 to Spurs.

A bursting Roberts run nearly made it 4-1 but it was Tony Galvin who scored Spurs' fourth with a header from Chris Waddle's right wing corner.

Barnsley were not done yet, with 23 minutes to go they scored again to make it 4-2 on the night and 7-4 on aggregate.

Clive Allen came on and within minutes he had scored Spurs' fifth goal with his strike from just outside the six-yard box. Barnsley were still not done and scored yet again a minute later but the game finished 5-3 on the night and 8-5 overall.

Result: Tottenham Hotspur 5-3 Barnsley
(Close, Hoddle 2, Galvin, C Allen)

Yes, there was some more ropey Spurs defending, but also an impressive attacking display that easily could've achieved more than the five goals they did net. Plus, it wasn't just goals from Clive Allen either. Tottenham were now drawn to play Birmingham City in the 4th round.

A few days later, the club announced that European football was returning to White Hart Lane.

Sadly, the UEFA ban on English clubs had not been lifted but Spurs had agreed to play a friendly match against the 1983 European Cup winners and German giants, Hamburg. The clubs were drawn together by a mutual connection - well, a brewery to be more precise. Holsten sponsored both clubs and, even with a competitive ban in place, hoped to recreate the famous midweek European game under the lights at White Hart Lane.

Hamburg had strong, recent European pedigree. In 1980 they lost the European Cup final to Nottingham Forest, but they managed to return three seasons later to beat Real Madrid and win European football's biggest prize. The game would be played at the start of November.

* * * *

Saturday 11th October 1986 – Anfield, Liverpool
(Att: 43,139)
Liverpool v Tottenham Hotspur
(TODAY League Division 1)

Tottenham went into their trip to Anfield in seventh place in Division 1. Champions Liverpool were not having the best start to their season and sat in third place behind Nottingham Forest and Norwich City.

They had been impressive in most games but faltered against teams you'd have not expected them to lose to.

Liverpool had been beaten at Filbert Street and The Dell, but they had stayed strong at home and Spurs had an awful record at Anfield.

Spurs had lost 4-1 last season but had actually won the season before, when Garth Crooks' strike was enough for Spurs to take all three points and historically become the first Spurs team to win at Anfield in 73 years.

Spurs would very much take a 1-0 today and to boost morale, Nico Claesen was available to make his debut for the club.

Spurs, in all white, lined up against Liverpool, in all red.

Omens were even better at the news Gary Stevens had returned to full fitness and he replaced Danny Thomas at right-back. Mabbutt came back in for Paul Miller and Clive Allen came in for Shaun Close. Nico Claesen replaced Ossie Ardiles and Spurs returned to a more conventional 4-4-2 formation with Claesen joining Allen up top.

Line up v Liverpool: Clemence; Stevens, Gough, Mabbutt, M Thomas; Waddle, Roberts, Hoddle, Galvin; C Allen, Claesen. Sub: P Allen.

Autumnal sunshine blanketed the Anfield pitch as Spurs started brightly. Clive Allen and Nico Claesen looking very sharp and very lively, and Spurs nearly took the lead after 11 minutes when Richard Gough rose high to head Hoddle's corner crashing into the Liverpool crossbar.

These moments visibly helped Spurs grow in confidence. Arguably, one of the most successful striking partnerships in English football history was kept quiet as Gary Mabbutt and Richard Gough defended stoutly. Kenny Dalglish and Ian Rush were struggling and Spurs went into half-time all square at 0-0. Arguably Spurs had been the better team too.

Within a minute of the restart Spurs had taken the lead. Waddle was the provider as he sent in a tantalising cross which found

Clive Allen goal side of the home keeper, Grobbelaar, to tuck home for 1-0.

Claesen thought he had scored on his debut, but the goal was disallowed and after that chances for Spurs were few and far between as it turned into a defensive masterclass. How often do you hear that about Tottenham!?

Paul Allen replaced Tony Galvin with 20 minutes to go and added some tenacious bite into Spurs' midfield. The final whistle blew, Anfield fell silent as the travelling Spurs fans went into a frenzy of celebration that was sprinkled with disbelief.

Result: Liverpool 0-1 Tottenham Hotspur (C Allen)

Now that was two victories in the last 75 years! What an excellent result and a genuinely strong performance that did not rely on luck.

The *Sunday Times* headline was, 'GLORY DAYS ON SPURS HORIZON' as the article firmly placed Spurs as genuine title challengers after that victory.

Two days later, *The Times* headline was, 'TOTTENHAM STORM NORTHERN BASTION' as it mused over the point that Spurs, and to some extent Arsenal, were about to challenge the 'northern dictatorship' that the Merseyside clubs had over English football. Special praise was directed at Richard Gough, "all the promise and imagination of Tottenham's forward play would have counted for nothing if their defence had not been so combative, so secure. Gough stood defiantly at the heart of Spurs; defence like General Custer".

Richard Gough remembers that game fondly, especially some of his Scotland teammates. "We kept a clean sheet which was brilliant, and I remember that being Nico's debut. He gave Gary Gillespie a hard time and I kept Kenny Dalglish quiet. A great win, I remember it well".

Chris Waddle was really starting to play well. A couple of weeks ago he was running rings around Everton's Derek Mountfield and today he was bewildering Liverpool full back Jim Beglin.

Tottenham had now beaten both Merseyside giants Liverpool and Everton in the space of two weeks. They were both favourites for the title and now Spurs had thrown their quality into the mix. Spurs had leap-frogged Liverpool into third place. Good times.

* * * *

Saturday 18th October 1986 – White Hart Lane, London
(Att: 26,876)
Tottenham Hotspur v Sheffield Wednesday
(TODAY League Division 1)

Tottenham fans turned up to White Hart Lane for the home game against Sheffield Wednesday in such a positive mood. It felt Spurs were in a good position to challenge for the title this year and, despite recent inconsistencies, the wins over Liverpool and Everton gave good food for thought.

Caution had been aired though when David Pleat spoke to *Spurs News* and stated that, despite beating Liverpool and Everton, "We haven't done anything yet". He continued, "Players are playing more solidly now but we must gain consistency".

Today was going to be Ray Clemence's 200th league appearance for Spurs and Clem had been solid all season. Ever the talker, he was now directing and leading his Spurs defence that had chalked up six clean sheets already.

I can remember there being such a buzz around the ground for this game. Having won at Liverpool was not a common feeling for Spurs fans so hopes were starting to rise. But, after the Everton victory, Spurs disappointed with a home draw against Luton. The fans hoped it would not happen again following on from such a brilliant performance over the league champions.

Wednesday were playing well though and had accrued 16 points from their opening ten games and were a point ahead of Everton.

The matchday programme had an image of Nico Claesen battling for the ball with Liverpool's Barry Venison during last weeks' superb win at Anfield. Claesen would be making his home debut today.

Wednesday boss, Howard Wilkinson had built a good footballing team and had some exciting talent at his disposal. Martin Hodge was one of the league's best goalkeepers and in front of him were two progressive full backs in Mel Sterland and Nigel Worthington. Young Gary Megson provided some craft in the midfield alongside winger Brain Marwood. Former England international Mark Chamberlain partnered the physical Lee Chapman up front, so they had enough firepower in their ranks to worry Spurs.

Wednesday's Nigel Worthington faced Chris Waddle only a few days before at Wembley Stadium. England hosted Northern Ireland in a European Championship qualifier. Hoddle and Waddle started. Gary Mabbutt returned to the squad again and this time was included on the bench. England won 3-0, a brace from Barcelona new boy, Gary Lineker. His first goal came from a Hoddle corner and England's second goal was scored by Chris Waddle. Waddle had been menacing all evening but his goal after 75 mins was built on a storming run by Steve Hodge before Beardsley took over and dinked the ball to Waddle who thundered the ball in with his left foot. Worthington was facing further torment today, we hoped.

Pleat only made one change from the Liverpool game. Tony Galvin came off injured at Anfield and was replaced by Paul Allen, who would start today. With Claesen playing closer to Clive Allen this saw Hoddle drop back into a more conventional central midfield role. This was more of a standard 4-4-2 formation.

Claesen would have been full of confidence too as he had netted a hat-trick for Belgium in their midweek qualifier against Luxembourg.

Line up v Sheffield Wednesday: Clemence; Stevens, Gough, Mabbutt, M Thomas; P Allen, Roberts, Hoddle, Waddle; C Allen, Claesen. Sub: Ardiles.

The sun was out once again as Spurs kicked off and playing towards the Park Lane end. Early in the game you could see that Wednesday came to compete. They battled for every single ball and were visibly making the lives of Spurs' creative midfielders difficult.

Where Claesen had looked impressive at Anfield, he looked a bit bewildered at the physicality of this game and, being honest, was largely ineffective on his home debut.

On the other hand, Clive Allen was flying into tackles and battling all over the place. This man was hungry to score. Chances were few and far between.

Despite Paul Allen not looking entirely at home on the left side of midfield, it was his left-wing cross that set Clive Allen up for his six-yard tap-in. It came from a Hoddle corner on Spurs' left, the ball made it to Roberts who played Paul Allen in to provide his third assist of the season.

This was Clive's thirteenth goal in twelve league and cup games already - staggering numbers.

Half-time came and Spurs didn't necessarily deserve the lead, but they were 1-0 up.

Where the first half began in sunshine, the grey skies gathered over White Hart Lane for the next period of the game, and Spurs' second half performance was just as grey. Wednesday equalised after 60 minutes. Mitchell Thomas had gone on a brilliant left wing run to see his cross being claimed by Wednesday keeper Hodge. Hodge threw the ball out immediately to his left wing and the counter was on. Gary Megson had been outstanding all afternoon. He had nullified any effectiveness Hoddle and Roberts dared to adopt and Megson was everywhere. And here he was now, sprinting the length of the pitch, he didn't break stride as a perfect square pass found him bursting in the box between Gough and Mabbutt to shoot into the back of the net.

Result: Tottenham Hotspur 1-1 Sheffield Wednesday
(C Allen)

Yet again, another goalkeeper was having an inspired game against Spurs. Martin Hodge was excellent and his swift throw for the equaliser was a bit of a turning point in the game. Speaking to Malcolm Winton in the *Sunday Times*, Pleat referred to some of his saves as 'world-class'.

Spurs were again wasteful, but in fairness, they didn't have the same thrust and vigour to compete with Sheffield Wednesday. Two points dropped.

Inconsistency, that word again.

* * * *

Saturday 25th October 1986 – Loftus Road, London
(Att: 21,579)
Queens Park Rangers v Tottenham Hotspur
(TODAY League Division 1)

Disappointment would inevitably have spread through the squad as they trained that week. They were not playing badly at all, but there always seemed to be the odd factor that stopped Spurs winning games and winning them convincingly.

Clive Allen was in rich form and on the Thursday, he was interviewed by Graham Miller on *Thames News*, where he stated that he was looking forward to returning to Loftus Road. Not just because he had good times there as a former player, but because Spurs had smashed five goals past them in one of the final games of last season. Allen was keen to point out that he felt now was the time the Spurs fans got to see his real potential as he was injury free.

Pleat still had close to a full squad to choose from. Tony Galvin came off in the Anfield win, a cartilage injury that would keep Galvin out of the side until the middle of December that year. Chiedozie was still out too.

Other notable absentees from the first team were Ossie Ardiles, Paul Miller and Chris Hughton. Ardiles was in and out of the first team whilst he was playing a fair number of games for the reserve team alongside Miller and Hughton. Clearly frustrating for those guys but good for the reserve team. Defenders Neil Ruddock and John Polsten had built a brilliant partnership in front of back up keeper, Tony Parks. They were still top of the Football Combination having conceded only six goals so far.

That said, Pleat went with the same eleven that drew with Sheffield Wednesday the week before. I wondered if this was the right choice. The Wednesday performance was limp and games at Loftus Road were always intense, I felt that Ardiles playing would've regulated our play so much more, but I imagine Pleat was keen to integrate Claesen and he was persevering with Roberts too.

Line up v QPR: Clemence; Stevens, Gough, Mabbutt, M Thomas; P Allen, Roberts, Hoddle, Waddle; C Allen, Claesen. Sub: Ardiles.

The game would be played on QPR's artificial pitch. A pitch, that most players referred to, as concrete. Hard and bouncy.

Spurs' last visit to Loftus Road had seen the away team run out 5-2 winners, Falco and Clive Allen both scored a brace with Hoddle making up the fifth. Results at Loftus Road were not too bad and going into this game Spurs were clear favourites.

Spurs changed their kit and performed in their all navy away kit. Still, to this day, one of my favourite Spurs kits and another winner by kit manufacturer Hummel. I would love to say that kit inspired a famous win, sadly not.

It was a turgid performance that saw QPR prevail as 2-0 winners. The game was also branded 'The Allen Affair', three cousins all playing in the same game. Clive and Paul Allen were the Spurs cousins who were up against another cousin, QPR midfielder Martin Allen.

It was a bit of a footballing dynasty. Clive's father, Les, was part of the Spurs 1961 double winning team and had also played at QPR and Chelsea. Martin's father, Dennis, had played professional football for Charlton, Reading and Bournemouth. Paul's father, Ronnie, played at non-league level but never achieved professional status.

Despite the goalscoring form of Clive, it was QPR's Martin that opened the scoring and shocking Spurs after only 9 minutes.

Yet another occasion that lacked the punch required to get back into the game. It slightly changed with half an hour to go when Pleat introduced Ardiles into the game. His tactical change saw Gary Stevens exit. Paul Allen slips into the right back role and allows Ardiles to take up his usual midfield berth. There were occasions when Spurs played some scintillating football but nothing cutting in the final third.

The Daily Telegraph's, Bill Meredith, wrote, "Ardiles arrival gave Spurs a touch of class, but it was not enough".

As Spurs tried to create an opening for the equaliser it was QPR who killed the game early into the second half. John Byrne scored with a turn and shot that gave Clemence no chance.

Claesen was the only one to test goalkeeper, David Seaman, but the young QPR and England U21 goalkeeper was having an excellent game. Everything he did was with the maturity of a seasoned pro. Even when Gary Stevens and Chris Waddle looked threatening, they shot wide whilst a towering Seaman bore down upon them.

Result: QPR 2-0 Tottenham Hotspur

This was Tottenham's third London derby of the season and they had taken only one point from a possible nine.

Spurs slipped to seventh in the table and to be honest the team were looking a little dis-jointed with Claesen's inclusion.

Maybe he still needed time to acclimatise but Hoddle and Waddle had not been as ineffective in the last two games either. The loss of Tony Galvin had affected the team too. Pleat preferred Waddle on the right but he could play left side too. Would Pleat dip back into the transfer market as the news on Galvin's injury was not a quick fix?

There had been one left-sided player that Pleat had been looking at. Probably time to talk to the chairman and see what could be done.

* * * *

Wednesday 29th October 1986 – White Hart Lane, London
(Att: 15,542)
Tottenham Hotspur v Birmingham City
(Littlewoods League Cup 3rd Round)

Pleat needed to inspire his team and get them back to their winning ways. A break from the league was a welcome tonic and the arrival of Division 2's Birmingham City gave Spurs an opportunity to get some form back.

On a more sombre note, the matchday programme announced the death of Club President, Sidney Wale. Wale joined the Spurs board back in 1957 and was a huge part of the Tottenham fabric during a time where he would see the club scoop nine major trophies in his tenure. Black arm bands were worn by Spurs players that evening.

Line up v Birmingham City: Clemence; Stevens, Gough, Mabbutt, M Thomas; P Allen, Roberts, Hoddle, Waddle; C Allen, Claesen. Sub: Miller, Ardiles.

Pleat had gone with the same side that lost to QPR and drew with Sheffield Wednesday. It seemed he was determined to make this group of players work.

Spurs did win the game and won it convincingly. It took 24 minutes for the scoring to begin when, from a Hoddle corner, Richard Gough powered in yet another header into the path of a Spurs attacker. This time it was Waddle who expertly guided the ball in for a 1-0 lead.

Gough was never one to really celebrate, he would sprint back to his centre-back position and lay ready for the next phase of the game.

Nine minutes before half-time, Hoddle split the visiting defence wide open and Clive Allen turned and struck the ball high into the top left-hand corner, 2-0.

Thirteen minutes into the second half, it was Clive Allen again. This time Paul Allen provided the assist straight from a corner. Paul's left-wing corner found Clive alone in the six-yard box to head home for Spurs' third.

Gough was to be the provider again when, five minutes later, another Spurs corner found Gough, who's challenge ricocheted to Graham Roberts who thumped the ball home from 25 yards. 4-0 to the Lilywhites.

Paul Miller came on to replace Mitchell Thomas and with here minutes to go it was Hoddle's turn to get in on the scoring. Hoddle had been brilliant all night and topped of a classic Hoddle performance with a 25-yard free kick that left the Birmingham keeper watching like a statue as he caressed the ball into the top left-hand corner. 5-0.

Result: Tottenham Hotspur 5-0 Birmingham City

A strong result against weak opposition, but 5-0 is still an impressive victory. Another brace for Clive and another clean sheet for Clem.

The good news continued that week as Tony Galvin had started to train again, it may not be a swift return but at least he was back training.

Two Spurs fringe players had also been put out on loan. Oxford United had a bit of a goalkeeping crisis, so Tony Parks joined them on a short-term deal. Young defender Tim O'Shea had also joined Newport County on loan.

Slightly sadder news, young midfield talent, John Moncur, had been on loan at Doncaster Rovers. In a game against Darlington, he broke his leg towards the end of the match. He would be out for some time, and he had now returned to White Hart Lane to start his rehabilitation.

Spurs had now played a dozen league games and were sitting in a disappointing seventh position having gained 19 points from near enough the first quarter of the season.

David Pleat had cited inconsistency being a concern amidst all the buzz around the victories over Everton and Liverpool. Spurs had to do better.

NOVEMBER 1986

Saturday 1st November 1986 – White Hart Lane, London
(Att: 21,820)
Tottenham Hotspur v Wimbledon
(TODAY League Division 1)

The arrival of Wimbledon at the start of November was another London derby.

Drawing with Arsenal and losing to QPR and Chelsea was not a great start to the 'league within a league'. In my opinion, London clubs often get a rougher ride due to the sheer number of London clubs, and therefore the number of derbies, to contend with. Spurs were still to play West Ham, Charlton and Watford. Seven London teams in total, fourteen games and 42 points up for grabs.

Wimbledon were visiting for a first league visit to White Hart Lane in their club's history. Newly promoted, Wimbledon began the season well and were top of the table after a few games but had slipped to fourteenth having gained only one win in the last seven league games.

That solitary victory came the week before where they beat Norwich City 2-0, in a home match at Plough Lane.

Elected to the Football League in only 1977, they would find acclimatising to the top-flight a bit difficult, but Wimbledon had some talented players in their ranks. They also had immense physicality to their game too.

Goalkeeper Dave Beasant had joined Wimbledon in 1979 from non-league Edgware Town. He had been a rock in their rise from Division 4, where they were champions in 1982-83, to Division 1 this season. In front of Beasant were the physicalcentre back pairing of Brian Gayle and Andy Thorn.

Where Wimbledon tended to hurt teams was up front. They would lead from the front. And they had a leader up front too in John Fashanu. Fashanu was the brother of former Norwich City striking legend, Justin Fashanu. He was not known for his goalscoring exploits but more for his dynamic, physical presence that made defenders' lives a complete and utter misery. He had been acquired from Millwall for £120,000 and was their most expensive signing to date.

Joining Fashanu in the forward line was the cunning Alan Cork and the direct Carlton Fairweather. Behind the attacking options were Lawrie Sanchez, Dennis Wise and Glyn Hodges. Sanchez and Wise were more than diligent footballers, but both had a ferocious bite to their game and they were supported by Welsh international Glyn Hodges. Hodges had a super left foot and was the most cultured footballer in their squad.

Manager Dave Bassett knew his teams' strengths and weaknesses. He didn't make them play above their stations, but he stuck to tried and tested tactics that were consummate with their physical prowess.

Pleat was, once again, looking to bounce-back after the poor result at QPR. Pleat started the same eleven for the fourth game in a row.

Line up v Wimbledon: Clemence; Stevens, Gough, Mabbutt, M Thomas; P Allen, Roberts, Hoddle, Waddle; C Allen, Claesen. Sub: Ardiles.

David Pleat's matchday notes welcomed Wimbledon and he wrote about dismissing newspaper 'gossip' that had been milling around a certain player's future at White Hart Lane. In truth, a fair bit of speculation had been doing the rounds about the future of Glenn Hoddle.

'*Spotlight*' on Gary Stevens was another full-page article within the programme. Stevens was talking about his latest injury comeback after damaging his knee at Leicester, then returning to the team for the victory at Anfield. Now playing at right-back he was impressed with Spurs defensively this season. "The whole back four has looked very strong in every game this season". Today, this strength would be put to the test.

This was the first game I had ever attended where I felt an opposition performance was completely unjust. Wimbledon came to White Hart Lane and 'beat up' this elegant Spurs side. Elements of the game turned into carnage as Wimbledon claimed their first ever away win in Division 1. I left that game feeling genuinely incensed.

Sunday Times reporter, Malcolm Winton, described this match as "Eighty minutes of drama and twenty minutes of mayhem". One hundred minutes of football you might ask, well yes, there was significant stoppage during the game that warranted the extra time.

Realistically, Wimbledon knew they could not match or compete with Spurs on a pure 'footballing' front, so they utilised their strength and intimidation skills. Even before the mayhem, Spurs had not played particularly well, the visitors dominated the game with a brash and dominant nonchalance that completely disarmed Tottenham. By the end of the game Wimbledon would have four men booked and one sent off. Spurs would have two men booked and two men stretchered off! Plus, one of the players stretchered off would also get a red card to add to his injury.

It was another defensive error that allowed Alan Cork to sneak in and score after latching on to a quick free kick. Wimbledon 1-0 up after 13 minutes.

Fashanu was definitely putting his weight about. Richard Gough recalls, "Before the game, Mabbsy told me to watch out for Fashanu as he will try to get into us early. I was used to physical football in Scotland but this was slightly different. Early in the game, Fash comes up to me and said, 'Oi, bastard. I'm gonna do you today'. I laughed it off and told him it was probably Mabbsy giving him verbals and not me". But Gough knew this was a battle.

Gough was also keen to point out that Glenn Hoddle was braver than people gave him credit for in games like that. Yes, Spurs were struggling with Wimbledon's physical presence, but Hoddle was not one to go missing.

There were only a few bright moments in the opening 45 minutes which saw Clive Allen, Glenn Hoddle and Nico Claesen go close, but Wimbledon held onto their lead at halftime.

Only observant fans will have noticed some of the niggly kicks and words that were being directed at one Spurs player in particular, Graham Roberts. In fairness to Robbo, he knew he was being targeted but he was keeping his cool very well. Hopefully that coolness would last into the second half.

As the second half progressed Spurs looked for an equaliser, but things were starting to bubble over. Roberts reacted angrily to provocation by Wimbledon midfielder Steve Galliers, but things started to worsen in the 54th minute when the visitors went 2-0 up.

Alan Cork launched in yet another cross to the Spurs penalty box. Clemence came out looking to claim it, but it looked odds-on for Gary Stevens to head clear. Steaming in from another angle was John Fashanu who leapt and clattered into Stevens whilst heading the ball home past Clemence.

Stevens went down in a heap and was not moving. The away team ran off celebrating as Clemence called for the physios. Several minutes were lost as Stevens was placed on to a stretcher and carried off.

Yet another injury for Stevens and even more galling as he had just fought his way back to fitness after getting injured at Filbert Street in September. Plus, Bobby Robson was about to announce his England squad for the upcoming euro qualifier versus Yugoslavia and this seemed Stevens would now not be available for selection.

I asked Gary how much he remembered of that moment and the challenge by Fashanu.

"I was knocked unconscious. It may have seemed that it was a bit of a misunderstanding with myself and Clem but as the ball looped in, I was about to head it away. Fashanu had got a run on me and his elbow smashed into me. It was an ideal opportunity for him to give someone a whack, and that somebody was me. So, I am unconscious in the air, and I came down like a deadweight and landed on my shoulder and fractured my collarbone. I spent the night in the North Middlesex hospital".

Stevens remembered that he once had a photo of that challenge but couldn't recall having it anymore, I informed him that the image was printed in the next matchday programme two weeks later. I sent the image to him at his request. He replied by saying he would share the image on his Twitter account. He posted the image along with the words, 'On the wrong end of a challenge back in the day. No wonder my memory is starting to fail me'. As ever, Gary was diplomatic in light of what was an outrageous foul on him.

The image tells the exact same story as how Stevens had seen it. Fashanu towering over him, elbow on him while Richard Gough and Carlton Fairweather look on in the background.

This was quite a powerful memory to recall, and it was underpinned with the fact he received another significant injury two years later at the hands of the same team.

In November 1988, Tottenham beat Wimbledon 3-2 at White Hart Lane. Stevens was playing at right back again and midway through the first half a right-wing cross from Wimbledon missed all the players in the area and was heading towards the far touchline for a throw-in to Spurs.

Fashanu and Stevens chased for the ball, Fashanu retrieved it, and Stevens came in to close him down. Stevens then managed to gain possession of the ball and with Fashanu falling all over him Stevens had no chance to see Wimbledon midfielder, Vinnie Jones, flying in with a ridiculous sliding tackle. Jones clattered the ball away, but he also took out Stevens' standing right leg.

Stevens was writhing on the pitch in agony, but the ref claimed Jones had got the ball. Stevens stayed on the ground and was stretchered away. An injury to his knee that would be the most significant of his playing career.

Gary Stevens is a very philosophical character; he sees the positive in nearly everything and you can sense that he holds no grudges.

Back to the game, Ossie Ardiles came on. Ardiles was never a player to instigate violence or strong, physical play, but he was also not one to shy away from it. Part of his game that day was to try and keep Robbo calm and controlled, but the provocation continued, and he would eventually lose that cool.

Not long after Stevens had been stretchered off, one of Roberts' main antagonisers, Lawrie Sanchez, dragged down Ardiles and Roberts got directly involved only for his teammates to haul him away from any serious trouble. But, at this point, the writing was on the wall, and you felt something was coming.

Roberts caught Sanchez with a late challenge, nothing too crazy but it was late. Sanchez reacted immediately by kicking Roberts in the right shin with such force the Tottenham hardman went down straight away. You could see he was in pain. Players were all now getting involved and a melee ensued. As Roberts was being treated, the referee gave Sanchez a red card. The right decision, especially if you add up all the other misdemeanours he had committed that day. However, for Roberts it looked like his game was over as he was placed onto a stretcher and heading off.

Whilst Roberts was heading off, the match referee, Mr Axcell, decided to show him a red card too for his involvement with Sanchez. David Pleat mentioned that he could feel the referee was about to brandish a card to Roberts, he felt that he didn't deserve it, but got the stretcher on in the hope he might avoid sending him off. Sadly, that didn't work.

When the players and the tension calmed a little, the game resumed. Despite Spurs not playing well at all they did provide a late onslaught of Beasant's goal. Mitchell Thomas grabbed his first goal for Tottenham after he scrambled home after 79 minutes from a cute Ardiles pass. Chris Waddle delivered a delicious cross that ran tantalisingly along the goal line, but no one was there to tap in and with a minute or so to go, Beasant pulled off a superb double save denying Clive Allen and the Claesen's follow up.

Having played nearly ten minutes of injury time, Mr Axcell decided to finally blow his whistle and end the game. Another loss and another London derby defeat.

Result: Tottenham Hotspur 1-2 Wimbledon

Fashanu and friends had bullied their way to gaining three points and in his post-match comments, David Pleat struggled to keep his anger in check. He told the *Sunday Times* that it was clear that Fashanu took out Stevens and knocked him unconscious. Wimbledon boss, Dave Bassett, saw it the other way. He told the *Sunday Times*, "Clemence and Fashanu and Stevens all went for the ball together and it was Clemence and Stevens who connected. Fashanu tried to get out of the way". Bassett would have done well to just say he didn't see it as the image showcasing the moment where Fashanu impacts Stevens.

Clemence was not even in shot. Even Fashanu came out and told the *Times*' Malcolm Winton, "Clemence and Stevens clashed, I don't want blaming for that". Poor from Fashanu, he tried turning himself into the victim.

Bassett did agree that Sanchez was out of order, deserved to be sent off and would be fined by the club. Two days later the FA announced they would look at and investigate the incident, and could extend both players automatic two-match ban. The FA were looking to crack down on these levels of serious foul play and both Spurs and Wimbledon were clubs that had been hauled up in front of the FA Disciplinary committee every season for the last five years.

* * * *

So soon after the disappointment and chaos of the Wimbledon loss, Spurs were facing their first European opponents since the recent summer tournament held in Barcelona. The game had been organised by Holsten; the official kits sponsor for both clubs.

Publicly, this was to give Spurs fans the chance to see European opposition during the current ban, but privately, the club would have seen this as a bonus revenue stream to assist them financially with the loss of European tie earnings.

Scholar and the board would have been disappointed to see only 5,095 fans turn up. Not exactly a bumper evening of revenue to be gained but still an enjoyable event, nonetheless. The club had marketed the game quite well, news of this match was in previous matchday programmes and the *Spurs News* periodical too.

Maybe the attendance was low due to an apathetic fan base that had not been inspired by the recent inconsistent results.

Anyway, this was another chance to see our heroes in action, and some new faces too.

Pleat gave starts to a couple of the fringe players and some youth too. Danny Thomas came in for the injured Gary Stevens and Chris Hughton came in for Mitchell Thomas to register his first senior start of the season. There was little change in the midfield and up front but youngsters Paul Moran, John Polsten and Shaun Close all joined Paul Miller on the bench.

Line up v Hamburg: Clemence; D Thomas, Gough, Mabbutt, Hughton; P Allen, Ardiles, Hoddle, Waddle; C Allen, Claesen. Sub: Miller, Moran, Close, Polsten.

The night proved to be a footballing success. Spurs were 2-0 at half time and won 5-1 after the 90 minutes. Hamburg were no mugs. They were second in the Budesliga and half of their team had played international football for West Germany. Five in the team were part of the European cup winning team of 1983 and they were led by coach Ernst Happel.

Happel was one of the finest managers in European football. The Austrian had successful spells at Feynoord and Club Brugge before taking control of the Dutch national side in 1977 where he guided them to the World Cup final in 1978 where they ultimately lost to Ossie Ardiles and Argentina. His career highlight was leading Hamburg's 1983 European Cup final success over Juventus and he was named 9th Greatest Manager of All Time by *France Football* magazine in 2019.

But the likes on Von Heesan, Kaltz, Grundel and Plessers had little impact in trying to control Clive Allen. Clive was on fire that night and scored a superb hat-trick, in only 38 minutes.

Clive;s hat-trick was followed up with goals for Claesen and Mabbutt and while Hamburg scored a late consolation it was nowhere near enough to dent the dominance Spurs exerted that night.

Result: Tottenham Hotspur 5-1 SV Hamburg

Pleat had brought on youngsters Paul Moran and John Polsten for their first senior starts in a Tottenham shirt.

Polsten was a gifted centre-back that had an elegance to his game. He read the ball very well, was an excellent distributor and in all honesty, he looked like a Richard Gough clone.

Paul Moran was a ridiculously fast wide midfielder. He was nicknamed Sparrow. As the years would go by fans would scream 'Roast'em Sparrow' as Moran pelted down the wing.

David Howells played a lot with Paul Moran, and I was keen to know where the 'sparrow' nickname came from. Howells revealed, "He got that nickname in the ball courts. He had these tiny, thin little legs and one day someone said 'Fucking hell son, you've got sparrow kneecaps there', so that was it. He was known as Sparrow from then on".

After the game, Scholar spoke to *The Times'* David Miller and admitted, "We knew it wasn't going to be much of a crowd, but we have to do something to win back our people. Since Brussels, the public has lost confidence in the game. If we sit and accept our exclusion from European football over the next few years, we could end up losing a generation of teenagers who know nothing of the thrill of football and will find something else to occupy their time". Scholar and Spurs, like with their family enclosure section, were at least trying to do something different, whereas most Division 1 clubs were not taking the lead in adapting to the Euro ban.

* * * *

Saturday 8th November 1986 – Carrow Road, Norwich
(Att: 22,139)
Norwich City v Tottenham Hotspur
(TODAY League Division 1)

Despite this mid-season soiree against European opposition there was still a stark reality that Spurs were terribly inconsistent. The 5-1 victory over Hamburg reminded the fans how good this team was, but after the second home league defeat of the season to Wimbledon, and sitting ninth in the league table, there was about to be a very significant change deployed by Pleat.

One of Europe's and England's greatest midfielders was dropped from the team that would face Norwich City. Glenn Hoddle was Spurs' footballing talisman and, in an age, when squads were very small and star players were even a smaller commodity, Pleat opened up to Joe Lovejoy in the *Independent* to explain why he was dropping Hoddle from the Spurs team.

The article came out on the morning of the game so fans would have known rather than Pleat dropping a bombshell when the team sheet was submitted.

Pleat said, "He (Hoddle) knows he is not playing well at the moment. He has had three poor games by his standards. I am prepared to sacrifice Glenn for this game because I feel I need greater strength in midfield. He is the most skilful player at the club, but he is not operating in the final quarter of the field as he is used to".

Lovejoy then surmised that this could be the writing on the wall at White Hart Lane for Hoddle and all the big European teams would be circling around the capture of his signature.

Speaking with Pleat, it was clear that even to this day he felt Hoddle was not being utilised accordingly and had visions of him operating in an advanced role without having any defensive duty. These further changes would actually occur in a few weeks' time, but Spurs were facing Norwich City who were fifth in the league and playing well.

It would be fair to say that David Pleat was under pressure. His team were inconsistent, and the Spurs board and fans were expecting better. During the week there had already been one high profile management casualty, when Ron Atkinson was sacked by Manchester United leaving them fourth from bottom in the league table. His replacement was Aberdeen's Alex Ferguson.

Ferguson was appointed United boss the day before Spurs trip to Norwich. Speaking to Derek Hodgson in the *Independent*, Ferguson announced his key objective. To win the European Cup! United had not won the league since 1967 so this was a bold statement. His final comment before taking his first day in office was 'Winning is important, but the manner of winning is important too'. Spurs would face United at Old Trafford next month.

In the ever-expanding files of the 'Ones That Got Away' we can insert this in section F. Ferguson had been speaking to Irving Scholar a couple of years before when Burkinshaw was about to leave Tottenham. In Scholars' *'Behind Closed Doors'*, he talks about the closeness of bringing Ferguson to White Hart Lane. "I had been talking to Alex Ferguson. These conversations had got to the point of agreeing personal terms and we shook hands on a deal. However, he then had second thoughts and decided not to accept my offer".

Scholar talks about how Ferguson was a good fit for Spurs' style and ethos. A huge importance on winning but they had to be entertaining too. But, as we know, Peter Shreeves was then given the reins for a couple of seasons before Pleat took to the helm.

Norwich City had been playing well. Manager Ken Brown had led Norwich to League Cup success in 1985 and, still to this day, he holds the club record for managing the club in more competitive matches than any other Norwich manager. Some key players from that '85 Cup win had just departed that summer when central defender Dave Watson had joined Everton and England goalkeeper, Chris Woods had joined Graeme Souness' revolution at Glasgow Rangers.

That aside, the other key component of that Cup winning team, Steve Bruce had remained. A superbly fierce and competitive centre back that was now leading a team full of promising youngsters.

They had just recruited a young Scottish goalkeeper from Aberdeen called Byan Gunn and Mike Phelan was also part of Brown's impressive defensive unit. But it was in the midfield and attack that Norwich mightily impressed. A young striker by the name of Kevin Drinkell was now the club's no.1 striker having already netted five league goals so far.

In midfield they had a slick and stylish winger in Dale Gordon. He had swift footwork and a superb eye for a cute pass. Former Spurs favourite, Garry Brooke, was also at the club but currently on loan at Gronigen. Another former Spur, Ian Culverhouse would have the daunting task of marking Chris Waddle today. Culverhouse, a diligent full-back, was yet another case study of Spurs' impressive youth system.

However, the most eye-catching player of Norwich's midfield, during the first quarter of the season, was Ian Crook.

Now, Crook joined Norwich from Spurs only four months before. A superb playmaker and he was laden with intelligence. Let's hope he does not do what Micky Hazard did to his former club when he returned to White Hart Lane and dominated in Chelsea's 3-1 victory over Spurs in September. Surely that will not happen again! Or will it.

With Gary Stevens side-lined, Chris Hughton returned at right back. Paul Miller returned to partner Richard Gough and that allowed Gary Mabbutt to take up Hoddle's midfield role.

Line up v Norwich: Clemence; Hughton, Gough, Miller, M Thomas; P Allen, Roberts, Mabbutt, Waddle; C Allen, Claesen. Sub: Hoddle.

Spurs continued with a 4-4-2 and a very combative midfield. Waddle the only real flair player on show and Pleat hoped this strength may see Spurs succeed for the first time in the league since winning at Anfield four league games ago.

The game was lively during the first 45 minutes. Some would say that it lacked Hoddle's finesse and touch, but it was still entertaining. As the half developed, it was quite clear to see that Ian Crook was getting a subtle, yet strong, hold on the midfield battle but, in fairness, Spurs were still in the game as it remained goalless at the break.

The second half began, Ian Crook began to orchestrate Norwich's dominance and in the 59th minute and they took the lead. And yes, it was Ian Crook who scored. It was a cool finish to a powerful Norwich attack and the former Spur had now opened his goalscoring account for his new team.

Pleat now feeling the pressure even more you would suggest. So much so, that he now turns to Hoddle to see if he can pull Spurs out of the jaws of yet another defeat. Enter Hoddle and enter Spurs' equaliser. In a flowing move from one end to the other, Hoddle identified Paul Allen darting forwards and placed a superb pass into his direction as Allen swept forward and brilliantly crossing low for Nico Claesen to score his first league goal for Spurs.

1-1 and game on.

Yet, Spurs were to go behind again only five minutes later. The euphoric reply was now cancelled out when Ian Crook lofted a wonderful free-kick on to the head of City's Shaun Elliott. Elliott headed home to put the hosts in front. Ian Crook, again.

Tottenham offered little in the final fifteen minutes and it was to be a third consecutive league defeat for Pleat and his players.

Result: Norwich 2-1 Tottenham Hotspur (Claesen)

Unsurprisingly, all the post-match reporting would focus on Hoddle's exclusion from the starting line-up.

The Daily Telegraph's Trevor Cook reported that Pleat had tried to explain his reason for Hoddle's omission in that he wanted to try out different options and combinations. He then got drawn into a statement around Hoddle leaving Spurs. "All I said was that everyone has a price, but I did not hang a FOR SALE sign on Glenn's shirt'.

It was evidential that from now until the end of the season, the future of Glenn Hoddle would be hot topic. Pleat and Spurs would not be able to avoid this cropping up on a regular basis.

In hindsight I had sympathy for Pleat on this point. Yes, Hoddle was not playing as well as he could, and this was perhaps because he had started the process of seeing who his next club was going to be. Sometimes dropping a player does them the world of good and motivates them to perform next time. Hoddle was not a troublemaker or toxic influence in the dressing room, but Pleat needed him to get back up to his usual standards. When Hoddle did, his game would bring the best out of the players around him. With Clive Allen seemingly playing as a lone striker it would be so advantageous for Spurs to have an effective Hoddle behind him pulling the strings. I'd imagine Hoddle's next move was impacting his personal life just as much, as something was very much on his mind.

A few days later, England manager Bobby Robson indirectly waded into the Hoddle debate too. England were about to play Yugoslavia in a European qualifier at Wembley and Robson had already announced two names that would definitely start. Peter Shilton was out injured, and this allowed Chris Woods to deputise. Robson also said Hoddle would start.

The Times' Patrick Barclay wrote that Hoddle had started twenty of the last twenty-one England internationals but the speculation over his England place, due to his indifferent form and Pleat's recent exclusion, would cast his England place into doubt. Barclay spoke to Robson who stated that "He'll (Hoddle) be worrying, and I want to ease his mind. What has happened at Tottenham does not bother me. If he had been playing in the reserves for the last few weeks it would be different, but Hoddle played really well last time out against Northern Ireland".

Barclay's piece glowed at the fact Hoddle was now one of the first names on the England team sheet and this should have been a regular occurrence over the last seven years since Hoddle made his debut in 1979. "The enigmatic midfielder, whose skills, unparalleled among Englishman of his generation, was relegated to the subs bench against Norwich". Barclays description was apt and the obviousness of his benching was galling for all to see.

The game against Yugoslavia on the Wednesday included a trio of Spurs players. Hoddle started alongside Chris Waddle. Despite Waddle not playing that well against Northern Ireland last time out, he was on the scoresheet that day.

Captain, and Manchester United midfielder Bryan Robson, was not fit enough to play. Spurs' Gary Stevens had occupied that central midfield berth a few times in the last year was sadly out injured, but Spurs' Gary Mabbutt was brought back into the midfield role and played alongside Hoddle to win his first England cap for three years.

England went 1-0 after 21 minutes thanks to Tottenham Hotspur. Hoddle took a left sided corner and swung the ball perfectly into the middle of the Yugoslavs penalty area to see Gary Mabbutt tower above everyone and direct his header into the bottom right-hand corner of the opposition goal. Mabbutt, wearing Robson's no.7 shirt, made his finish look like a classic Bryan Robson goal as he then ran off to celebrate with Hoddle and his England colleagues.

England started the second half in dominant fashion. Both Hoddle and Waddle set up Lineker who was denied by the visiting keeper on both occasions. Then in the 57th minute it was a North London connection that put England 2-0 up.

What was fair to say is Hoddle was at his majestic best. Picking up the ball in the middle of the Yugoslav half, Hoddle chipped an inch perfect ball into Beardsley whose first-time touch found Waddle. Waddle then centred a delightful cross for Arsenal's Viv Anderson to head home. A wonderful team goal and England looking strong.

The game meandered for a while until the final ten minutes when there was a sickening clash of heads between Hoddle and Aston Villa's Steve Hodge. The game was stopped for some time as Hodge was stretchered off, but Hoddle returned with his head in bandages.

The final whistle came, England were victors and Hoddle was instrumental in the whole game. A good response by Hoddle to Pleat's benching four days earlier.

The media focus after the game was more on Mabbutt's uber-diligent deputisation for Bryan Robson. Speaking to Colin Gibson in the *Daily Telegraph* Mabbutt said, 'I have always tried to play like Bryan Robson. He is a player I truly admire'. There has never been any doubting Robson's capability and contribution to the national team and was always held in such high regard by his peers, but Gibson's headline of 'MABBUTT TAKES OVER ROBSON'S ROLE' was clear testament to how well Mabbutt played.

Saturday 15th November 1986 – White Hart Lane, London (Att: 22,139)
Tottenham Hotspur v Coventry City
(TODAY League Division 1)

When Saturday came, it was to see Spurs host Coventry City. Mixed fortunes against the Midlands club last season saw Spurs triumph 3-2 away from home but lose 1-0 at home in February 1986 which was the final defeat in a wretched run of form for Shreeves' team.

In fact, Spurs had only lost once in their last nine league encounters with Coventry and only had two league defeats to them, home and away, throughout the entire 1980's so far. It is fair to say, this is a team Spurs liked to play against.

However, Spurs were languishing in eleventh place and Coventry excelling up in sixth position.

Clive Allen was still in good form, that was a fact. But Spurs needed more goals from elsewhere and to tighten up defensively.

Coventry had only lost three times in their opening fourteen league games. The dual leadership team of George Curtis and John Sillett seemed to have built a very strong, resilient and tough team.

Defensively, they had the third best record in Division 1 having conceded only 10 goals. Big keeper, Steve Ogrizovic, had already kept six clean sheets this season and he had a tough tackling group in front of him. Centre backs Trevor Peake and Brian Kilcline were a compatible partnership and with the tough tackling Lloyd McGrath and the industrious Welsh international, David Phillips, dominating midfield it was clear to see they were a tough nut to crack.

Going forward they had the wonderful right-wing wizardry of Dave Bennett. Bennet, sporting a superb 80's perm, was adept at bamboozling full backs. His delivery would often be met by the mercurial talent of Cyrille Regis. Regis had been a thorn in Spurs side before over the years during his time at West Bromwich Albion and he had now formed a new, strong partnership with Keith Houchen. Houchen was a lower league journeyman having joined Coventry in the summer of 1986 following spells at Hartlepool, Leyton Orient, York City and Scunthorpe United.

I am afraid to say that Keith Houchen features later in the story of Spurs' season, and not in a great way I may hasten to add.

Suffice to say, I was lucky enough to spend some time talking with him and to recall his first season at Coventry. He opened our conversation by revealing that he was a closet Spurs fan!

Houchen admitted, "As a kid I loved the Tottenham kits, plus I loved the way they used to play. Even after I retired, I would always look forward to watching Spurs on *Match of the Day* due to the way the played football". High praise indeed, but that praise had little effect on the amount of carnage he and Regis were about to bestow on Tottenham that season.

Houchen remembers joining Coventry that summer and hooking up with Regis. "I was mates with Ogrizvoic and had played against the likes of Mickey Gynn, Dave Bennett, Brian Kilcline and Trevor Peake. But Cyrille was an icon. He was such a lovely man and brilliant around the dressing room. But he was then one that we sat there in awe of".

Houchen continued, "I didn't get into the team straight away and had people saying that two big centre forwards couldn't play together, but we ended up having a brilliant partnership".

Houchen had a few injuries in his early months at Coventry and did not feature in the game at White Hart Lane. There was a young midfielder who started for Coventry that day, his name was Steve Sedgley. This 17-year-old lad hailed from Enfield, he was on the books at Spurs as a schoolboy before moving to Coventry. He made his league debut in Coventry's 2-1 win over Arsenal in the August of 1986. Spurs fans would get to know him even better when he would eventually move to White hart Lane in 1989. But today, he was up against his boyhood club.

Pleat knew Coventry would be tough. Pleat also knew it was time tor recall Hoddle after his superb show for England midweek.

Spurs took to the field in all white. This was the Lilywhites versus the Sky Blues. However, the Sky Blues were in their away strip of all yellow. Please keep that point in mind, ALL YELLOW.

Paul Miller had been replaced by John Polston. Young Polston was about to make his senior competitive debut alongside Richard Gough and this allowed Mabbutt to stay in the middle of midfield alongside a returning Hoddle. The only notable omission was Graham Roberts. Roberts had not even made the bench as that spot was not occupied by Ardiles.

Line up v Coventry: Clemence; Hughton, Gough, Polston, M Thomas; P Allen, Mabbutt, Hoddle, Waddle; C Allen, Claesen. Sub: Ardiles.

Pleat's pre-match programme notes congratulate Messrs Sillet and Curtis on their excellent start to the season, but he then laments his team's recent defeats to Wimbledon and Norwich. Pleat held most of his unhappiness at the Wimbledon loss. Pleat was unhappy at how Lawrie Sanchez and John Fashanu had claimed there were not responsible for the Roberts sending off and the Stevens injury. He claimed that Spurs had video evidence that would be gladly sent on to Plough Lane so they can see the reality for themselves.

Pleat concluded, "I do not begrudge Wimbledon their win. They should enjoy that, but why defend players who dent their club's reputation?". He had a valid point, but as the years will go by it is all too evident that part of Wimbledon's brand was to 'ruffle feathers'. They knew they didn't have the talent to compete toe-to-toe with the top teams and the top players, but they found a formula that would give them success.

Anyway, onto the Coventry game.

Things started ominously for Spurs. The right back position seemed to be cursed with injury this season as Chris Hughton, in for the injured Gary Stevens, twisted his knee after only three minutes. Hughton had already been in and out with injury so far this season, so this was another blow for him.

Ardiles replaced Hughton which saw Paul Allen convert to right back. With John Polston making his debut it was fair to say that Cyrille Regis may target the fresh-faced 19-year-old defender.

Paul Allen was up and down the right-wing like a man possessed and delivering wonderful balance of defensive responsibility and attacking prowess. Allen carved out Spurs opening goal after 21 minutes. It was Paul's low cross for Clive to side foot home for 1-0. A great move and once again, Paul Allen with another assist. This was Paul's fifth assist of the league season already and his numbers were well ahead of the usual suspects in Hoddle and Waddle.

The Sunday Express described it as, 'It was a goal worth the entrance money alone'.

Sadly, that was to be the only goal of the game as Coventry jousted with Spurs for possession and territory over the remaining seventy minutes of the match.

Spurs were easily worth their victory and Hoddle was close to being back to his best with another consummate midfield display.

The dominance and control of the midfield came from Ardiles. The 34-year-old midfielder seemed to be back to his best. His substitute cameos this season had always received rave reviews from the media so it was a shame we could not see him starting more. Hughton's injury was Ardiles and Tottenham's gain on this occasion, and let's not forget John Polston's clean sheet debut.

Polston looked relatively seamless alongside Gough that day. Clemence did not have too much to do but he did get concussed, and a bashed nose, in a late goalmouth onslaught by City. But Spurs were back to their winning ways and a clean sheet.

Result: Tottenham Hotspur 1-0 Coventry City (C Allen)

The Daily Telegraph's Brian Stater's headline was 'CLIVE ALLEN – AGAIN'. Despite the obvious plaudits for Clive Allen, Stater did provide just praise to Ray Clemence, Paul Allen and debutant, Polston.

That win only allowed Spurs to move one place up to tenth in the league. To stay in touch, Spurs needed to put a run of games together. Liverpool were not running away with the league as they usually did and with Arsenal, Forest and Everton all up there, surely Spurs could compete with that crowd.

Back to winning ways, Pleat started to plot his plan for the next league game away to Oxford United. This was to be a game that would turn Spurs' season around and be a factor that would become a talking point with Spurs fans for many years to come.

Saturday 22nd November 1986 – Manor Ground, Oxford
(Att: 12,143)
Oxford United v Tottenham Hotspur
(TODAY League Division 1)

Speculation of Hoddle's future was now being discussed by all football journalists across the United Kingdom and even Europe. The November edition of *Spurs News* also ran its front-page headline of 'GLENN TO GO?'.

Pleat told *Spurs News* that, 'Glenn already had an agreement that if the right offer came in, he could go'.

Not everyone knew that Hoddle had already agreed to give Pleat one final season but it was now time for Pleat to avoid the speculation and focus on how he could get the best out of Hoddle in his final several months at Spurs.

Many players have spoken of this game and this moment that appeared to be a catalyst for change in the season. Pleat often gets asked if he decided to change Tottenham's formation because of how he was impressed with the Belgium team that got to the World Cup semi-final in Mexico or the France team that won the 1984 European Championships.

Pleat said, "Perhaps Belgium was in the back of my mind but honestly I say this, I don't want to be too humble but we did stumble across this change. We had to do something to change and we had to so something to release Glenn. We needed to somehow release Glenn from this arduous task of having to work back and then repel any criticism of the fact he might not appear to be working as hard as the others. He had wonderful passing ability with both feet and we needed to utilise it".

Pleat was about to move away from the conventional 4-4-2 formation that had been embedded in English football for years and favoured by so many managers.

He wanted to utilise his main assets and his strengths. They were his midfielders.

Mark Falco had clearly fallen out of favour with Pleat and Nico Claesen had not made a huge impact up top alongside Clive Allen. Pleat wanted to load his midfield with quality and allow Clive to operate up front on his own.

He wanted to deploy a 4-5-1 formation. This formation, and variants of it, had been used across the continent. France won the 1984 Euro's by playing Platini is a very advanced midfield role that allowed him to split Bellone and Lacombe wide as they played up front. It was a system that fed into Platini's skill set and brilliance.

Belgium were similar too. Enzo Scifo was their advanced playmaker, and he would play just behind Jan Ceulemans who occupied a lone role up front. Claesen and Veyt would support wide, but this system allowed Belgium to get the best out of Scifo.

Even Argentina's success was based on a similar principle. Maradona playing in the advanced central midfield role and feeding in between Burruchaga and Valdano.

In England, the favoured 4-4-2 formation would require two central midfielders to be box-to-box. All action and dynamic but not a huge requirement for a cultured playmaker.

Hoddle could tackle and get involved. Richard Gough was very keen to point this out too. "Glenn would not go missing. People gave him that reputation, but he would always get stuck in".

This system might just allow Hoddle to operate in his happy place, the middle and final thirds of the pitch. The system would also allow penetrative wide midfielders to support Clive and Glenn. Tailor made for Chris Waddle and Nico Claesen.

In Clive Allen's *Up Front*, he talks about a meeting the day before where this new formation was discussed by Pleat and his players. "Ray Clemence said that they had tried it at Liverpool, it didn't work, it's a system that isn't right for us. Glenn and a couple of others had their say too, but David was adamant".

The idea was a good one. It fed into the capabilities of such talented midfielders that Pleat had at his disposal, now let's see if it works.

Paul Allen was outstanding at right-back in the Coventry win, so Pleat kept him there. Polston maintained his centre back berth which meant Mabbutt stayed in central midfield, no place for Roberts again. Not even on the bench as Danny Thomas was the spare man this week.

The line up also included Ossie Ardiles in his first league start of the season. Many a game had he come on as a very effective substitute but now he was starting alongside Gary Mabbutt in the heart of Spurs' midfield.

Line up v Oxford United: Clemence; P Allen, Gough, Polston, M Thomas; Claesen, Mabbutt, Hoddle, Ardiles, Waddle; C Allen. Sub: D Thomas.

Spurs took to the field in their all-white strip. Rain had been pelting down for quite some time but hopefully Spurs would put some shine on this occasion.

Oxford were managed by Maurice Evans. He was the man who brought Steve Perryman to the Manor Ground and he had also taken Tony Parks there recently on loan due to a goalkeeping availability crisis. Former Spurs striker, Dave Leworthy, was also on show against his old club, let's hope he doesn't do what Hazard and Crook have done to Spurs already this season.

Up front Oxford were very strong. John Aldridge scored for fun and was being eyed by many of the top Division 1 teams. Just behind Aldridge was Irish international Ray Houghton. He too was catching the eye of various clubs around the league, they were an attacking force indeed.

In true Spurs style they went 1-0 down early. Two minutes in it was not John Aldridge but, you guessed it, former Spur Dave Leworthy.

As those next five to 10 minutes passed, players were looking over to the bench to see if Pleat would revert back to 4-4-2 but he was not to be convinced in such an early change. He had belief in this formation and wanted to see how it panned out over the 90 minutes.

On 11 minutes Pleat was partially justified when Spurs equalised through, ahem, Clive Allen.

Some neat interplay between Mabbutt and Hoddle saw Allen finish clinically from the edge of the box. The new system was noticeable and so too was Chris Waddle. He had an excellent first half and on 25 minutes he combined with Hoddle brilliantly. Hoddle lofted in a delightful ball to Clive Allen to volley home his second of the day. That was Hoddle's first league assist since the September victory away at Leicester.

Spurs went into the break 2-1 up. Despite some delicious attacking play, there were a fair few vulnerable moments at the back but luckily Clemence was in excellent form too.

Richard Gough remembers that game well, "We went 1-0 down quite early but we quickly got into our stride. Clive equalised and then we took control. We had so many good midfield players that the system confused most teams from then on".

Gough was not wrong as halfway through the second half Spurs' dominance was rewarded as Chris Waddle scored his first league goal of the season. Waddle and Clive Allen's smart interchange saw Waddle stroke home to put Spurs 3-1 up.

Waddle was really starting to stamp his authority on the game and he was now playing with his usual swagger and dynamism.

Gary Briggs dragged one back for Oxford in the 74th minute but Spurs' were flowing now. Claesen was replaced with nearly ten minutes left, Danny Thomas came on at right-back and allowed Paul Allen to move forward even more.

The game was sealed with several minutes to go when Waddle got his second of the game. Following a pass from the excellent Ardiles, Waddle ran the length of the Oxford half to then curl his shot into the top corner for Spurs' fourth goal of the day.

Referee Keith Cooper blew the full-time whistle, and the travelling Spurs fans were elated. It was the first time Spurs had scored more than three goals since the opening day win over Villa, fifteen games ago.

Post-match, David Pleat was full of praise for his players. He was also complimentary on the pitch that Oxford had prepared. Speaking to the *Daily Telegraph*, Pleat praised the Oxford groundsman for giving us a 'passing pitch'. This fed perfectly into Spurs' style and its new midfield five.

Ardiles had played his first 90 minutes of the season, and the 34-year-old had enjoyed it too. Speaking to Brian Oliver in the

Telegraph, Ardiles said, "There was a time when I wondered if I'd ever get back into the first team, but now I am feeling fitter than ever. I haven't missed a day's training all season and I really enjoyed this game".

A few newspaper articles did not make much of this formational change, in fact, I am not sure most of them had seen Pleat's change. Oliver's description of a 'revitalised and attractively balanced midfield' was an ode to how well the midfield played, but Pleat was pleased to see Hoddle thriving and operating in the final third. Hoddle was excellent.

Result: Oxford United 2-4 Tottenham Hotspur (C Allen 2, Waddle 2)

The sun had popped out on a couple of occasions during the game, but it was heavy rainfall that most supporters remember from that game. Spurs took 3,000 fans to that match and there were only 12,000 spectators in the whole stadium! One of the fans that day was Norman Jay MBE.

Norman Jay is one of the UK's superstar DJ's that emerged in the mid 1980's and was awarded an MBE for services to music in 2002. He began watching Spurs nearly twenty years before as a young West London boy and had been seduced into travelling across London and following Spurs by his love for Jimmy Greaves.

Music was Norman's love, his trade and part of his soul. He cites as London being 'the place to be' growing up. But he also had a passion for Tottenham Hotspur.

He was lucky enough to go to the League Cup final wins in 1971 and 1973 and also highlights the genuine disappointment of relegation in 1977. Jay said, "In a perverse way, that relegation year was dread, but a year in the second division was fantastic. I went to more grounds than I'd ever been to, lots of British market towns and it was a fantastic time traveling and following the club. I was at Southampton when we won promotion after a 0-0 draw. I remember going to Bolton twice that year, losing in the January game covered in snow. It was good times".

Norman also mentioned getting sacked as he was so intent on getting himself to the 1981 FA Cup Final replay against Manchester City. That sacking was clearly worth it to see Villa's wonder goal and Spurs' first FA Cup since 1967.

Style is also a huge part of Norman's life and his personal brand. The Spurs kits over the years were another area that piqued his interest. "Don't ask me to comment on the kits of today, I wouldn't want them for free. But I had a friend who once showed me a picture of an old Spurs kit. Navy shirt with a white cockerel worn by former Spurs player Roger Morgan many years before. Anyway, my friend found out the original shirtmakers were based in Preston and got a batch made up. He gave me one and I put no.8 on the back (after Jimmy Greaves), and everyone was asking me where I got it from but before he could get any more made up the club put an injunction on him. It was a shame, but Spurs were the first club to have a really cool retro shirts". Norman cites that the style of the football and the style of the kits were part of the Spurs appeal.

During this time his career had really started to take off. He was a regular face performing at the Notting Hill Carnival every year and he was DJ'ing more and more around the UK. This meant he found Friday and Saturday nights were his busiest times. In 1985 he had also founded KISS FM. "During that time a few friends of mine wanted us to start our own black, pirate radio station. We felt inner city London was not being represented and there were huge waves of black music that wasn't being played or spoken about and we wanted to give it a platform. I often spent time in New York where the style and club culture was pretty vibrant and the music coming out was amazing. In the summer of '85 we began, and we borrowed the name from KISS FM in New York".

Norman admitted there was a risk in using this name; "It was a brainstorming session with Gordan Mac and the late, great George Power where we decided to go with KISS FM. We thought, they are so far away, let them come to London and sue us. We would just come off the air and disappear".

And so, KISS FM was born. Jay's career was on an upwards curve, he was a very busy man but he did manage to get time for the odd game during the 1986-87 season and away at Oxford being one of them.

"I remember the game; I don't remember much of the tactics, but I remember it was wet. I drove to the game, and I parked my van. I used to have this blue escort van, and I parked it outside a pub near Headington just off the A40. It was a ten-minute walk to the old Manor Ground. I came back after the game and I'd seen that some Oxford fans had put a brick through my windscreen, and I had to drive all the way back like that in the rain".

For the record, there was no evidence to suggest it was Oxford fans, but Jay jokingly concludes, "I've never forgiven Oxford for that".

Even fans like, Norman Jay MBE, who were at that game may not have noticed the formational change but the players knew and Pleat knew. Deep down Pleat was satisfied that his plans had come to fruition, and he was now able to deploy his key assets at the same time.

Wednesday 26th November 1986 – Abbey Stadium, Oxford (Att: 10,033)
Cambridge United v Tottenham Hotspur
(Littlewoods League Cup 4th Round)

Having dispatched Birmingham in the previous round, Pleat took his team to the Abbey Stadium to face Division four side Cambridge United. The hosts had only been re-elected back into the football league six months before and were loitering around mid-table of the football league's lowest division.

Spurs should not allow complacency to set in though. The great win at Oxford was one thing, but Spurs struggled in the second-round league cup win at Barnsley so they could not afford to approach this in any other way but focused and determined.

Pleat had most players to call upon, except Nico Claesen. Claesen was replaced late in the Oxford game due to a hamstring injury. His return may not be too swift, so Pleat needed a slight tweak of personnel.

The team was near enough the same that featured last Saturday but John Polston had been demoted to the bench and Graham Roberts was back in. Mabbutt reverted back to his defensive pairing with Gough and young striker Shaun Close came in to make his second senior appearance.

Close was an out and out striker and it appeared he would partner Clive Allen up front as it looked like Pleat may have reverted back to a conventional 4-4-2 formation. But as the early minutes ticked by, it was clear to see that Close was playing wide right in the role Claesen was used to filling.

Cambridge had no evidential household names lining up for them. They did have a promising young striker called Mark Cooper leading the line and just like Spurs had two Thomas's and two Allen's, that Cambridge had two Kimble's. They were brothers Garry and Alan.

Alan Kimble was a strong left back who then found himself in the topflight of football a few years later when he joined Wimbledon. Today he was up against one of Spurs' brightest talents in Shaun Close.

Line up v Cambridge: Clemence; P Allen, Gough, Mabbutt, M Thomas; Close, Roberts, Hoddle, Ardiles, Waddle; C Allen. Sub: Polston, D Thomas.

It was a bit of a raucous atmosphere and an impressive crowd of over 10,000 contributed towards an entertaining evening of football. Spurs went into an early lead when Clive Allen pounced after four minutes. Paul Allen and Close combined superbly well down the right to then see Close play the ball into Hoddle. Edge of the box, Hoddle chips the goalkeeper and beats him, only to see his effort rebound off the crossbar for Allen to then acrobatically volley home.

Good start for Spurs and Close.

Spurs' lead only lasted four minutes when Mark Cooper equalised for the hosts when winger Garry Kimble floated in a superb cross to find Cooper, who had found some space and headed into the top right hand corner. Brilliant goal in truth.

Maybe this goal stayed in Pleat's memory as Mark Cooper would sign for Spurs on transfer deadline day in the spring of 1987. One for the future apparently, but sadly he never played a single game for Spurs and was sold to Gillingham several months later.

Spurs spluttered for the remainder of the first half and worryingly Richard Gough limped off to be replaced by Polston before the break.

Spurs managed to grapple back the lead seven minutes after the restart. Mabbutt released Waddle down the left wing and he carved out a cross to the near post that Clive Allen flicked on to find Shaun Close who nodded home with ease, 2-1 to Spurs and a justified lead too.

With 28 minutes to go Spurs went 3-1 up. Waddle was having a superb evening popping up on both wings and linking well with Hoddle and Clive Allen. It was from a Hoddle short corner with Mitchell Thomas that saw the Spurs full-back lay on a simple pass to Waddle who was just inside the Cambridge area, still very left-side, and he lofted the ball over the keeper into the far corner for a lovely goal.

Was it a cross or was it a shot, who cares, it was a lovely goal. Hoddle came close to making it 4-1 just before the end, but the Cambridge keeper saved his late penalty to keep it as a 3-1 victory for Spurs.

Spurs had now reached the Quarter Final stage of this year's Littlewoods League Cup.

Result: Cambridge United 1-3 Tottenham Hotspur (C Allen, Close, Waddle)

The cup draw was to pit Spurs against their London rivals West Ham United. West Ham had just beaten Oxford 1-0 in this round and were currently sitting fourth in Division 1. The Hammers would fancy their chances as the game had been drawn in favour of a West Ham home tie, at Upton Park.

Personally, this would be my first visit to Upton Park and I couldn't wait!

Saturday 29th November 1986 – White Hart Lane, London
(Att: 30,042)
Tottenham Hotspur v Nottingham Forest
(TODAY League Division 1)

Things may be on the up for Pleat and his team, but the league position was not great news being sat in tenth position.

But the good news was that, even though Clive had scored again against Cambridge, it was Waddles third goal in two games and along with a couple of assists, things were looking brighter for the former Newcastle winger having disappointed in many games so far this season.

Brian Scovell, in the *Daily Mail*, headed his Cambridge report with 'WADDLE TURNS ON THE MAGIC', let's see if that continued as Spurs' inconsistency seemed to link with Waddle's inconsistency too.

Nottingham Forest were visiting and they were second in the table behind George Graham's high-flying Gunners.

Led by Brian Clough, Forest were a juicy mix of pure talent and pure graft. If Clive Allen was leading the scoring charts on 14 league goals, then Forest striker Gary Birtles was not far behind on 11 goals coming into this game. Midfielder Neil Webb had also scored 11 times this season and Birtles strike partner, young Nigel Clough, had scored six goals.

All together Forest had scored 35 league goals so far and Spurs had scored only 19. On the flip side, Forest had conceded 22 goals already this season, Spurs only 16.

In goal for Forest was Hans Segers, he had been hampered by injuries during the last league campaign but was fully fit this season. In years to come, Segers would be on the coaching staff at White Hart Lane, but today he was looking to keep his seventh clean sheet of the season.

Maybe one of the reasons Forest were shipping in a fair number of goals, was due to their youthful back four. Chris Fairclough, Des Walker and Stuart Pearce were all in their early twenties, but they were unbelievable talents and the times would improve for them all.

Back to the 'Ones That Got Away' files, and filed under W is Des Walker. Walker was a Tottenham schoolboy and, rumour has it, he was released by Spurs' former manager Bill Nicholson because he wouldn't adhere to club's standards and get a haircut! I am not sure how accurate that story is, but it's a hell of a way to exit a future world class talent.

Walker had already played several times for England U21s, and he would win his first full cap for England in 1988 against Denmark. Walker would play over 50 times for his country, play in a World Cup and also spend time with Sampdoria in Italy. His pace was legendary and would've been a wonderful asset at White Hart Lane.

Clough, who had an eye for younger talent, plucked him in 1980 when he became an apprentice at the City Ground, Nottingham.

His central defensive partner was Chris Fairclough, he had also represented England at U21 level and within a year, he would actually find himself plying his trade at White Hart Lane. But more of that later.

Left-back Stuart Pearce was the one making most of the headlines. This powerful and hugely committed player was the one player pushing Arsenal's Kenny Sansom to keep his England place. Sansom was an England stalwart, but young Pearce was not just knocking on the door, but he was running straight through it.

Born in West London, Pearce schooled in Northwest London and joined non-league Wealdstone FC as a youth. He played for the Harrow based club for five years until Coventry yanked him into professional football. Two seasons at Highfield Road was enough to tempt Clough to grab him, and what a signing he turned out to be. During his early days at Forest, Pearce would advertise his electrician services in the matchday programmes! He offered complete household rewires, repairs and maintenance and his estimates were free - oh and all work guaranteed of course. Suffice to say, they were not paid the big bucks that footballers get nowadays.

Pearce would make over 400 appearances for Forest, winning a few trophies along the way and being one of the most pivotal players for England during the next 10 years.

Earlier in this book I referenced Chris Waddle's penalty miss for England in Turin during the 1990 World Cup. Pearce was the other penalty taker who missed during that heart-breaking June evening in four years' time. Pearce would become so well known for his brilliant free-kicks and assertive penalties but sadly he was remembered for one he missed.

The man redeemed himself beyond belief during Euro'96 though. He had a brilliant tournament, that saw England reach the semi-finals, and he will be forever known for the emotion that flowed through his being when he netted his penalty against Spain in the quarter final of that tournament.

Neil Webb was the midfield sensation of the season so far. A playmaker that always seemed to have time on the ball, but he had had scored 11 goals already this season, an amazing return for yet another England U21 international. His full caps would come soon too.

Another player that was soon to join Tottenham was Johnny Metgod. Metgod lined up alongside Webb and the Dutchman was a strong and very direct midfielder who complimented Webb well.

Metgod was more commonly known for his wonder goal against West Ham the season before. With the ball 35 yards out, Metgod's straight long run up saw him hammer the ball like a dart into the middle of the West Ham goal. On commentary Tony Gubba's words were, "Didn't he drive it well! What an amazing goal by the Dutchman". He was my vote for BBC's goal of the season, but he lost out to Bryan Robson's superb volley for England against Israel in Tel Aviv.

Today Pleat was facing Brian Clough, one of the greatest managers in the history of British football.

In Irving Scholar's book *'Behind Closed Doors'*, Scholar remarks about how he felt Pleat was obsessed with Clough and that he wanted to be like him. Pleat would easily disagree and simply say how much he respected everything Clough had done in the game.

Line up v Nottingham Forest: Clemence; P Allen, Polston, Roberts, M Thomas; Close, Mabbutt, Hoddle, Ardiles, Waddle; C Allen. Sub: D Thomas.

Spurs took to the field with only one change from the team that started against Cambridge. Richard Gough was replaced by Polston and Roberts would partner him in the centre of defence today.

On a high from the Oxford game and fresh from the professional win over Cambridge in the week, Spurs were confident going into this game, but a very poor start was what they got.

Forest had only arrived at the ground at 2.30pm due to travel difficulties but less than a minute into the match they took the lead. Sadly, it was young Polston's error that led to the goal.

Clemence, ball in hand, rolled it out to Polston at the edge of the box who moved forward. Polston was looking to play a simple five-yard pass to Paul Allen but was brilliantly intercepted by Nigel Clough. Clough racing towards Clemence was moving at such speed that Clemence had little chance to get to the ball and brought Clough down.

Penalty to Forest and who steps up to lash the penalty into Clemence's top left-hand corner? Yep, Stuart Pearce. 1-0 Forest.

Spurs did gain control quite quickly though and over the next 30 minutes Clive Allen could have quite easily, yes easily, had a hat-trick. Brilliance from Hoddle, Waddle and Mabbutt on those occasions amounted for nothing but Clive did get Spurs' equaliser on 36 minutes.

Mabbutt was chasing a fifty-fifty ball with Stuart Pearce and the deflected pass fell into Allen's path and he superbly slotted it past Segers in the Forest goal. 1-1 and more than deserved by Spurs.

Waddle missed a couple of opportunities to put Spurs in the lead and just before half-time and when Graham Roberts slid into Nigel Clough from behind to give away a silly free kick on the edge of the box it looked like Forest may take the advantage.

Luckily Metgod struck his free-kick wide, but this was a case-in-point made by Bill Nicholson to Pleat, about Roberts and giving away free-kicks. There had actually been a bid for Roberts during that week by Rangers, that Pleat had initially turned down. Roberts had not been involved much in the last few weeks and maybe Pleat was considering his options.

1-1 at half-time. Decent for Forest but Spurs should've been in front.

So, half-time. Is that half-time entertainment I hear you say? Well of course, and who better to provide on-field entertainment but Chas n Dave!

The cockney pop duo had delighted Spurs fans over the years with their niche Tottenham cup final songs of 1981 and 1982. They did have other songs in their locker too and there they were.

Chas Hodges on his joanna and Dave Peacock on his drum set in the middle of the pitch blasting out '*Ain't No Pleasing You*' to a crowd of men who had left the wives, and respective partners, at home while they enjoyed the game. The song was about a man whose wife didn't appreciate him no more! It's a hard world lads, ain't it?

This was stuff of the eighties alright!

Sadly, Chas Hodges died back in 2018 but Dave Peacock keeps the songs going. He still plays live and still does the speaking circuit on Spurs Legends events.

I was lucky enough to catch up with Dave to get some of his viewpoints on spending time at White Hart Lane.

Dave recalls playing on the pitch during the Forest game, "That was to film footage for our Christmas TV special that year, the final cut had us playing on a bus on our way to White Hart Lane. We'd already played on that pitch a few times before, against

Nottingham Forest in 1983 and against Liverpool in 1986, so it was just something we did. Always exciting playing at the Spurs though".

There would be high hopes that Chas n Dave could do another Cup Final song this season but there was a long way to go, despite being in the League Cup quarter final, the FA Cup had not even started yet.

Dave still remembers the powerful connection with Spurs supporters and their music from back in 1981: "One memory that jumps out was when we were at a match about a week after '*Ossie's Dream*' came out in 1981. It suddenly dawned on us that the crowd were all singing the song (when it was only a week old!) - it was a very special feeling to have White Hart Lane singing something we'd written, and of course they continue to sing it when (if!) Spurs go on a cup run these days".

The players had come out onto the pitch for the second half as ground staff hurried Chas, Dave and their equipment off the field of play. The second half was about to begin.

Following on from their dominance in the first half, Spurs went into the lead after 58 minutes when Spurs had a freekick that was positioned mightily close to Spurs right wing corner flag.

Hoddle and Waddle stood over the ball, this time Hoddle wandered off and Waddle swung in a beautiful cross for Clive Allen to get in front of Chris Fairclough and head past Hans Segers. 2-1 to Spurs and this was well deserved by the home team.

Then eight minutes later, a poor error saw Spurs give up their lead.

Clem played the ball to Roberts near the edge of the box for Roberts to return and Clemence to pick up ready to launch the ball forward. Nigel Clough raised his arms in the air and the linesman flagged.

Clemence's pass had not gone outside the penalty area when Roberts passed it back. This was a schoolboy error and one that Roberts should have known better. An indirect free kick given to Forest just inside the Spurs box.

The Spurs wall was lined up, Metgod touches the ball to Pearce who drives a bullet shot past the ball only to see Clem parry the ball away just in front of him. Forest defender was the first to react and reached the ball before John Polston and tucked it past Clemence for Forest's equaliser. 2-2 and all Spurs hard work was diminishing.

Hoddle was close to putting Spurs in front with around ten minutes to go but it was Forest who grabbed a winner when a battling Birtles carved out an opening for Neil Webb as he saw his sweet left foot shot fly past a helpless Clemence.

3-2 to Forest and a couple of minutes left was not enough time for Spurs to create anything more to salvage an equaliser in a game they should have won.

Result: Tottenham Hotspur 3-2 Nottingham Forest
(C Allen 2)

Two errors. Spurs had played really well against a team who were just off top spot, but two errors were to cost them three points. Polston's lazy pass and Roberts' lack of concentration were pivotal points that not only kept Forest in the game but saw them win it.

The *Sunday Times'* Brian Glanville wrote, "Clive Allen continues to be prolific, but Spurs lost a game they seemed likely to win".

Disappointingly Glanville lay most blame at the feet of Spurs' youngsters Polston and Close. He highlighted Polston's error and Close's ineffectiveness in the final third as key to the defeat.

In *Spurs News*, Pleat came to their defence, "Their goalkeeper was brilliant today and John Polston is learning hard lessons, but that is what the first division is all about. I did think that Polston and Close battled bravely".

Danny Thomas came on for Ossie Ardiles, but in hindsight, Thomas should have replaced Shaun Close. Paul Allen would have moved into the wide right role and Danny just behind him. That would have given Spurs more penetration and presence up against Stuart Pearce who had a marauding game for Forest.

Well, two steps forward and one step back. This was the story of our season so far as we crept into December.

DECEMBER 1986

As the club entered the final month of the calendar year, around a third of what would be the season's total games had now passed. By the end of the season, Spurs will go on to play 57 matches and, to this point, 21 games had been completed. Attendances had been an issue and Scholar highlighted this the previous month when arranging the Hamburg friendly.

Attendances had been dwindling. Lack of European competition was one thing, but this period was underpinned by the continual hooliganism problem that had stemmed from the 1970's and continued bleeding into the 1980's.

1986 was still at the height of Thatcher's Britain. Moving away from the economic struggles of the 1970's, the 1980's started off in ominous fashion with continuing high unemployment levels and poverty-stricken areas rife across the UK. Our industrial output was diminishing, and Thatcher was gradually shaping Britain into a more finance-driven, entrepreneurial world with the rise of privatisation and professional services being key to national economic growth.

The mid-80's saw the emergence of the 'Yuppie'. These were young, middle-class folk that were paid well and driven by financial success that brought along material reward. The age of excess was evident on both sides of the Atlantic with London and New York becoming even more powerful as financial hubs. The excess also brought a lack of compliance and regulation in many different sectors and industries, which added to the world of excess among some and started to create even more of a divide between rich and poor.

Football was not considered a rich man's sport. Foundations of the game were embedded within the working classes and over the years attendances were mainly made up of that demographic. The rise of hospitality and sponsorship perks were on an upward curve within top clubs in the topflight of football. The hooligan element was a major contributing factor towards low attendances. It created a lack of diversity in football support and even though the European football ban was lamented by many, a grip was not being tightened on this rogue element.

Organised crime is usually associated with the criminal underworld and mafia-type exploits. But hooliganism was criminal behaviour plus it was organised. Most clubs had a 'firm' associated with their support and this would make the to'ing and fro'ing from games a massive headache for normal, law-abiding supporters. Nearly every football fan that went to professional football matches in the 70's and 80's will all have a hooligan related story to tell.

It was hard. It was always a worry on your mind, especially when travelling to away grounds to follow your team. The government would continually condemn these unruly behaviours, but nothing would really change until the 1990's began and things would gradually start getting better.

Average attendances in Division 1 during the 1960's were 26,954. There was a 46% decline in average Division 1 attendances during the 1970's. That average of 14,322 was a huge drop as struggles in society and the economy were significant factors in that massive drop in attendances.

Up to the start of this season, 1986-87, the average attendances in the opening half of the 1980's were up to 21,242 in Division 1. This was already a 48% increase on the previous decade, but things had been in decline over the last season or two.

At the end of the 1984-85 season the average attendances were 27,774 which was the highest since 1967-68. Sadly, that season ended in the Heysel stadium tragedy, resulting in a European ban on English clubs. The following season, 1985-86, the average attendances in Division 1 had declined by 17% to 23,101.

Going to football was not as alluring as some of the great football that was being played and that was simply due to the hooligan element, declining standards of stadiums and the Euro ban.

Spurs were no different. Despite playing some brilliant football and winning trophies in the early 80's, the White Hart Lane attendances were also dipping.

Up to the start of December 1986, Spurs had played 11 home league and cup games to an average crowd of 23,175. This was a slight increase on the same figure a season before (84-85) when Spurs had played 12 league and cup games to an average crowd of 22,193. Compare this to the same time period in the 1983-84 season when Spurs won the UEFA Cup. Spurs had played 11 games to an average gate of 33,683 up to the start of December 1983, that's a 31% decline in only a couple of years.

Spurs and every other club couldn't control hooliganism. The only control clubs had was to make the in-stadium experience enjoyable by making supporters feel safe but ultimately putting on a super show of football. Scholar and Pleat were gradually doing that this year.

Nowadays, topflight professional footballers are among the highest paid people in the UK. They have the money to live in a world of excess every single day of their lives. Back in 1986 this was a different story. Footballers were nowhere near being some of the nation's top earners.

Different revenue streams were gradually being developed by most clubs and this was also the time when some football chairman would start to learn from the lucrative models used in American sports.

Television would be a powerful tool in attracting fans and revenue that was craved by the football administrators.

Television was one of the first areas that English football started to see as a money maker. Nowadays, televised football is delivered at such an excess that it has lost the same razzmatazz you felt when your team were on the box. For me, this is also one of the reasons why the FA Cup has declined in its importance to us as the FA Cup Final day was possibly the 'event' of the year in most households.

That aside, television would start to rule the roost as the next few years would pass. In a week's time, Spurs would travel to Old Trafford which would be the first live televised match of the season.

It wasn't just about getting bums on seats. You had to entertain! Pleat was starting to shape a team that was doing just that. A few days before, Pleat had lost to Brian Clough's Forest. Spurs were the better team and should have bagged at least four goals and maybe even five or six. Pleat felt that things were about to click as they faced a busy Christmas month that had a packed league schedule along with a trip to the Caribbean and also taking part in a relatively new footballing entity up in Manchester called the Guinness Soccer Six tournament.

* * * *

Sunday 7th December 1986 – Old Trafford, Manchester
(Att: 35,267)
Manchester United v Tottenham Hotspur
(TODAY League Division 1)

Spurs had a week's rest between the Forest defeat and their visit to Old Trafford. Alex Ferguson was the new boss at United and his tenure started with a defeat at Oxford. The last few weeks had seen his team lose at Wimbledon, draw against Norwich City at Carrow Road and his only win was a home victory against QPR.

For the Manchester United career he would go on to have, this was a poor start.

United were just above the relegation zone and they needed a win in a game played on the Sunday and was Live on BBC1.

Line up v Manchester United: Clemence; P Allen, Gough, Mabbutt, M Thomas; Waddle, Roberts, Hoddle, Ardiles, Galvin; C Allen. Sub: D Thomas.

For the fourth time this season, Spurs lined up in white shirts, navy shorts and white socks as they took to a chilly Old Trafford.

John Motson was in lead commentary position alongside Lawrie McMenemy as they prepared viewers for a footballing treat. I was overjoyed at the chance to speak to John about this season, he was generous with his time and his recall was outstanding. I spoke to John a few months before his unfortunate death in early 2023.

"I remember covering that game", Motson recalls. "It was one of a few live games that season, and it turned out to be a cracker, both United and Spurs had some brilliant players on show and this was our first chance to really see the famous Spurs 5-man midfield".

Motson was spot on with all his observations. Despite Spurs having Hoddle, Waddle and Ardiles in midfield. United had Bryan Robson and Remi Moses battling in their midfield. They also had had mercurial wide-midfielder Jesper Olson on show too. Olson was part of the dazzling Denmark team that wowed the recent World Cup in Mexico.

Pleat had brought back Richard Gough and a now fit Tony Galvin, but also moved Mabbutt back to partner Gough and Roberts into the heart of the midfield. Things were rumbling in the background when it came to Roberts and changes were afoot with the Spurs UEFA Cup winning captain.

Clive Allen was up front on his own. Fresh from his brace against Forest, Allen was now up against Paul McGrath and Kevin Moran. These were uncompromising competitors and both Ireland internationals.

Clive Allen struck the post in the first minute but it was United that took the lead after 12 minutes. A well worked United free-kick found Scottish midfielder Gordon Strachan all alone to centre his right-wing cross to Norman Whiteside who side-footed home.

Whiteside was a wonderful talent. Traditionally know as an attacking midfielder, he was more of a centre forward today.

Whiteside's strike partner put the hosts 2-0 up after 36 minutes. Peter Davenport benefited from an almighty mix-up between Paul Allen and Gary Mabbutt to see United take a 2-0 lead into half-time.

Spurs did have some chances, but this was not at all impressive. Roberts was ineffective in the middle of the park and Ardiles and Hoddle could not gain any traction at all.

Pleat needed to change things. It was not that the 4-5-1 was not working but there needed to be a tweak. Ardiles was removed and replaced by Danny Thomas. With Thomas joining the fray this allowed Paul Allen to join Hoddle in the middle of midfield.

Now most people highlight the five-man midfield being the key to Spurs' great football that season. But, for me, this was the moment it really kicked on.

Danny Thomas would go on to play 18 consecutive games in the right back role and Paul Allen would now play 33 consecutive games in his central midfield role. This change, alongside this 4-5-1 formation, allowed both players to thrive over the coming months and especially for Paul Allen who would be possibly one of the most influential players of Spurs' whole season.

Speaking on the *The Spurs Show* podcast in 2018, Roberts recalls that game. He stated that just before the game started, Graeme Souness had the nerve to tell him that Rangers were making an offer for him this week. Not the type of thing you want to hear just before a game, and then with Spurs being 2-0 down at half-time, Roberts recalls Ray Clemence grabbing him in the tunnel and told him, "Don't leave this football club playing as you are!".

Roberts and his teammates turned things around sharply and were level 14 minutes after the restart!

On 57 minutes, Gary Mabbutt scores possibly his best ever Spurs goal. Spurs had a corner on their right flank. Hoddle took the set-piece with his right foot and swung it towards the penalty spot region. Then all of a sudden, out of nowhere, Mabbutt throws himself at the ball like a leaping salmon and smashes his header home past a hapless Chris Turner.

Only moments before, Motson and McMenemy were lamenting Spurs' approach play and then Mabbutt steps forward with that.

On commentary Motson screams Mabbutt's name followed by, "That is a terrific goal, and this player is all-purpose". It was an apt nod to how versatile this player was, and he'd headed Spurs back into the game. The Hoddle corner to Mabbutt's head was the same combination for England's opening goal against Yugoslavia a few weeks before.

Only two minutes later Spurs equalised. Kevin Moran scored an own goal, but it was via the genius of Glenn Hoddle. Hoddle won the ball in the middle of the United half and he shrugged off challenges to see his delightful chip nearly beat the United keeper but his fingertips only directed it into the path of a hapless Moran. Spurs were back in the game.

Spurs were chasing down everything and asserting pressure on a regular basis now. Paul Allen won a corner and from a short corner with Waddle and Hoddle. Chris Waddle looped a cross into the far post and under extreme pressure Clive Allen headed home to put Spurs in front. He ran off celebrating, although clearly looked in discomfort.

Spending time with Clive Allen was an absolute pleasure. Having recently written his own book, Clive's recall is very good and this game was no different. Especially that goal.

Clive smirks as he remembers, "I broke my nose that day scoring our third goal. It was a wee Scotsman, Gordon Strachan, that booted me in the face as I dived in to head it, I probably wasn't renowned for my bravery but when it came to scoring goals, I used to do some crazy things. This game was a thriller and people still talk to me about it today as there was not too much football on telly back then".

Clive ran off then fell to the ground, clearly in pain. Spurs' physio John Sheridan ran onto the pitch to make his assessment. Blood pouring from his nose, you can clearly see Clive saying, "I'm alright, I'm alright". There was no way this man was going to come off!

His team were now in the driving seat. 2-0 down and now 3-2 up.

Spurs continued to play on the front foot, but with two minutes to go Strachan threaded a pass into the Spurs box where Bryan Robson burst through only to be challenged by Danny Thomas who had appeared from nowhere. Robson went down and penalty to United.

Thomas' challenge looked clumsy but still to this day Danny feels the Robbo made a meal of it; "I gave that penalty away, Robson came running into the area and I think he dived to be honest". Thomas' cheeky grin as he said that was followed up with, "It was a shame as it meant we had thrown two points away".

The game finished 3-3 as Davenport converted the penalty kick. Both Danny Thomas and Clive Allen agreed that a point at Old Trafford was not a bad result, but Spurs had done the hard work to win it.

Result: Manchester United 3-3 Tottenham Hotspur (Mabbutt, Moran og, C Allen)

The papers had a field day with this all-action 3-3 thriller. Patrick Barclay wrote in his *Times* column the following day; "A labyrinthian plot, played out with an unpredictable mixture of slapstick and wit, was given its final twist two minutes from time when Davenport scored to snatch United from the jaws of defeat". Alex Ferguson told Barclay that their efforts on the first half should have seen United four of five goals up.

But David Pleat spoke to *Spurs News* and said, "You don't normally get back from being 2-0 down, but United were shot. We had them completely on the run and we were much fitter and stronger". Pleat sounded satisfied having come back from 2-0 down, but it was yet another game where points had been lost from successful positions.

* * * *

On the Wednesday of that week, there was more action for Spurs players in a new tournament that was catching the eye of football fans up and down the country. Spurs were the current holders of the Guinness Soccer Six trophy and sent a very strong squad up to Manchester to defend their crown in the G-Mex arena.

As holders, Spurs were placed in the final group games that would take place to determine who would compete in the final. The evening before, Arsenal had won their qualifying group to make this evening's final group games and yes, they were placed into Spurs' group.

Tottenham Hotspur, Sheffield Wednesday and Arsenal made up the first group and Manchester United, Chelsea and Oxford United made up the second.

The games were played on a plastic pitch which was around half the size of a normal football pitch. The playing area was sectioned into three zones, teams could only score in their final third so no long-range efforts were allowed, and one man must always remain in the opponent's half. It promoted continuous play as there were no throw-ins with plastic boardings around the edge of the pitch which allowed players to utilise them when need be.

Spurs took a very strong squad up to retain their crown: 1. Parks, 2. Paul Allen, 3. Mitchell Thomas, 4. Danny Thomas, 5. Ossie Ardiles, 6. Steve Smart, 7. Graham Roberts, 8. Gary Mabbutt, 9. David Howells, 10. Chris Waddle.

Steve Smart and David Howells were the youthful addition in a squad that consisted of many strong senior players.

Spurs won their first game 2-1, beating Sheffield Wednesday with goals from Chris Waddle and David Howells. This set up a showdown with Arsenal where Spurs needed a win to see them through despite the fact Arsenal were still to face Sheffield Wednesday.

Spurs went 1-0 in the first half through a David Howells strike. Spurs were playing in their all navy away strip and were in control for most of the match. In the second half Arsenal brought on one of their promising youngsters, Paul Merson, and his inclusion was a positive impact for the Gunners. With Spurs looking to keep their slender lead, it was Arsenal who equalised with a couple of minutes to go. The goal scorer was Ian Allinson - and this name would be haunting Spurs in a few months' time!

With 23 seconds to go, the Spurs defenders switched off and Gus Caeser slipped in to score the winner for Arsenal. Final Score, 2-1. Yes....2-1! Disappointing to say the least.

Arsenal went on to beat Wednesday and make the final where they lost out to Oxford United.

Clive Allen was part of the team that won the previous Soccer Six trophy but did not feature in that tournament. "I didn't make that trip as my nose had been broken a few days before" he mentions.

But David Howells recalls being part of that squad, "I'm not really sure something like that could happen in the middle of a season nowadays, but I loved playing in that tournament. The surface was very hard, and I remember it was televised which was not too common back then. I remember losing to Arsenal, but until now I couldn't remember the score and their scorers".

Howells was right, the evening's action was televised on *BBC's Sportsnight* where Steve Rider introduced the tournament concept and commentary was delivered by John Motson. During the Spurs-Arsenal game, Motson highlighted that in early January 1987, Arsenal would visit White Hart Lane in the first live televised game of the new year.

* * * *

Towards the end of that week, Donald Saunders in *The Daily Telegraph* reported on an article that had been written the day before in *El Pais*, a Spanish newspaper. The morning Spanish paper had spoken to Diego Maradona, who had recently joined Napoli, and mentioned that he would like to spend a couple of seasons at Real Madrid and then honour a "long standing commitment to an English Club".

Saunders highlighted that even though Maradona did not identify the English club, his disclosure immediately led to speculation that he would eventually like to join Tottenham. Saunders then made links with Ardiles and Maradona playing at Spurs in May for his testimonial match.

Saunders even approached Pleat who told him that he was unaware of any agreement with Maradona.

It would've been a huge coup for English football, whoever he wanted to join. Yet the reality was, who could afford him?

Saturday 13th December 1986 – White Hart Lane, London
(Att: 23,137)
Tottenham Hotspur v Watford
(TODAY League Division 1)

The following Saturday Spurs faced Watford at White Hart Lane. Chas n Dave were back at the Lane, entertaining the crowd and recording more material, this time for a Benny Hill Christmas special.

Watford were one place below Spurs in eleventh and of their 18 games so far, they had won seven, lost seven and drawn four. During the season they had thumped four past Aston Villa and Charlton Athletic and a few weeks ago they had swept aside Leicester City by five goals to one.

Most impressively, the week before they beat Liverpool 2-0 at home. One of their top scorers this season was Luther Blissett. Blissett was already a Watford legend and in his second spell with the club. He made his debut in 1975 and scored 95 goals in 246 league games before making a dream move to AC Milan in 1983. Sadly, that move to the Rossoneri only lasted one season where he scored five goals in 30 league games before heading back to Vicarage Road, Watford.

This season he had scored six league goals so far but was not top of his clubs scoring charts. That record belonged to former Spur Mark Falco. Falco had not long been at the club, but he had made a great start and had already netted seven league goals in this campaign.

Would this be yet another case of a former player coming back to haunt us like Micky Hazard, Ian Crook and Dave Leworthy had already done so this season?

David Pleat's matchday programme notes welcomed Graham Taylor and his team he praised his charges for a wonderful game at Old Trafford but then highlighted that we were giving away too many goals of late and that we should maybe "take a leaf out of the book of our 'mean' North London neighbours".

Arsenal were top of the league and had conceded nine goals in 18 games. Spurs were in tenth and had conceded 22 in 18 games. Pleat was not wrong.

Spurs had to be aware of today's opponents. Defensively they were not too bad but going forward was where Taylor's men impressed. They had scored 33 league goals already this season which was right up there with the top clubs. Falco, Blisset and the skilful John Barnes would give Mabbutt and co. headaches today. Watford's attack was also fed by the wonderfully talented Kevin Richardson.

Line up v Watford: Clemence; D Thomas, Gough, Mabbutt, M Thomas; Waddle, Roberts, Hoddle, P Allen, Galvin; C Allen. Sub: Ardiles.

Pleat kept the same eleven that finished the game at Old Trafford. Ardiles dropped to the bench and Paul Allen kept his midfield spot as well as Danny Thomas at right back. This was the fourth consecutive game where Pleat had stuck to his 4-5-1 formation too.

Unbeknown to the fans, this was to turn out as Graham Roberts' last game for Tottenham Hotspur.

Playing all in white, Spurs got off to a great start. Tony Galvin's simple pass found Hoddle on the edge of the area to see his right footed shot curl into the bottom right had corner. An elegant strike and Hoddle's first league goal of the season.

Spurs made it 2-0 just before the break when Richard Gough scored his first goal for the club. Yet again, Hoddle was the architect. A corner on Spurs' right side, saw Hoddle swing the ball into the penalty spot region and Gough got free of his markers and towered above everyone to head home. He ran off, right arm in the air and sprinted back to his centre back position.

Gough recalls that goal, "We had a corner from the right and Hoddle put it right on my head for me to score. I was surprised though that it had taken me until December to score as I scored a lot of goals in my time at Dundee United".

I also asked Richard why he always sprinted back to his position after venturing up for corners and free kicks. He admitted, "It's something I always did. I hated defenders ambling back so I wanted to get back into position as quickly as I could, it was urgency you know".

Spurs went into the break 2-0 up and in complete control. Clemence had nothing to do, and the midfield was dominant.

The second half began a bit more sedately and this was something to play into Watford's hands.

Pleat had mentioned in his matchday notes about not conceding and being more 'mean' like Arsenal. That meanness disappeared with twenty minutes to go when Watford pulled one back. From a seemingly innocuous Watford cross, Mark Flaco leapt higher than Gary Mabbutt and Mitchell Thomas to head Watford back into contention. Yes, Mark Falco, another ex-Spur scores against us.

This then saw Spurs fluster and panic over the final twenty minutes which allowed Watford to control and dominate. They could not find a winner and Spurs scraped home 2-1 winners.

Result: Tottenham Hotspur 2-1 Watford (Hoddle, Gough)

Some of the attacking football Spurs played earlier in the game was outstanding, but the mentality when things got a little close was an alarming outcome to games they were in control of.

This was something that visiting manager Graham Taylor noticed when speaking to *The Daily Mail's* Jeff Powell. Taylor said, "There is something in Spurs' psychological make-up which gives the opposition a chance. It nearly worked in our favour".

When David Pleat emerged from the dressing room, he told reporters that he had tried to correct that attitude. Powell reported Pleat's words of, "I've had a go at our lads. I've had to talk to international players who insist it's impossible to maintain good form for the entire match. I'm not accepting that, Ardiles even argued that even though Watford got back into the game they had very few shots at Clemence. I had to point out that Watford worked the ball well across our goalmouth often enough to have turned us over from a winning position".

Pleat concluded, "It's vital we stop that from happening".

This was an outburst of frustration from Pleat and even more surprising was that he told the press this too. I am not sure this would've gone down well with some of those players.

However, the 4-5-1 was still progressing. So much so, Graham Taylor praised Hoddle in his attacking free-role. He said "Our team had no idea how to handle Hoddle in the first half. He is intelligent as well as skilful, I had no option but to man mark him in the second half".

A tactic for Taylor that seemed to work too. He nullified Hoddle in the second half. Hoddle and Spurs would need to work out an antidote for that tactic in future.

The win had only seen Spurs rise one place to ninth.

So, after three league points gained, what do you do next? Go to Bermuda of course!!!

* * * *

Not long after the Watford game, Spurs flew 3,500 miles southwest of London to Bermuda.

They had been asked to play a friendly match against a Bermuda eleven at Somerset Cricket Club which was in Somerset Village, South Bermuda.

Pleat did not make the trip and Trevor Hartley was in charge for this one-off match. The players saw this as 'warm weather' training as they left the chilly, grey United Kingdom behind.

Paul Allen remembers that trip, "We left on the Sunday after the Watford game and it was a very relaxing break, we had played a lot of games and this break was a good ploy as when we returned, we went on a very good run of form".

The players spent time on the golf course during their brief stay. There are even rumours that Mitchell Thomas commandeered and wrecked a golf cart! All speculation of course.

The Bermudans were using this game to prepare themselves for the Pan American Games that were coming up next year. It's fair to say that Spurs probably got rewarded handsomely for sending over their star squad and the warmer climate was a very well received tonic for them all.

Richard Gough has fond memories of Bermuda too, he said; "I found it weird that in the middle of a season we go to Bermuda to play a friendly, but it was a fantastic break. Great weather and blue skies, I'd not been to Bermuda before, and come to think of it, I've not been back since!"

Spurs won the game 3-1. The hosts took a very early lead, but Clive Allen equalised barely a minute later.

Worryingly, Clive Allen limped off halfway through the first half with an ankle injury and young Shaun Close came on to replace him. A 25-yard Hoddle screamer put Spurs 2-1 up after 53 minutes and Chris Waddle made it 3-1 from the spot having converted a penalty won by Mark Bowen.

The result was 3-1 to Spurs. It mirrored the result the last time Spurs had ventured to Bermuda. In June 1979, Spurs travelled to Hamilton to play a Bermudan National team and a wave of injuries meant Spurs did not have a full eleven. It turns out that Club Secretary, Peter Day, and club physio, Mike Varney, turned out for Spurs that day. Spurs also had goalkeeper Milija Aleksic playing outfield that day too. Bizarre, but true!

Clive Allen remembers that Bermudan experience well, "Trevor Hartley took the team, and he said that David (Pleat) wanted us to relax and have a quiet week. On the Friday, I remember coming back to Heathrow and getting on the team bus. A few of us said that we should at least go for a jog around the ground as we were playing Chelsea the next day and we hadn't done a lot of training since the Bermuda game".

"We didn't see David until 1.45pm at Stamford Bridge just before the Chelsea game the following day and said he hoped we had a nice week away and felt refreshed, but this is how we are going to play today. A few of the lads said we had done little training since the game on Tuesday, and we haven't prepared that well. But we went out and gave one of our best away performances of the season!"

Saturday 20th December 1986 – Stamford Bridge, London
(Att: 21,576)
Chelsea v Tottenham Hotspur
(TODAY League Division 1)

Perhaps one reason David Pleat did not join his players in Bermuda was due to player transfers.

It appeared time was up for Graham Roberts and, with the links growing stronger of a move to Glasgow Rangers, it was not surprising that Roberts was left out of the matchday squad that visited West London.

It was evidential that Roberts and Pleat did not get on that well, so his departure was not a shock to people and players within the club.

Back in their all-white kit, Spurs were looking to avenge their home 3-1 defeat from early September. Pleat made a couple of changes from the team that had beaten Watford, bringing in Ardiles for the now departing Roberts and Tony Parks made his first appearance of the season in place of a flu ridden Clemence. Polston was the spare man on the bench.

Line up v Chelsea: Parks; D Thomas, Gough, Mabbutt, M Thomas; Waddle, Ardiles, Hoddle, P Allen, Galvin; C Allen. Sub: Polston.

Chelsea had recently lost 3-0 to Liverpool and 4-0 to Wimbledon. Manager John Hollins was under extreme pressure to turn results around and despite his defensive frailties he still had some impressive attacking talent in Kerry Dixon, David Speedie and Pat Nevin.

However, Tottenham dominated from the start and the midfield was where that dominance was applied. Chelsea's midfielder Nigel Spackman was brilliantly dispossessed by Danny Thomas near the centre spot and the ball found its way to Hoddle. Surrounded by Chelsea midfielders, Hoddle races towards the Blues penalty area only to check back and then deliver a delicious back-heel into Clive Allen's path and Allen struck the ball with venom into the top of the Chelsea goal for Spurs' lead.

Spurs were going into half-time fully justifying their lead, but just before the break, Tony Parks clumsily clatters into Chelsea's Joe McLaughlin and it seemed a penalty was a surety. Amazingly the referee disagrees, and Spurs got away with that.

The winter darkness descended over Stamford Bridge as the second half went on. The warm Bermudan climate was now a fading memory, but Spurs continued to play with sunshine brilliance. The dynamic between Waddle, Hoddle, Galvin and Paul Allen was relentless for Chelsea to try and get a handle on.

The game got a tad scrappy, and some ugliness slipped in when Joe McNaught elbowed Gary Mabbutt in the face. McNaught received a booking but that made Mabbutt, who had a great game up to that point, become even better and on 61 minutes he expertly broke up a Chelsea attack and set a sweeping counterattack in motion where Spurs ran the length of the pitch. Via the brilliance of Hoddle and Waddle, they colluded to set up

Clive for his second goal of the game. The Spurs fans were ecstatic. Stamford Bridge was hushed to a quiet as all you could hear were the jubilant away fans.

Chelsea threw everything they had a Spurs in the final 20 minutes, but Gough and Mabbutt were unbeatable. By far their best game as a pairing.

Result: Chelsea 0-2 Tottenham Hotspur (C Allen 2)

This was yet another brace for Clive Allen. He had now scored 24 goals in the season, and we hadn't even hit Christmas yet. 19 goals in the league and that was five goals ahead of his nearest rival Ian Rush on 14 league goals.

Clive remembered the win more than his goals. "I know we won up at Anfield, but we blew Chelsea away and should've scored four or five".

Clive himself missed a good chance near the end to grab his hat-trick and Brian Scovell in *The Daily Mail* reported just that. His headline was, 'ALLEN GIVES THE BOOT TO HIS BOOTS'.

According to Scovell's article, Clive had thrown his boots into the bin in fury at missing his hat-trick chance. Pleat told him not to do it and then Allen told Scovell, "The old pair were living on short time. They had gone in the toe after 30 games and after I had turned my ankle in Bermuda, I thought it was time I used the new pair I'd broken in".

Scovell was marvelling at Spur's 'Mexican World Cup Style' five-man midfield that was contributing to Allen's amazing goal tally. Allen told him, "Our midfield players make it easy for me. If you give the ball to Glenn Hoddle and move off, he'll put it on a sixpence for you".

* * * *

Tottenham were now up to fifth place in Division 1 and only three points behind Liverpool and Everton who were joint third on 35 points. Spurs had now won four of their last six league games and arguably could have been better. The point at United should've been a win and the home loss to Forest should've been avoided if it were not for some base errors.

Spurs were on the up and to make their Christmas even better, they were about to announce the signing of Steve Hodge, the England and Aston Villa midfielder.

In *The Daily Telegraph*, Colin Gibson asked for Pleat's thoughts on seeing Roberts depart for Glasgow Rangers. Pleat's parting shot was "He has kicked a few people in England and perhaps he will kick a few more in Scotland. We will live without him, and I am sure the referees won't miss him. I am happy with my central defensive partnership of Richard Gough and Gary Mabbutt".

Gibson also reported Roberts' retort, "If that's what they think of me after seven years then I am glad I'm going".

In *The Independent* newspaper, David Livingstone reported that Roberts was hurt by the public criticism and said, "I've always wanted to go to a bigger club, and now I have". Ouch, that comment hurt Spurs fans too Graham.

Roberts continued, "Spurs seem glad to be rid of me. Apparently, I am only good for kicking people now, even though they were saying last week I was their best player".

Roberts was another high-profile addition to Souness' Rangers Revolution, and he mentioned that a visit to Scotland several weeks before helped him see the passion for the club. Roberts said, "I came up with Richard Gough (in October) to see the Rangers-Celtic Skol Cup Final and it was amazing to see the Rangers support. I'm impressed. I'll play anywhere; I played every position for Spurs, including goalkeeper, so it doesn't matter to me".

Speaking with David Pleat now, does he regret saying that about Roberts, of course he does. But the fact of the matter is Pleat was keen to see his team go in a different direction, and sadly that did not include Roberts.

Roberts left the club in a manner that was not comparable to the excellent service he had given to the club and its supporters over the years. But this is football.

From a Spurs supporter point of view, the only disappointing thing was it seemed that Roberts was not willing to let his grudge towards Pleat and the club go. Even to this day, you still feel that it rankles him when he is ever interviewed about this period in his Spurs career.

Roberts would go on to win the League Championship with Rangers that season. STV made a documentary about Rangers' success that season and Jim White, now with Sky Sports, interviewed Roberts after the 1-1 draw with Aberdeen at Pittodrie which saw Rangers clinch the title.

He asked Robbo if he had any regrets joining Rangers, Roberts replied, "No not at all, this is the best day of my life, honestly".

Listening to that, I am not sure if he still felt bitter about his Spurs exit, but some may struggle to believe that was a better moment in comparison to when he lifted the UEFA Cup for Spurs three years earlier. But again, not great to hear if you are a Spurs fan.

That week, Steve Hodge joined for a fee of £650,000 having seen Roberts depart for £450,000. Hodge was an excellent, industrious attacking midfielder that had broken into the England set-up several months before and was pivotal in the success England had in Mexico.

Speaking with Steve it was clear to see that he felt joining Spurs would be a definite career boost and he recalls the opening day of the season when Spurs came to Villa Park and played them off the pitch with a 3-0 win back in August.

"I remember that 3-0 defeat well, it was like men versus boys. But when Spurs came in for me that December it was an easy decision to make. I would be joining a club with a proud history, top manager, fantastic playing squad, iconic stadium and a great fan base".

Hodge joined Spurs just before the Christmas Day break and that meant he would be available for selection for Spurs' next home game against West Ham United on Boxing Day.

Friday 26th December 1986 – White Hart Lane, London (Att: 39,019)
Tottenham Hotspur v West Ham United
(TODAY League Division 1)

The memories I have of this game are very strong. It was a morning kick off, 11.30am to be precise, and there was a beautiful winter sun that blanketed the playing surface at White Hart Lane.

This turned out to be the most enjoyable game I had experienced at White Hart Lane since the 5-0 crushing of Arsenal back in 1983. The crowd were so bubbly and hopeful but also a bit wary as West Ham had a very good side. I felt that Pleat had finally assembled a side that he felt was his own.

Spurs had been playing some great football in the last 4-5 weeks and expectations were high when West Ham visited, especially with the addition of England international, Steve Hodge, to the team.

The Hammers were only one point behind Spurs, and they had a very impressive team that had slightly underperformed so far this season.

Their last league campaign had seen them challenging Everton, and eventual winners Liverpool, for the league title. They had finished third, only two points behind Everton and four points behind the champions Liverpool. They lost to Everton in the final league game of last season which saw Everton claim runners up spot.

This season, West Ham had lost a bit of consistency from their game.

Making his debut for West Ham as a second half substitute in a recent defeat to Newcastle was a young Paul Ince. Ince was a tough tackling and dynamic central midfielder that had been brought up through their youth system. Ince would go on to have significant success with Manchester United, Inter Milan and Liverpool. He would also be a key player in England's impressive tournament showings during Euro'96 and France'98.

However, today he would struggle to shift West Ham midfield stalwarts Alan Devonshire, Alan Dickens and George Parris.

Manager John Lyall had a wonderful strike duo in Tony Cottee and Frank McAvennie. They had scored 16 goals in 20 league games between them already this season and both players had a good record against Spurs.

Pleat's matchday programme notes concluded with, "Enjoy the game – I hope you have all enjoyed your Christmas and that this morning we will see a game to remember".

You're not wrong there David! It turned out to be an absolute belter of a game and an extra Christmas present for all Spurs fans who were there.

Line up v West Ham United: Clemence; D Thomas, Gough, Mabbutt, M Thomas; Waddle, P Allen, Hoddle, Hodge, Galvin; C Allen. Sub: Ardiles.

Hodge came in for Ardiles who dropped to the bench. Pleat kept Galvin wide on the left and Waddle wide on the right. He set up Hodge to play alongside Paul Allen in the middle of midfield just behind Hoddle.

Paul Allen and Steve Hodge would go on to run absolute riot today.

This game would be the best footballing performance I had seen at Spurs produce since we demolished Arsenal 5-0 back in 1983.

With the playing surface bathed in that low, winter sun Spurs were out of the blocks early. Swift, cutting football that seemed to have West Ham running in circles.

In fairness, West Ham did well to wait until the 14th minute when they conceded Spurs' first goal. Spurs had a corner on their right-hand side in front of the Paxton. Hoddle swung the ball out to the penalty spot again and Richard Gough rose high to create a near carbon copy of his goal against Watford. This time his header fell to Clive Allen whose left foot hook volley beat Steve Hodge who was trying to head home with a flying header. Allen scores yet again and Spurs are on top.

Spurs swarmed forward and West Ham were struggling to cope with this onslaught of attacking football. They held it to 1-0 at half time though.

On 53 minutes, Hodge capped a wonderful debut with a superbly taken goal. Paul Allen noticed his run into the box and his pass saw Hodge spin and shoot past Phil Parkes for Spurs' second goal of the game.

One minute later it was probably the goal of the game. Hodge, in a central role played a pacey pass into the feet of Clive Allen who saw his first-time pass fall into the path of a charging Chris Waddle who struck it first time with the outside of his left foot over Parkes and in the net for Spurs' third. What a classy, swift move. The Hammers were shell-shocked.

The scoring concluded 14 minutes later when Hodge, yet again, performed a superb 1-2 with Hoddle and saw his cross fall into the path for Clive Allen to score. Yet another Allen brace!

Clive Allen raced off towards the West Stand and slid on his knees like a kid at a school disco. Arms aloft as his teammates came to embrace him.

Clive Allen, two goals and one assist. New boy Hodge, one goal and two assists.

Result: Tottenham Hotspur 4-0 West Ham United (C Allen 2, Hodge, Waddle)

Hodge recalls; "My debut could not have gone any better, but I was nervous before that game. It was special to score on my debut and also to score past the great West Ham goalkeeper Phil Parkes".

Tottenham could have quite easily bagged four or five more goals over that 90-minute showpiece, but four goals were more than adequate, and a consecutive clean sheet. Cottee and McAvennie were kept quiet by the brilliant Gough, Mabbutt and the excellent covering full backs, Danny and Mitchell Thomas. Clem had next to nothing to do all day but just occasionally re-adjust his baseball cap to keep the sun out of his eyes.

When reviewing this game with Clive Allen, he has nothing but golden memories when this match gets mentioned. He said, "This is my greatest game for any club side I have played for, it's the greatest team performance that I've played in. I remember the 11.30am Boxing Day kick off, it was Steve Hodge's debut as well and he was sensational".

Clive went on to say, "We could've scored ten that day the way we were playing, and West Ham could not cope with us. It was unbelievable, my best performance of the season".

The newspapers were gushing over Tottenham following that performance. Brian Scovell in *The Daily Mail* penned a headline, 'SPURS SPARKLE'. He wrote, "Tottenham are striding into 1987 as genuine title challengers for the title they last won 26 years ago". Praise indeed.

He also highlighted that Clive Allen had now scored 26 goals in 26 games and cheekily joked that he was now in danger of being reported to the monopolies commission having scored 21 goals out his team's 32 league goals so far this campaign.

In *The Independent*, Joe Lovejoy's headline went with, 'PLEAT'S MEXICO WAY'. Lovejoy led with, "The sponsors were Weetabix, and with the match kicking off in the morning, Spurs could be said to have had West Ham for breakfast".

Lovejoy emphasised that English football seemed to have learned little from the Mexico World Cup, but Spurs were the exception. He praised Pleat's five-man midfield and lone striker by highlighting its flexibility and it being a way of maximising his team's attacking potential.

There were positive words across all newspapers and *The Times* sharply wrote, "Tottenham were very much the toffs, shaming the Eastenders with a performance of elegance that was all of the four goals superior as West Ham suffered their worst defeat to Spurs in 19 seasons".

A memorable day and also the day that a future Spurs captain was born. Goalkeeper Hugo Lloris was born in Nice on Boxing Day 1986. He enjoyed playing in behind some wonderful footballers just like Clem had done during this game.

A great result, but sadly no time to really appreciate it as Spurs needed to travel North to face Coventry at Highfield Road, less than 24 hours later!

Saturday 27th December 1986 – Highfield Road, Coventry
(Att: 22,181)
Coventry City v Tottenham Hotspur
(TODAY League Division 1)

In today's football, managers and players would be up in arms having to play two games in two days. But Spurs headed to Highfield Road in excellent form and maybe slightly giddy from some of the outstanding football they had been playing.

The giddiness had clearly got to the kit men, Wallis and Reyland, as they were confronted by a referee when they were settling in at Coventry's Highfield Road. He was not happy with Spurs' shirt colour choice and stated they had to wear another colour to avoid clashing with Coventry's home kit.

With limited options to appease the referee, Spurs ended up wearing Coventry City's away shirt, all yellow! Now yellow is not too alien to Spurs players or fans. Some of our away kits in the 1970s and early 1980s were yellow. A favourite that always springs to mind is the 1977-78 yellow shirt which had two navy blue sashes over the chest and was manufactured by Admiral. It was very stylish, and I can always imagine Terry Yorath or Steve Perryman when I think of that kit.

Our FA Cup win over QPR in 1982 was in a beautifully simple all yellow kit, another stylish manufacturer produced that superb strip, Le Coq Sportif. Even after the 1991 FA Cup success I had a penchant for the away yellow jersey made by Umbro.

The Coventry away shirt was all yellow with blue neck and sleeve edges. It was sponsored by Granada Social Clubs. I wonder what Holsten made of that scenario?

The Sky Blues eleven was similar to the team that faced Spurs back at White Hart Lane in November. There was one significant change that saw Keith Houchen partner Cyrille Regis up front. Former Spur, and still only 17-years-old, Steve Sedgley also lined up in midfield against Spurs' glamourous five.

Mitchell Thomas came off during the West Ham win with a slight knock to the knee and oddly, Pleat deployed Tony Galvin at left back. Ardiles came in and had taken the number 3 shirt, but it was Galvin that lined up behind Hodge of the left side for Spurs.

Line up v Coventry: Clemence; D Thomas, Gough, Mabbutt, Galvin; Waddle, P Allen, Hoddle, Ardiles, Hodge; C Allen. Sub: Claesen.

Spurs took to the field in yellow shirts along with a navy short and sock combo and this turned out to be one of the games of the season. Spurs took the lead, and it was late in the first half when Clive Allen scrambled home from an Ardiles corner on 38 minutes.

Four minutes later, Keith Houchen equalised when he converted a deep right-wing cross with a superb header. He seemed to shrug off Richard Gough quite easily and headed past Clemence from around the penalty spot.

Spurs took the lead again not long after, just before the break. Danny Thomas' throw-in found Ossie Ardiles. The Argentinian darted a super cross-field pass to Clive Allen on the far side of Coventry's penalty box, Allen dropped his shoulder and onto his favoured right foot where he powered a low shot past Ogrizovic's left hand and in off the post. A brilliant strike.

Into the second half and Coventry equalised just before the hour mark when they scored a Spurs-esque goal. Bennett won the ball in the middle of the pitch and set up a swift attack that saw one touch into Houchen who laid if off to Regis. Bennett had not stopped running and Regis slotted the ball into his path to see Bennett shrug off a Gough challenge and slip underneath Clemence.

Three minutes later Coventry took the lead. Houchen flew in with a flying header only to see his effort hit the post and bounce back to Bennett who smashed home for his second goal of the game. The crowd were going crazy, what a game this was turning out to be.

Spurs had to dig deep but kept pressing with some wonderful attacking football. Pleat sacrificed the excellent Ardiles and threw on Nico Claesen, and with six minutes to go that switch paid off.

On 84 minutes, Hoddle was just inside the right touchline when his powerful low cross found Clive Allen on the edge of the box.

Without breaking stride, Allen volleyed the ball low and hit Ogrizvovic's left hand post only to see Claesen poach the rebound home. 3-3 and fully deserved by Spurs too.

Just hold it now lads.

Sadly, that was not the case. The six-goal thriller was now a seven-goal thriller when, with two minutes to go, Regis leapt between Mabbutt and Gough to had a cross onto the crossbar past a stretched Clemence. Regis' momentum meant he was the first to react and he slotted the ball past a recovering Clemence. 4-3 to Coventry and Highfield Road had erupted.

When the final whistle rang out, the Spurs players looked rightfully dejected. Apart from a few moments when some defenders might have been a little more assertive, Spurs would have got something out of this game.

Evidentially, it was also plain to see that Regis, Houchen and Bennett were thorns in Spurs' side. They were relentless all game and with the Regis/Houchen physicality it was a tough trip for Mabbutt and Gough.

Result: Coventry City 4-3 Tottenham Hotspur 4-0 (C Allen 2, Claesen)

A couple of Spurs players forgot they had worn the Coventry away shirt that day, Steve Hodge did remember, "Yes, I remember we had to wear Coventry shirts as there was a kit clash, the game was thriller despite us losing!" Welcome to Spurs, Mr Hodge.

Keith Houchen has fond memories of that game, a goal and two assists, plus the bizarre shirt story. He recalled, "There were two teams playing in Coventry strips, that was a bit of an anomaly. It was a great game and I felt I was about to score the winner, but Cyrille flew in with his header and when he's coming through like that you just get out of his way".

Houchen wore the number ten shirt for Coventry, and I delightfully pointed out that Glenn Hoddle was wearing his other number ten during the game in Coventry's away shirt. Houchen remembers, "I was used to wearing number nine, but that was Cyrille's shirt, and I took on the number ten. So, Glenn wore my shirt that day did he! I used to love watching Glenn in those early 80's cup finals".

The newspapers were gushing over the game at Highfield Road, a wonderful footballing spectacle. Brian Marshall's *Sunday Telegraph* headline was: 'REGIS SHATTERS SPURS'. He labelled Coventry's win as being courageous and determined.

In *The Sunday Times*, James Wilson lauded the game with the headline, 'MAGNIFICENT – ALL SEVEN'. He penned that Spurs' triumphant recent run of form had been interrupted with a superb Coventry second half display. He gave Coventry credit for their no-nonsense and direct approach which clearly rattled Spurs but labelled it 'an afternoon of continuous excitement'.

In comparison to October and November, this had been an excellent month for Pleat's men.

Up to this point they won three, drawn one and also competed in the Guinness Soccer Six AND a trip to Bermuda too.

Spurs went into the New Year 6th in Division 1 and ten points behind leaders Arsenal. They were facing a League Cup quarter final against West Ham and in just over a week they would kick off their FA Cup campaign at home to Scunthorpe United.

At the top, Arsenal had scored 33 and conceded 11 goals. Spurs had scored 35 goals and conceded 27.

15 of the 35 goals scored were in the first 45 minutes of each game and 20 in the second half. They had led at half-time in 10 of those matches but had only gone on to win seven of them despite being ahead at half time.

Spurs had conceded nine first half goals and 18 goals in the second half of those league matches played. The second forty-five was where points were being lost. With seven goals conceded in the last fifteen minutes of matches, and the regular errors. It was not surprising to see why Spurs were not doing better.

However, it now seemed that Pleat had stumbled across a back four that was a bit more settled and working well, despite the recent three goals conceded. With his back four, his midfield five and Mr Allen up top on his own, it finally felt like Pleat had a team he was happier with than maybe two months before.

The calendar year was ending. Nigel Mansell had won the 1986 Sports Personality of the Year beating Javelin hero Fatima Whitbread and Liverpool's Kenny Dalglish to top spot.

Back to the Future, *Top Gun*, *Aliens* and *Rocky IV* topped the UK film box office charts in 1986 and John Cleese's *Clockwise* the most successful British film released that year.

The festive period revealed that the coveted Christmas no.1 single was '*Reet Petite'* by Jackie Wilson and the album charts that year were dominated by Madonna's *True Blue* and Paul Simon's *Graceland*.

Christmas TV was won by the BBC and their Eastenders two-part Christmas Day special.

Eastenders, the East London soap-opera, was still in its relative infancy but the nation was captured when main character, 'Dirty' Den Watts, concluded the festive special by issuing a divorce letter to his wife Angie and shocking the estimated 30 million people who had tuned in to watch. Great 80's TV drama.

The New Year was now upon us and many people were keen to see the back of a year that had witnessed the NASA's *Challenger* exploding in the Space Shuttle disaster, the nightmare and widespread panic caused by the explosion of a nuclear power plant in the Russian town of Chernobyl and the madness of Mad Cow disease that had hit UK cattle.

But for English sport fans, the year had finished well as Mike Gatting, and his England Cricket team, had regained the Ashes on Australian soil when winning the Boxing Day Test match in Melbourne. Before the end of 1987 though, Australia would have their revenge when they beat England in the fourth World Cup Final in Eden Gardens, Calcutta.

Back at White Hart Lane, 1987 would be a big test for Scholar, Pleat and the Spurs players and staff. Still in with a shout for all three trophies, could the Lilywhites bring home the first major silverware since the UEFA cup win back in 1984?

JANUARY 1987

December seemed to be a long, yet varied month for Spurs and with Pleat's team looking a little more settled during that period, one reality had been gradually sinking in - this would be Glenn Hoddle's last season at Tottenham Hotspur.

During the three-day break in Bermuda, Hoddle had spoken to the media and announced this would be his final year at Spurs.

Colin Gibson in, *The Daily Telegraph,* wrote, "I believe this will be my last season at Spurs. I would not have said this at the start of the season, but I know I must make the break. It will be one of the biggest regrets in my life if I don't play abroad and discover just how good Glenn Hoddle is".

So, with this now being Hoddle's final fling with his boyhood club, he would hope that he goes out with a bang. This process would start in an away New Years Day fixture at Charlton Athletic. The next few months would see Spurs play a total of 31 more games, it will be fast and frenetic, and we'd be stupid not to expect a fixture pile-up at some point!

Thursday 1st January 1987 – Selhurst Park, London
(Att: 19,744)
Charlton Athletic v Tottenham Hotspur
(TODAY League Division 1)

Charlton Athletic were ground sharing with Crystal Palace at Selhurst Park, South London. Charlton had left their home stadium, The Valley, in autumn 1985 and had struck an agreement with Crystal Palace to share their stadium and facilities while The Valley was being redeveloped.

Charlton had been promoted that season and Spurs' last competitive game against the South London outfit was two seasons before when they had knocked Charlton out of the FA Cup in a 3rd round replay.

They had been flirting with the relegation zone all season and going into today's match they were one place above the relegation places. The had beaten Manchester City 5-0 at Selhurst Park a few days before but that was their first win in nine league games.

Scoring goals was a problem for Charlton though, only 19 goals were scored before the unexpected five goal haul against City. A solution would present itself in a few months' time when Charlton sign ex-Spurs legend Garth Crooks on the 1st of March 1987, but for now Jim Melrose and Colin Walsh were the men to lead the line for Lennie Lawrence's men.

Today, Spurs were wearing their all-pale blue away kit and with Mitchell Thomas still out injured, as well as Chris Hughton,

Pleat decided to utilise Paul Miller at left-back for his second league start of the season. Plus, Claesen was back in the starting eleven after his late strike a few days before at Coventry.

Line up v Charlton: Clemence; D Thomas, Gough, Mabbutt, Miller; Waddle, P Allen, Hoddle, Claesen, Hodge; C Allen. Sub: Galvin.

There was one significant moment just before kick-off. The referee was greeting both team captains to toss the coin for choice of ends. This time it was Richard Gough in the centre circle and not Ray Clemence. This little moment went unnoticed by most and it wouldn't be until the Scunthorpe matchday programme, in several days' time, that Pleat would reveal why this change had happened.

It was a chilly and grim New Years Day saw Spurs remain in control throughout the most of this game.

The back four were rarely troubled at all and for Paul Miller this would turn out to be his last game for Tottenham Hotspur. Oddly enough, today's opponents will be the club he next joins, but today he performed diligently and contributed towards a well-received clean sheet.

A huge number of Spurs fans travelled south of the river to pack out the majority of the Holmesdale Road end as Spurs took a 14th minute lead when some neat midfield play between Chris Waddle and Glenn Hoddle saw the latter thread a pass through to a speedy Claesen who raced on, slipping the ball neatly underneath Charlton keeper Bob Bolder.

Spurs went into half-time 1-0 up and they could've extended their lead both sides of half time with good chances for both Clive and Paul Allen.

Tony Galvin was introduced as a second half replacement for Steve Hodge and that would prove to be a shrewd change for Pleat as the game went on. Amazingly, Clive Allen did not appear on the scoresheet today, but Cousin Paul was the difference when he carved out a great opening for Spurs' second and final goal of the game.

Picking the ball up just outside his own area, Allen pelted forwards but had little support. Galvin was running just ahead, and Allen slipped the ball into his path while being taken out by a Charlton midfielder. After this passage of play, Allen would come off the field with concussion and leaving Spurs with only ten men on the field for the final few minutes of the game.

The ref waved play on and with Galvin still in his own half there was a fair bit of work to do.

Socks down, Galvin steams towards the Charlton penalty area only to realise he is as good as alone. He cuts back in on his right foot and unleashes an absolute belter of a shot to nestle into the top right-hand corner of the Charlton goal! What a strike.

Before any of his teammates can reach him to congratulate him, Galvin had stooped down in front of the away support and shook his fists in celebration at his adoring fans. 2-0, game over.

Despite this being Paul Miller's last game for the club, this turned out to be Tony Galvin's last goal for the club....and what a goal it was.

Result: Charlton Athletic 2-0 Tottenham Hotspur
(Claesen, Galvin)

Spurs had now scored a mighty 14 goals in their last five away league games.

Telegraph reporter, Donald Saunders, headlined his Spurs piece with, 'GALVIN'S GRANDSTAND CLINCHER' as a direct nod to Galvin's late wonder strike at Selhurst Park. He said, "Galvin's spectacular late goal clinched it for Spurs and put them back on track for the 1987 league championship".

Charlton manager, Lennie Lawrence, told Saunders, "We don't score enough goals. It is touch and go whether we stay in the first division, we do not have the quality".

Lawrence will end up signing Garth Crooks and Paul Miller, these players will ultimately prove to be quite inspirational signings as Charlton will go on to keep their Division 1 status in a dramatic end of season 'play-off' win over Leeds United.

* * * *

The January 1987 edition of *Spurs News* had new signing Steve Hodge as front-page fodder.

Hodge shared his delight at joining Spurs and an inside article also had a photo of Hodge alongside his England colleagues

Hoddle, Waddle and Mabbutt. It pointed out that this was in fact, the midfield four that Bobby Robson had deployed in the most recent England international against Yugoslavia back in November. I doubt even before, or since, can Spurs boast a whole midfield made up of their own players.

Spurs News also reported that former club captain, Steve Perryman, was included in the recent New Years honours list by Her Majesty Queen Elizabeth II. He would be invited to Buckingham Palace to collect an OBE for services to football, mainly services to Spurs in truth.

Another award, albeit not as prestigious as Perryman's, was Ray Clemence being named the Spurs Supporters Club Player of the Year for 1986. Clem was still good enough to be in the England party that went to Mexico last summer, but he was clearly enjoying his time at Spurs and playing so well.

Awards aside, Spurs now needed to focus on a huge game. On Sunday they would play in their second live televised match of the season when they host league leaders, and rivals, Arsenal at White Hart Lane.

Sunday 4th January 1987 – White Hart Lane, London
(Att: 37,723)
Tottenham Hotspur v Arsenal
(TODAY League Division 1)

Spurs were now in sixth position, but they remained ten points behind Arsenal who had beaten Wimbledon 3-1 on New Years Day keeping them top.

This would be the 100th league meeting between these rivals and I can still recall walking to this game full of excitement but also some unease as there seemed to be so much riding on this game.

Music is a wonderful trigger for memories. Still to this day there is a song that always reminds me of this match.

London pop band, Curiosity Killed the Cat, had released a great track in readiness for their album launch in April 1987. *Keep Your Distance* would go on to be one of the best-selling albums of that year and reaching the Top 10 that week was their second single released from that album. *Down to Earth* is a catchy, soulful track that would spark their success and this is the song that reminds me of this game.

I remember listening to it on my Walkman as I walked to the Lane, loving the song but praying that the song title would not be an accurate reflection of Spurs' current good form.

There had been a few false dawns this season already, and a loss to Arsenal today would bring us back *Down to Earth* as the track title suggests.

The matchday programme Ray Clemence was quoted as saying, "North London matches Merseyside for emotion". A perfect response from someone who has played in both, and he cunningly avoided saying any one derby was bigger than the other.

Hodge had not recovered from the knock he received at Charlton, so Galvin started on the left-hand side and Ardiles joined Paul Allen and Glenn Hoddle in the middle.

Paul Miller made way for the returning Mitchell Thomas at left-back and Pleat must've felt quite confident in the eleven that took the field in white shirts, navy shorts and white socks. Nico was dropped to the bench despite his two goals in two games.

Line up v Arsenal: Clemence; D Thomas, Gough, Mabbutt, M Thomas; Waddle, P Allen, Hoddle, Ardiles, Galvin; C Allen. Sub: Claesen.

Live on BBC1, pundit Trevor Brooking highlighted the need for Spurs to win today and bridge that 10-point gap with Arsenal. Jimmy Hill was firm on Arsenal winning today. John Motson was joined in his commentary position with England World Cup winner Bobby Charlton as his dulcet tones took the armchair fans through this North London battle.

Did Spurs turn up? Did they heck. From early on in the game you got the feeling that today was not going to be the home team's day.

That irksome feeling came to fruition when Arsenal's young centre back, Tony Adams, put the league leaders ahead after only six minutes when Spurs failed to clear a ball into their box and Adams scrambled the ball home after a 50-50 with Clemence.

Awful defending and an awful start for Spurs.

It was yet another grim, grey, drizzly day and things would get worse for Spurs just before half time when Paul Davis put the visitors 2-0 up. An outstanding move by the away side saw Martin Hayes race clear and heading for a showdown with Ray Clemence. Danny Thomas flew in from nowhere and gave away a freekick on the edge of the box. Nowadays Thomas would be sent off straight away, but Hayes was certain to make it 2-0.

From the resulting freekick Paul Davis struck the ball through the Spurs wall, in between the legs of Galvin and Paul Allen, which left Clem stranded. Clem was livid, absolutely furious, but Spurs were floundering here.

Just before the break Spurs did pull one back. Spurs swept forward and Hoddle fired across a low pass to Ardiles who was all alone in the Arsenal box but couldn't reach the ball. Nor could the Arsenal keeper Lukic, but scampering in at the back post was Mitchell Thomas who slid in and struck the ball into the back of the net for his second strike of the season.

Spurs did not necessarily deserve that goal, but half time meant it was time to regroup.

The second half had no more goals, but more concerning was that Arsenal did not look uncomfortable for the remainder of that game. The home midfield had plenty of the ball, but Spurs were limp in the final third, a testament to Arsenals defending more like.

Result: Tottenham Hotspur 1-2 Arsenal (M Thomas)

Spurs were now in seventh position and 13 points behind leaders Arsenal who were now four points ahead of Everton in second place.

This was Spurs' fourth home defeat of the season, and it seemed that all the good form that had led up to this game had disappeared at the point of a pressure match.

One player who had been very inconsistent since the start of the season was Chris Waddle. There were odd games where he was exquisite to watch, but Pleat needed more consistency from the England winger. There were moments in this game that I recall the crowd getting on to Waddle a little bit. Waddle was very much a 'head-down' player when things were not going that well, this did not help and we needed the real Chrissy Waddle back.

In *The Independent*, Patrick Barclay rightly pointed out that "Paul Davis dictates the centenary derby as Gunners point the way in the title battle".

Pleat was a touch more philosophical than the performance suggested and told *Spurs News*, "I am convinced that if we scored the first goal then we would have won, but we will never know". With a statement like that, as fans we must question the mentality of the players once more, it was an inability to be resilient when they went down so early in the game that seemed to be the key factor here.

Anyway, the game is gone and Spurs had to look forward to their FA Cup encounter with lowly Scunthorpe United next Saturday.

It was a week to reflect and for Pleat to get back to the training ground with his team. But, back to *Curiosity Killed the Cat*. Yes, we had been brought back *Down to Earth* as the track title so annoyingly pointed out.

Saturday 11th January 1987 – White Hart Lane, London
(Att: 19,339)
Tottenham Hotspur v Scunthorpe United
(FA Cup – 3rd Round)

Everyone loves the FA Cup and Spurs have an affinity with this trophy. Seven times a winner, with this record Spurs fans felt like the FA Cup belonged to them.

This campaign would begin on a bitterly cold Saturday afternoon. I still think this is the coldest I have ever felt going to a Spurs game. But the freezing temperatures aside, a win was needed, no exceptions.

Hodge was painfully missed during the Arsenal defeat, but he would be back today.

Lining up for Spurs today was of course, Hoddle and Waddle. I was always amused that one of Scunthorpe's midfielders that day was called Broddle. Julian Broddle was not a household name, nor were the rest of his teammates to be honest.

In Pleat's matchday programme notes he explained the change in captaincy on New Years Day, "Before the Charlton game I made Richard the new team captain. Ray Clemence has been a splendid goalkeeper, captain, ambassador for this club, but I have to look ahead. Ray has been an excellent guide to me over the first few months and will still be much involved. Richard has the potential to be a fine captain from an area with closer contact to the bench, referee and players".

Personally, I have never been a fan of goalkeepers as captains and preferring to see a centre back or central midfielder in that role. Saying that, goalkeepers Dino Zoff and Hugo Lloris were both captains of their respective World Cup winning teams so, what do I know!?

Visiting Scunthorpe manager, Frank Barlow, had been at the helm since 1984 and this was his club's first ever visit to White Hart Lane. Journeyman Steve Johnson was their main threat up front, but Spurs were still favourites to come through this game unscathed.

Line up v Scunthorpe United: Clemence; D Thomas, Gough, Mabbutt, M Thomas; Claesen, Waddle, P Allen, Hoddle, Hodge; C Allen. Sub: Ruddock, Ardiles.

With Hodge back on the left, Claesen came in on the right-hand side which meant Chris Waddle tucked in centrally.

It was a centrally placed Waddle that carved out Spurs opener after 19 minutes. Waddle, in a left-central midfield position, swung in a left-footed cross behind the Scunthorpe defence to find Gary Mabbutt lurking and hit a superb half-volley for Spurs' opener.

FANTASTIC DISAPPOINTMENT

The away team equalised three minutes later when Steve Johnson beat a poorly organised Spurs offside-trap, to run through and score past Clemence. Once again, Clem did not look happy, especially against the club where he began his professional career.

The crowd were not liking this at all. Grumbles and groans all-round as the half wore on. Half-time came and Spurs trudged off at 1-1.

The second half started off quite bland too. It was only boosted into life just before the hour mark when a poorly hit Hoddle corner managed to somehow find its way to Nico Claesen who crept in to put Spurs back in front. 2-1.

With 12 minutes to go the game was won.

Chris Waddle had another fairly quiet game and you sensed the crowd unrest was not making him feel any better. Spurs were moving forward, and that ball was played to Waddle on the right side of Spurs' midfield. Danny Thomas flanked to his right, Clive Allen darted into the box, but Waddle dropped his shoulder and came inside on his left foot and unleashed a ferocious shot from 30 yards out. It sped into the top right-hand corner for his sixth goal of the season.

He immediately turned to the West Stand and defiantly raised his arms aloft in what seemed like anger. Head down despite scoring an absolute peach of a goal. Could this be the turning point for Waddle's season.

Spurs only had another ten or so minutes to see the game out, but with three minutes to go, Scunthorpe midfielder, Ken De Mange, skipped through Spurs' midfield and struck the ball past Clemence from 25 yards out.

Another goal conceded, another 'switched off' moment and I am sure Pleat would not have been happy.

Result: Tottenham Hotspur 3-2 Scunthorpe United (Mabbutt, Claesen, Waddle)

The 4th Division club had given a good account of themselves. In Sue Mott's *Sunday Times* article, she highlighted how well Scunthorpe had done with Spurs winning unconvincingly. She was also right to point out that Scunthorpe had strong alumni having produced three England captains in Ray Clemence, Kevin Keegan and Ian Botham!

After the game, Scunthorpe boss Frank Barlow admitted that Chris Waddle's goal was 'worth the entrance fee alone' and in *Spurs News*, Nico Claesen admitted he was surprised at the quality of 4th tier clubs in England. He said, "When we play a 4th division side in Belgium, the score is usually 4 or 5-nil. I think the standard in England is higher!" Nico was also pleased with his current form having scored now in both league and cup games.

The crowd attendance was around half of what had turned up for the previous home game when Spurs thumped West Ham 4-0 on Boxing Day. Maybe the fans were getting bored of the inconsistency as much as Pleat was getting annoyed by seeing it.

But Spurs had won, through to the next round where they had been drawn at home to Division 2 highflyers, Crystal Palace.

With Spurs still being involved in both cups, there was a good chance that a fixture pile-up would ensue. With that in mind, Spurs would now find themselves with two weeks until their next competitive game. It would be at home to Aston Villa on the 24th of January as the scheduled league game away at Newcastle, on the 17th January, would be postponed due to severe weather conditions.

Last month they jetted off to Bermuda, the team were not so lucky this time as they would be heading to Northern Ireland for a friendly match against Linfield. For the record, there is nothing wrong with visiting Belfast, but it's not as warm or sunny as Bermuda in January, is it?

On the injury front, Chris Hughton, who underwent a cartilage operation in November was still a few weeks away from training again, but Gary Stevens had played his first 90 minutes in a friendly against Charlton at Cheshunt. It was his first outing since his breaking and dislocating his shoulder against Wimbledon last November.

* * * *

The day after the Scunthorpe victory, there was an interesting article written by Brian Glanville in the *Sunday Times*. It headlined, 'DO FOOTBALLERS NEED A COUCH OR A COACH?'. Glanville was reporting on the rise of psychology within the game.

His article focused on two key areas. The 1982 Italian World Cup winning manager, Enzo Bearzot and British psychologist, John Syer.

Firstly, he spoke about an interview that Bearzot had given to Italian television a few weeks before where he still struggled to understand how his team were knocked out of the 1986 World Cup when France, the current European Champions, beat his 1982 World Cup holders 2-0 in their Second-Round tie.

It was an underwhelming defence of their title and Glanville viewed the implications of his comments as 'breath-taking'.

Bearzot said, "I still don't understand the cause of our failure in Mexico. Certainly, it is absurd that it should have been up to me, after every game, to calm the team down. There should have been people there ready to do that job. I often asked the doctors what was going wrong, and their response was always the same; there are problems of a psychological nature. And, unfortunately, I am a football manager, not Freud".

Bearzot had acquired a group of players that were physically exhausted and largely demoralised from the pressures and strains of the Italian Championship. He felt that he had worked tirelessly to create what he called "an atmosphere of disintoxication". Bearzot was essentially saying that dealing with the player's psychological state was not his job and that specialists were required.

This brought Glanville on to the second phase of his article, the British psychologist, John Syer.

Now, Spurs fans may know of Syer. He had been working with Spurs in the Burkinshaw years and Glenn Hoddle had always spoken highly of Syer's interventions with him and his teammates during his tenure with the club.

Syer had just released a book called, 'Team Spirit; the elusive experience'. Glanville felt that Bearzot's comments fed into 'people like' Syer. He described his book as 'muddled, ill-written and intellectually diffuse' and claimed that, even though Spurs did well in the five years when Syer was with them, he doubted how much of that was actually down to Syer.

Glanville described some of Syer's methods as 'sometimes original and sometimes banal' it was clear to see that the *Sunday Times* columnist was not a fan of this 'performance' tool. Glanville highlighted that managers like, Bill Nicholson, Herbert Chapman and even the current Forest boss, Brian Clough, may not have favoured this type of intervention with their players. However, he did concede that they all had their ways in getting the best out of their players which could very well have been a psychological intervention.

Nowadays, psychology in sport in an absolute necessity when creating high performers and high performing teams. I believe Glanville failed to grasp that this was the next stage in the evolution of elite sport and this tool would soon be deployed across all sports as the years would pass by.

Nevertheless, Glanville did point out that Syer had previously worked with Steve Archibald to 'harness' his aggression and then use it wisely on the football field. The essence of sports psychology was to understand the player and to 'take into account' his mental and emotional state as this could benefit his and the team's performance if managed or coached effectively.

The New Zealand Rugby team (All Blacks) have a simple formula to create their high-performance culture. It is *High Performance = Capability x Behaviour*. The All Blacks were not just after players who were exceptionally good at playing the game, it also required players that had a resilience when things were not going that well or even an emotional strength to deal with hostile atmospheres and scenarios. There were elements of attitude, conduct and behaviour that needed to be in place for players to be part of a high performing team in a high-performance arena. A large ingredient in the All Blacks, and other successful sporting teams, tends to be down to the environment that is created to enhance the skills that each team member brings to the group. Culture is key.

The fact of the matter is, managers and coaches had been utilising psychology for years already, some consciously and others less consciously. Maybe it was the overt nature of this as a discussion point now that people may have disagreed with but managing the psychology of a player was not a groundbreakingly new concept.

Two weeks after that article, Syer was invited to take part in a *Thames TV* talk show, hosted by Mavis Nicholson, on the subject of '*Psychology in Sport*'.

Syer was joined on the programme by former England Cricket captain, Mike Brearley and current manager of Wimbledon FC, Dave Bassett.

Brearley was no longer playing professional cricket and was now a psychoanalyst. Around a year before, he had published *'The Art of Captaincy'*, which was a wonderful insight into captaining first class and test match cricket by understanding his approach and mindset. This was a 'go-to' book for many managers, leaders, captains and coaches for some time.

Bassett was enjoying his first season in Division 1 having seen his Wimbledon team propel up the league ladder in the last few years. It was fair to say that Bassett and Brearley were chalk and cheese, but there would be a few common denominators between them that we would ascertain whilst watching this programme.

Nicholson jumped right into it by asking Syer to explain the three main areas that had resonated from his book, *Team Spirit*. They were; high synergy, high cohesion and positive confluence.

It was clear to see quite early on that Brearley and Bassett viewed these as 'buzz' words and things they tried to avoid in their professional arenas. Syer was merely pointing out that these were recognisable traits that successful teams had and they contributed to high 'Team Spirit'.

He highlighted that synergy was when a group was working well together, it provided an energy that was 'extra' rather than just individual energy, which then contributed towards enhancing team success. He mentioned when things were going well at Spurs, it felt like there was a twelfth man on the field due to the team working so well together. Today, we class the crowd as the twelfth man too!

Confluence was the feeling of being part of something greater than yourself and where things meet. In some ways, when team strategy and planning pays off, alongside players performing then this is the outcome.

Finally, cohesion. Simply, when teams stick together. Again, nothing new but areas that are being unpacked so it can be understood among the collective.

It was interesting to read the body language of the guests while Syer made his opening statement. Brearley looked to his right and appeared to be ostentatiously listening to what Syer was saying and Bassett had his eyes fixed on the presenter and not on Syer.

Bassett was polite but didn't really want to analyse the depth of these words in team spirit among his team. It was fair to say that Bassett had created a culture at Wimbledon that suited its personnel. Spurs, and other teams in Division 1, had already experienced that this season, and Bassett knew his players approach was to psychologically effect their opponents both mentally and physically since their technical skill set may not match the likes of Spurs, Liverpool and Everton.

Brearley agreed the three words were alien to him, as much as they were to Bassett, but not the concepts. You could sense

Brearley wanted to buy-in but you could see he wasn't too sure where the whole conversation was going. The host Nicholson even referred to Syer as an 'outsider' compared to the two other guests.

Over the remainder of the programme, both Brearley, Bassett and host Nicholson all started to discuss and debate these points and started to conclude this was accurate to creating effective team environments.

Brearley even spoke of a reflection he had a few years before when skippering England fast bowler Bob Willis. Willis was struggling with his run-up approach and his physicality was not the same as he was coming to the end of his career. Players would tend to laugh and make fun, but Brearley's reflection made him realise that this was affecting Willis psychologically as he couldn't perform like he used to. The laughs and the jokes would not have helped.

Bassett mentioned that he didn't want to consume the players with too many specialists, but Syer spoke about small interventions, giving the players something to think about when they were at home or away from the game. Focusing on developing a player's psychology will contribute towards the physical and technical training that tended to get the most focus.

Bassett was astute enough to see the signs though. He spoke about John Fashanu being the star of his team and the fact the media liked him, but he knew that the team would suffer if he spent more time on his media interests than his footballing ones.

Bassett knew that would hamper his team's spirit and he kept an eye on it.

As the programme concluded, it was refreshing to see that Bassett and Brearley realise these were fundamental benefits to player and team performance and had probably been doing this unconsciously. Brearley seemed to be more on board as his studious and tactical mind had helped him so well for Middlesex and England over his career.

They all agreed that player nerves and apprehension was a huge part of the game and understanding each player helped a manager, captain or coach understand that each player dealt with these scenarios in their own way. Allowing the uniqueness of human nature in some ways.

Syer concluded that he felt it was the manager or coach's responsibility to manage and harness team spirit, but his role would have been to just add an 'extra extra' that would help the players develop even more. Bassett nodded positively as Syer said this.

So, even 30-plus years later, it is fascinating to see that the foundations of such a huge part of sporting success nowadays was dismissed by some and welcomed by others.

Personally, I am very much entrenched in the Syer/Brearley camp. Psychology in any performance arena is key. Whether it be elite sport, corporate business or even charitable volunteering groups, there is always a requirement to get the best out of who you work alongside. This can be done by getting to know people.

FANTASTIC DISAPPOINTMENT

Understanding good day behaviours and bad day behaviours gives you the opportunity to get the best out of your colleagues and peers and helps to create environments where people want to achieve and perform at their optimum level. Not everyone is the same, so their motivators and blockers will be different, but when you have that level of awareness you are more likely to be an effective coach, leader, influencer or even just a friend.

So back to Glanville's original headline of wondering if footballers need a coach or a couch, the real answer is that they need both. The evolution of elite sport is a fascinating subject.

* * * *

A few times over the season, the mindset and psychological state of this Spurs team and some of the players had been questioned already. Clearly a talented group but also a group that needed to have shown a touch more resilience, cohesion and mental strength when various goals were conceded and points lost.

It is fair to say that Pleat was an excellent tactician and had superb knowledge of the game, but perhaps his individual man-management may not have been as strong with every player. His right-hand man, Trevor Hartley, would also have been technically strong but maybe some of those soft skills, like emotional intelligence, might not have been as strong as his technical and physical coaching skills were.

One person whp did deploy these 'psychological' skills was club physio John Sheridan.

Sheridan was medically qualified, so that obviously covered the technical requirements of the job. Another huge part of his skill set was his ability to be emotionally intelligent with the players. When dealing with injured players or players going through a stage of rehabilitation, Sheridan would also act as a counsellor, therapist, psychiatrist and even a friend.

Sheridan was not medically trained in these areas, but he knew that this was an important balance to deploy in his game that was essential in keeping players mentally strong during these tough times of being out of the team.

He would sometimes deal with things that therapists and counsellors were known for. I have spent time talking to John about his first year at White Hart Lane and he highlighted this as one of many things that he brought to the role. He said, "Guys would speak freely in front of me. They would talk about many things, and they trusted me completely. Players would be unhappy, especially if they are out of the team, and sometimes they'll use the treatment room to talk. Generally, they'd want someone to put an arm around them and look after them but being there was a great help".

John also stressed the fact that Pleat and Hartley were still relatively new to many of the players, so it took time for relationships and understanding to build. Come January, some of these elements started to fall into place as Spurs went on a superb run of form.

* * * *

Spurs travelled to play Linfield in Belfast in honour of Roy Coyle who was one of the most successful players and managers in the club's history. Tottenham were invited to take part in his testimonial match to celebrate his tenure at Linfield and as one of the most successful managers in European club football.

There was a link with Pleat and Linfield. One of Pleat's first major signings at Luton Town in 1978 was bringing defender Mal Donaghy to the Bedfordshire club. Donaghy has legendary status even to this day at Luton Town and Pleat still regards him as one of the best, if not the best, defender that he has worked with during his career as a manager.

Spurs played the game as Manchester United, who were originally due to play the game but pulled out at the last minute. For Spurs this was a good decision in light of the recent postponement of the Newcastle away game.

Spurs won the game 3-2. Gary Stevens played 65 minutes on his return from injury and the winning goal was scored by Danny Thomas, yes Danny scored the winner!

Clive Allen puts Spurs ahead after 20 minutes from a penalty and the home side equalised just before the break. Chris Waddle's good form continued when his slalom through several players resulted in a wonderful left foot strike put Spurs 2-1 ahead.

The goal of the game was scored by full-back Danny. With 16 minutes to go a superb move was masterminded by Waddle and Paul Allen, the ball made its way to Danny who ran several yards then struck home for his first, albeit not competitive, goal of the season.

Linfield pulled one back after 82 minutes, but the game was won. A good run-out for Pleat's men in readiness for the Aston Villa game in four days' time.

Not known for his goals, I asked Danny his memory of that wonderful goal. Danny replied, "Did I? I don't recall scoring in that game, it must've been Mitchell!". It was only when I sent Danny the *Spurs News* article that he realised he was the one to score the winning goal.

Saturday 24th January 1987 – White Hart Lane, London (Att: 19,744)
Tottenham Hotspur v Aston Villa
(TODAY League Division 1)

It was disappointing to see that near enough the same number of spectators came out to watch the Villa game that had watched the Scunthorpe game. Since the thirty-nine thousand crowd against West Ham, this was now the second consecutive home game where the attendance was half in comparison to that Boxing Day encounter.

Maybe the fans were frustrated at the inconsistency, or in fact the good December form had trickled away, or even because the weather that January was cold and grim. Things needed to get better and today they really did.

Pleat deployed a strong eleven that oozed attacking class and the same eleven that beat Scunthorpe last time out.

Line up v Aston Villa: Clemence; D Thomas, Gough, Mabbutt, M Thomas; Claesen, Waddle, P Allen, Hoddle, Hodge; C Allen. Sub: Galvin.

Tony Galvin returned to the bench as Spurs welcomed the team, they had dispatched so brilliantly on the first day of the season. Interestingly, it was only Steve Hodge's second league game for Spurs, against his old employers. By all accounts, the Villa supporters were not happy with Hodge leaving for Spurs as he stated he needed to leave Villa to consolidate his England place.

Villa were still struggling in second from bottom position in Division 1. They were now led by Billy McNeil who had left Manchester City earlier in the season to join Villa after they had sacked previous boss Graham Turner.

McNeil had already been to White Hart Lane back in September when his City team frustrated Spurs in a very tight 1-0 win for Pleat's men. Today he arrived in wretched form with only two league wins in the last 12 games dating back to the start of November.

Spurs were in control for most of the game and ran out as easy victors.

Steve Hodge would be the clear man-of-the-match for his new team as he dealt with the hisses, boos and jeers from the Villa support every time he touched the ball.

Luckily for Hodge and Spurs, it was the former Villa man that opened the scoring on 13 minutes. Hoddle won the ball in midfield and a short pass saw Paul Allen release Hodge down Spurs' left. Looming closer to the penalty area, Hodge looks up to cross to Clive Allen but cuts inside the Villa defender and struck a low right-foot drive inside Spink's near post. An excellent goal but the Villa fans would've been tearing their hair out.

Spurs dominated the midfield but carved out few chances. They led at half time and only four minutes into the second half Spurs doubled their lead and once again, it was Steve Hodge.

Not necessarily known for his heading ability, Hodge rose above everyone when Hoddle swung his corner into the Villa penalty spot region where he outjumped Martin Keown to head into the top left-hand corner. Hodge ran off, arm in the air and celebrated his first brace for his new club.

In Joe Lovejoy's *Independent* article, he reported that the Villa fans baited Hodge throughout with cries of 'what a waste of money' and 'we hate Hodge'. Sadly, these chants did not affect Hodge and only seemed to inspire him if truth be told.

The game was finally up after 70 minutes when Hoddle grabbed his second assist of the game when he fed Nico Claesen in to score his fourth goal in his last five games.

Result: Tottenham Hotspur 3-0 Aston Villa
(Hodge 2, Claesen)

Despite Villa's league position, it was an excellent team performance and another clean sheet. It had moved Spurs up to fifth place and Pleat told Lovejoy that Spurs were still in the title race. Pleat said, "It's still wide open, it just needs a team within the pack to put together a run of 10 or 11 good results which Liverpool proved last season".

Lovejoy's headline was, 'HODGE PROVES HIS WORTH'. A spot-on assessment which contradicts the Villa fans' 'what a waste of money' jibes.

The league form seemed to be back on track, still in the FA Cup and in a few days' time they would head to the cauldron of West Ham to contest a league cup quarter final.

Tuesday 27th January 1987 – Upton Park, London
(Att: 28,648)
West Ham United v Tottenham Hotspur
(Littlewoods League Cup 5th Round)

The league cup quarter final showdown with West Ham promised to be an intense affair. Two very good footballing teams and despite Spurs playing well and higher in the league than West Ham, it was still a home game for the Hammers therefore they would be a force to battle.

This was my first trip to Upton Park. Over the years I have visited most London grounds, but more than any other time, I recall the nerves and apprehension going to this game and not from a footballing perspective. With violence still rife amongst rival supporters, this fixture had thrown up many stories of trouble over the years. I was a teenager and I recall my dad telling me that if something kicked off, just run! I was a pretty good athlete and at the time I had recently joined Shaftesbury Harriers running club so felt confident I could pelt it out if there was trouble.

However, I don't think my dad and brother were pretty fast runners, so I genuinely feared for them more than me. That aside, I do recall a few tussles here and there, but I did not experience anything major. This added to the spice of a London derby and a place in the League Cup semi-final at stake.

Upton Park was buzzing that night, a chilly January evening that had a warmth resonating from a raucous crowd. Spurs were in their pale blue away strip and Pleat had no major selection worries to consider when naming his eleven.

Steve Hodge was cup-tied which meant Ossie Ardiles came back into the team. Claesen dropped to the bench which meant Galvin also returned to balance the left-side of midfield in Hodge's absence. Good news too - Gary Stevens returned to the bench for senior team involvement for the first time since his horrific clash with John Fashanu back in early November.

Line up v West Ham: Clemence; D Thomas, Gough, Mabbutt, M Thomas; Waddle, P Allen, Hoddle, Ardiles, Galvin; C Allen. Sub: Stevens, Claesen.

Spurs were close to taking the lead in the first 15 minutes and were the team who looked more in relaxed and poised.

Midway in the first half Tony Galvin was a lucky man. A midfield clash between Galvin and Mark Ward saw both players fall to the ground and Galvin kicked out to see his studs go straight into Ward's chest. Bizarrely Galvin received nothing, and Ward got a booking for the original foul. Minutes later Galvin was booked, for a blatant barge on a West Ham defender.

But Spurs seemed more in control as the half went on despite there being mostly end to end football.

Highlights of the game were shown on ITV later that evening, the inimitable voice of Brian Moore commentating on this swashbuckler of a derby.

David Pleat had taken a position in the stands for the first half, he was flanked with Chairman Scholar one side and reserve team coach Doug Livermore the other.

With seven minutes to half-time Spurs took the lead. Spurs won a corner and the resulting set-piece saw intricate play between Ardiles and Waddle that allowed Paul Allen to storm into the box and slip a lovely cross into Clive Allen who put Spurs 1-0 up. Pandemonium in the away end.

Tottenham deserved the lead and went into the break happier than their hosts. Spurs already knew that victory tonight would see them face Arsenal in the semi-final as the Gunners had beaten Nottingham Forest in their quarter final match a week before.

West Ham equalised early in the second half. A scrappy goal to concede and a lack of cohesion between Gary Mabbutt and Mitchell Thomas allowed a scuffed shot to fall into Tony Cottee's path to tap home.

That goal galvanised West Ham and they controlled the game from then on. They had a few chances but nothing clear cut. Spurs rarely ventured forward after that and a 30-yard Hoddle rocket that went just over the bar was possibly the highlight of the half for Spurs.

Despite West Ham's onslaught Richard Gough and Gary Mabbutt were in excellent form.

1-1 it finished, a replay at the Lane and yet another fixture juggle for Spurs to deal with.

Result: West Ham United 1-1 Tottenham Hotspur (C Allen)

Clive Allen was now edging towards 30 goals for the season, but this was also Paul Allen's 9th assist of the season. Allen was now relishing his central midfield role and was proving to be a wonderful source for Clive's goals.

The Sun described the encounter as, "This was as good as a cup-tie you could possibly wish to see, a classic confrontation between two fine sides".

Pleat told *Spurs News*, "I was pleased with the game as a whole and nobody can go away feeling they have been sold short".

Essentially Pleat highlighted that it was a fair result and a superb advert for football.

The Daily Telegraph kept us in focus with their headline, 'COTTEE AND ALLEN KEEP THE CUP TIE BOILING'. Colin Gibson's article reminded us that we would be back to see these two sides slug out a replay, and on evidence of tonight, we should be in for a treat.

And believe me, as Spurs fans, we will be!

Saturday 31st January 1987 – White Hart Lane, London
(Att: 29,603)
Tottenham Hotspur v Crystal Palace
(FA Cup 4th Round)

With the league form picking up, a quarter final league cup replay coming soon too, it was time to re-focus on the FA Cup with the visit of Crystal Palace to White Hart Lane.

Palace were flying high in Division 2 and had some wonderfully slick attacking talent in their ranks. Managed by former England and Manchester United winger, Steve Coppell, Palace had brilliantly knocked out Brian Clough's Forest in the previous round.

They had also strengthened their defensive unit this month too when they signed former Spurs defender, Gary O'Reilly, for £40,000 from Brighton & Hove Albion.

They had a wonderful attacking duo in Mark Bright and Ian Wright. Ian Wright was unfit for this match, but he would go on to score ten goals that season. He would then go on to score nearly 20 goals every season until he got a high-profile move to Arsenal in 1991. Mark Bright would have a similar record before he made a successful move to Sheffield Wednesday in 1992.

Another impressive young talent that supported the Palace strikers was Andy Gray. Gray had been plucked from non-league Corinthian Casuals in 1984 and was making waves as one of the most sought-after midfielders in the second division. Like Wright and Bright, he too would make a move away from Palace and would eventually join Spurs in 1992 having had a spell at Aston Villa.

Club Captain and strong defender Jim Cannon would play alongside O'Reilly, and they had the unenviable task of keeping Clive Allen quiet this afternoon.

Line up v Crystal Palace: Clemence; D Thomas, Gough, Mabbutt, M Thomas; Waddle, P Allen, Hoddle, Hodge, Galvin; C Allen. Sub: Stevens, Claesen.

With Hodge returning from being cup-tied Ardiles was the player to miss out. Galvin stayed left-side of midfield and Hodge played just inside him alongside Paul Allen. Waddle hugged the right wing and Hoddle took up his now familiar position just behind Clive Allen.

Palace battled well in the first 25 minutes and looked comfortable against their top-flight opponents, but it was the unlikely source of Gary Mabbutt who opened the scoring for Spurs, just like he did in the previous round against Scunthorpe.

The architect of Mabbutt's goal in the last round was Chris Waddle, today it was Hoddle's turn. From a Hoddle corner, Mabbutt caused enough confusion to baffle the Palace goalkeeper and put Spurs 1-0 up.

A few minutes later Spurs scored again when Chris Waddle saw his powerful low drive take a slight deflection off a Palace defender and the home side had doubled their lead. Waddle could not claim credit for this goal, this was a Gary O'Reilly own goal. Whereas ex-Spurs players usually score against them, today it was an ex-player scoring for them. Poor Gary.

Half-time came and went. It was a competitive cup-tie but only Spurs were carving our chances. Things kicked into life when Nico Claesen was introduced as a 69th minute replacement for Tony Galvin. Claesen, unlucky to be on the bench despite his good scoring form, nearly scored a couple of minutes after his introduction when his 25-yard shot just drifted over the Palace cross bar.

With ten minutes to go, Chris Waddle tracked back fantastically well and dispossessed a Palace attack deep in his own half. He then immediately turned and went on another mazy dribble, passing defenders on his way to tripped in the box by a clumsy Tony Finnigan challenge. Penalty given and converted by Clive Allen for his 30th goal of the season and we were still in January!

Palace had a flurry of late efforts but to no avail and it was Claesen, at his bustling best, popping up after 87 minutes to score Spurs' fourth goal. The goal was orchestrated by Hoddle and Waddle, as Waddle's direct run into the Palace box saw him stop and back heel the ball to Hoddle who slung a low cross in for Claesen to tap home from five yards.

Glorious football and both Hoddle and Waddle had been exemplary as their midfield dominance didn't give Palace a chance to deploy their swift, attacking football that had taken the second division by storm this season.

Result: Tottenham Hotspur 4-0 Crystal Palace (Mabbutt, O'Reilly og, C Allen, Claesen)

With Clive Allen racking up his 30th goal of the season it was just as encouraging to see that Spurs had now scored 37 goals in their last 14 league and cup games. Fourteen of those goals were from Clive Allen which highlighted 23 goals from other sources like Claesen, Waddle, Hoddle and Steve Hodge.

This was a significant difference from the first two months of the season when Spurs struggled to score. This was also their fifth clean sheet in nine games, an improvement on the three clean sheets in the nine games before that.

Spurs' five-man midfield was getting praise and plaudits from fans and media alike. With Pleat still liking the balance that Galvin, Hodge or Waddle could give from wide areas it was a struggle for Nico Claesen to get a starting spot in the team.

In *The Daily Mail*, Trevor Haylett's headline read, 'RIVALS BURNING WITH AMBITION' as he wrote that Spurs' romp over Palace was matched by Arsenal's demolition of Plymouth Argyle by a 6-1 scoreline. He remarked on Spurs' continental style that was serving Pleat and his players so well, yet Claesen was now seen as a bit of a casualty of the 'one striker up' front formation. Haylett wrote that being on the bench left Claesen unhappy and restless. Claesen said, "I am not happy at sitting on the bench. Maybe it's wrong of me to say that, but it's how I feel. I want to play and enjoy football, it's not about money".

Claesen was clearly frustrated, his unhappiness would probably subside slightly in the coming days as Spurs would face West Ham in the league cup replay. With Hodge suspended, Nico may get another starting berth. For Pleat though, he was able to call on two World Cup internationals in Nico and Gary Stevens as substitutes - that's strength.

One other noticeable result over the FA Cup weekend was Coventry's brilliant 1-0 victory over Manchester United at Old Trafford. The midlands club had been picking up some good results in recent months, not to mention their 4-3 thrilling win over Spurs one month ago, but they were also in the fifth-round draw. Spurs were drawn to play Newcastle at home, Coventry were rewarded with a tricky tie away at Stoke City whilst big-hitters, Arsenal and Everton, would face Barnsley and Wimbledon respectively.

FEBRUARY 1987

Monday 2nd February 1987 – White Hart Lane, London
(Att: 41,995)
Tottenham Hotspur v West Ham United
(Littlewoods Cup 5th Round Replay)

Just 48 hours after the home win over Crystal Palace in the FA Cup, Pleat and his men were turning attentions back to the League Cup with a quarter final replay against West Ham.

This would be the highest attendance at White Hart Lane this season as nearly 42,000 fans were about to witness a stunning night of football under the White Hart Lane lights.

Only a handful of weeks before, Spurs had dispatched West Ham with a ravenous performance on Boxing Day and Spurs fans were hoping of the same again. Surely it couldn't happen again or could it.

Pleat brought Claesen and Ardiles in for the cup-tied Steve Hodge and Tony Galvin. Galvin had limped off during the Palace victory, so this saw Waddle switch to the left, Claesen stayed right side and Ardiles joined Paul Allen and Hoddle in the middle.

Gary Stevens was again on the bench alongside reserve team dynamo, Mark Bowen. The reserves were top of the Combination League at this point and Bowen had already netted 11 goals in his attacking midfield role behind David Howells and Shaun Close.

Line up v West Ham United: Clemence; D Thomas, Gough, Mabbutt, M Thomas; Claesen, P Allen, Ardiles, Hoddle, Waddle; C Allen. Sub: Stevens, Bowen.

This is a game that sticks fondly in the memory of Paul Allen. Paul said, "When I speak of games in my career, this one always stands out for me. It was such a brilliant team performance and great game for me. West Ham were a very good side, but we played like a dominant European team that night. We played out from the back, kept the ball really well in midfield and then you had Clive up front".

Paul would register two assists and win a penalty this evening and he ranks this in the top three games of his career. "The 1991 FA Cup semi-final and 1991 FA Cup final were also other games that were most memorable but the way we played that night epitomised that 1987 team. It had a continental feel and it's a shame there was a European ban around that time".

In the matchday programme there was a 'Spotlight on Paul Allen' article written. Paul speaks about his early years at West Ham, some of the recent encounters with his old club and that tonight was going to be a difficult test. Paul said, "It will be tight and there won't be a lot in it, but it should be quite a good game". Well Paul, it was a cracker and Spurs were dominant.

West Ham fielded their usual eleven with only 40-year-old Billy Bonds being the only potential weak-link. Due to a bit of a fullback crisis, Bonds was making his first appearance for West Ham in around 18 months. Surely Chris Waddle would test him strenuously.

In fact, it was Billy Bonds that nearly scored the opening goal. The 40-year olds' left foot volley was tipped over the bar for a corner by 38-year-old Ray Clemence and showing very much that there was still life in these old dogs yet.

After six minutes Spurs went in the lead. The goal was scored by the apparently 'unhappy' Nico Claesen, and, for me, this goal typifies what Nico brought to the team and possible his most memorable goal for Spurs.

Centrally Ardiles had skipped past his midfield marker, looked up and floated in a perfectly weighted diagonal pass to Claesen who's pace saw him shoot past a beleaguered George Parris, chest the ball down before volleying past Parkes who had zero chance of stopping the Belgian netting his sixth goal in his last eight games.

Ossie's pass though - now that was pure artistry.

An explosive goal and an explosive start. After that the rest of the first half was relatively even as both sides were battling for possession, territory and ultimately midfield dominance.

The second half felt more in Spurs' favour than their visitors but after 71 minutes the game would turn. The next 20 minutes would be relentless and savage from Spurs as they spanked West Ham out of sight.

A superb team goal that saw Clem roll the ball out to Mitchell Thomas who then threaded a ball through to an advancing Waddle who's sublime first touch found Paul Allen. Allen weighed up his options and saw Hoddle was clear to receive the ball in a central position around 25 yards from West Ham's goal. Then boom. Unchallenged, Hoddle lined up his shot and pinged a right footed dart into the bottom left-hand corner of the Parkes' goal. The crowd went loopy, and Hoddle and his teammates did too. What a goal it was, accuracy beyond belief, this was a Hoddle classic.

Nine minutes later, West Ham had a corner that simply fell into Clemence's hands. Swift thinking by Clem saw him throw the ball to Spurs' right wing were an unmarked Claesen gathered the ball and set off at his speedy best. The crowd were buzzing as Nico approached the Hammer's box and his simple centred pass found Clive Allen who shot first time and the ball looped high and into the Hammers goal. Cue pandemonium in the stands again.

3-0 up and West Ham out of sight. What a great night. However, it did not stop there.

Four minutes after Clive Allen's strike Spurs would go 4-0 up. Paul Allen had just set up Claesen with a great chance having played a sublime one-two with Hoddle. But Paul was not done yet.

West Ham were in possession 15 yards outside their box, Paul Allen muscled in and brilliantly dispossess before running into the box like a man possessed. Alvin Martin could not cope with his momentum and brought Allen down. Chris Waddle hugs Allen immediately to recognise what a superb run that was. Penalty won and duly converted by Clive for 4-0.

Not long after, Paul sprayed a superb pass out to Claesen who's run and shot whistled just above Parkes' crossbar. Paul was on fire.

With a minute to go, the 'Allens' were still not finished. Clive scored to register a nine-minute hat-trick and once again, it was built by his industrious cousin, Paul. Hoddle picked the ball up 15 yards outside Spurs' penalty area. He passed to Paul Allen who was surrounded by West Ham midfielders, Allen spun away and started yet another attack on West Ham's shell-shocked defence.

Taking on all-comers, he swept the Hammers aside and saw his pass reach Clive Allen who was all alone and happy to side foot home his third of the night before sprinting off and performing a knee-slide in front of the West Stand fans.

The cousins embraced but Clive then held Paul's two arms aloft to showcase that he was the real hero of this evening, despite scoring a hat-trick himself. Hoddle, Waddle and Ardiles were all excellent.

Nico Claesen was outstanding, his best performance in a Spurs shirt so far. But Paul Allen, wow, it was an absolute masterclass from him. An utterly stunning midfield performance.

Result: Tottenham Hotspur 5-0 West Ham United (Claesen, Hoddle, C Allen 3)

Luckily for Spurs and football fans who were not able to get to White Hart Lane, highlights of the game were played on BBC1s *Sportsnight* the same evening. Commentator, Tony Gubba, could hardly catch his breath from this Spurs performance and it sent shockwaves through the league at the type of devastating football Pleats men could produce.

In *The Independent*, Patrick Barclay lauds Allen's hat-trick but mentioned Hoddle's goal as the spur that sparked a crazy final twenty minutes. Disappointingly Barclay referred more to Clive's goals than Paul Allen's performance. In *The Daily Telegraph*, Colin Gibson was a tad more observant when describing Paul 'demoralising' West Ham with his all-round game.

The Daily Express noted some powerful words too, "Last's weeks Upton Park encounter might have been a close-fought classic, but this was simply a slaughter".

Even to this day, all the players I have spoken to, backroom staff or even members of the media, still remember this match for its sheer class and quality.

Clive Allen remembers the game fondly too, he said, "Clearly, I can never forget a nine-minute hat-trick, but Paul, wow. Well, that was my cousin's best game for Spurs. He was sensational that night. Oddly, West Ham played quite well that game, but we literally blew them away".

Spurs had now scored nine goals in two games against West Ham over a six-week period, Clive jokingly concluded, "I don't think they liked playing us that season".

For manager David Pleat, it was like all his plans had come to fruition with this performance. Spurs had been brilliant several times this season already, but this evening was special and would remain in Pleat's memory still to this day.

Pleat remarked, "It is a game that everyone still talks about. Over those two games we played some remarkable football. The West Ham manager, John Lyall, wrote me a letter after the game. He praised the team that had been built and the fantastic performance that he had witnessed. A lovely man John, and it was a lovely letter to receive".

Pleat also recognised Paul Allen's performance that night, "Brilliant, terrific energy. He did a lot of donkey work for us in that midfield, a wonderful team-player".

Spurs had now scored 42 goals in their last 15 league and cup games. Defensively this was also their third clean sheet in the last four games, Gough and Mabbutt were looking so in-sync in the middle and the speed and athleticism of Danny and Mitchell

Thomas contributed effectively to both defensive and attacking tactics too.

All good signs going into the biggest game of the season so far. Away at Arsenal in the first leg of the League Cup Semi-Final.

Sunday 8th February 1987 – Highbury, London
(Att: 41,306)
Arsenal v Tottenham Hotspur
(Littlewoods Cup Semi-Final 1st Leg)

The league game against away at Manchester City had been rescheduled due to this cup encounter. Along with the recent move of the Newcastle away game, this meant Spurs now had two games pushed into March.

Pleat and his men couldn't focus or control a potential fixture pile-up, they needed to focus on the next match. Playing at Highbury was never easy, but Spurs had not lost there for the last two seasons and had already notched up a goalless draw in September.

With the game being broadcast live on ITV commentator Brian Moore and recently sacked United manager, Ron Atkinson, would watch George Graham's league leaders Arsenal battle with the attacking force of Pleat's Tottenham.

Before the game, Pleat spoke to ITV and said, "They are to be respected here. They are unbeaten at home in all competitions and only conceded four goals. If we get a result here, we will be highly delighted".

Tony Galvin returned from injury to sit on the bench alongside Gary Stevens. Sure enough, Pleat had gone with the same eleven that annihilated West Ham six days before.

Line up v Arsenal: Clemence; D Thomas, Gough, Mabbutt, M Thomas; Claesen, P Allen, Ardiles, Hoddle, Waddle; C Allen. Sub: Stevens, Galvin.

Spurs, playing in white shirts and navy shorts, were attacking the North Bank end in the first half and it would be a game that would see Chris Waddle in supreme form. Luckily for Spurs, right-back Viv Anderson was suspended for this game and Gus Caesar came in to replace him. Waddle gave him a torrid time over these 90 minutes.

In Chris Waddle's 1997 biography, he recalls this match and how he gave Caesar the run around. So much so, Waddle felt that he dominated Caesar significantly enough that it started a decline in his Arsenal career!

Waddle said, "At most clubs you play, there's one performance you remember more than most. Playing to the best of your ability and seeing a lot of the ball you'll give the defending full-back a difficult time. On that day I had a good game and Gus had a bad one. I never set out to make an opponent look foolish, but I do try to entertain".

Waddle continued, "I can't say I felt sorry for Gus at the time. If he'd marked me out of the game, he'd have been doing his job and I was just doing mine".

Also suspended for Arsenal was in-form midfielder, David Rocastle. He would be replaced by relatively new signing Perry Groves. Groves joined Arsenal back in September and I caught up with Perry to discuss his memories of the game.

Groves said, "We were confident going into that game. We didn't focus too much on the opposition as we concentrated on getting our 4-4-2 to work for us. We knew Spurs played with width and we had a process of channelling the wide players inside more. So, someone like Martin Hayes would show Chris Waddle inside, but he would be straight into Steve Williams, if Waddle got past him, he'd be straight into Paul Davis. So, we used that tactic to stunt elements of their attacking play".

The first half ebbed and flowed both ways while Danny and Mitchell Thomas were having superb duels with Martin Hayes and Perry Groves just like Waddle and Claesen were worrying Caesar and Kenny Sansom too. The middle of the park was congested, and this suited Davis and Williams. Caesar was incredibly lucky not to be booked for a poorly timed tackle on Mitchell Thomas.

Several minutes before half time Clive Allen, who had been quiet up to that point, saw his 25-yard pile driver tipped over the bar brilliantly by Lukic and led to a Spurs corner. From the resulting corner Spurs went 1-0 up.

Hoddle, left footed, curled the ball into the heart of the Arsenal box and the ball found its way to Richard Gough who mishit it into the path of Gary Mabbutt. Mabbutt's shot found its way to

Clive Allen who volleyed home. His strike was similar to his finish at Upton Park in the 5th round game against West Ham, but Spurs had the lead as half-time appeared.

The early part of the second half was controlled by Spurs. Gus Caesar went into the book for a rough tackle on Mitchell Thomas and possibly should have been off considering his first half challenge. Seconds before his foul on Thomas, Caesar's elbow caught Waddle in the head too which put the Spurs man down. Arsenal's right back was walking on thin ice.

Arsenal did come more into the game during the second half and it was Spurs who nearly scored again when, from a wonderful Hoddle pass, Clive Allen raced through to score past Lukic, but he was ruled out for offside.

Nico was largely ineffective during the game; it seemed the high-tempo physical nature of the game wasn't his cup of tea and he was replaced by Tony Galvin who took up position on the left hand side.

Hoddle had a couple of long-distance efforts go close, but the score remained 1-0 to a jubilant Spurs and their away support.

Result: Arsenal 0-1 Tottenham Hotspur (C Allen)

After the game George Graham claimed that both Claesen and Allen were in offside positions when the goal was scored but on balance, Spurs did deserve their win.

Watching the game back, I must say that Gus Caesar didn't have as bad a game as Waddle claims. Waddle was brilliant yes, but Caesar won 3-4 duels with him and when Galvin came on Waddle roasted Kenny Sansom just as much on the other flank. I'll go all out and say, I have seen Waddle have significantly better games than that during his Spurs career. I recall a game at White Hart Lane in 1988 against Aston Villa when Waddle was unplayable, he followed up his wizardry with two goals that night too. Sorry Chris, just saying.

In *The Daily Telegraph*, David Pleat was quoted saying that the key to this victory was his side's ability to defend as a unit. It was a third consecutive clean sheet. He said, "We have a lot of attack minded players, but the team defended solidly and restricted Arsenal to a few chances".

Clive Allen had scored his 34th goal of the season. In his *Independent* column Patrick Barclay wrote, "No attacking side can be more difficult to deal with than Spurs at the moment and it was a typically swift and inventive move that led to Allen's opener".

Barclay felt there was little doubt that Allen would be called up to Bobby Robson's squad and travel to Madrid for an upcoming international friendly against Spain in ten days' time.

Barclay also felt that Spurs had edged the game and Arsenal offered little going forward but felt that with Rocastle and Anderson returning for Arsenal, the second leg promised to be another cracker and the tie was not dead.

Whenever they were on the telly, Spurs did not disappoint. Roll on the second leg.

Saturday 14th February 1987 – White Hart Lane, London
(Att: 22,066)
Tottenham Hotspur v Southampton
(TODAY League Division 1)

Training at Spurs Lodge during this time must have been buoyant. I'd imagine that Pleat would have been especially pleased with his defensive quartet. Since the start of 1987, they had notched up four clean sheets in the last seven games, and things were going to get even better over the coming weeks.

On the injury front, John Chiedozie was still nowhere near a return to fitness and Chris Hughton had experienced the flu which had hampered his return. But the squad seemed strong and eager to push on.

This would be their first league game for three weeks having just played four league and cup games. They had dropped to seventh place but had a few games in hand.

England wide-man Steve Hodge would return to the team which meant Claesen dropped to the bench again. Claesen was ineffective versus Arsenal, and you couldn't deny Hodge and Waddle on each flank was a mouth-watering prospect.

Southampton were two points off the relegation places and having a disappointing season. Manager Chris Nicholl still had some strong players at his disposal, but they needed a string of results to boost themselves to mid-table safety.

They had conceded the second most goals in the league and that was surprising when they had England internationals Peter Shilton and Mark Wright playing.

Bizarrely, they had scored the same amount of league goals as Spurs had at this point, both teams with 41 goals for. Colin Clarke led the line with 16 league goals.

Line up v Southampton: Clemence; D Thomas, Gough, Mabbutt, M Thomas; Waddle, P Allen, Ardiles, Hoddle, Hodge; C Allen. Sub: Claesen.

Spurs took to the field in all-white and brimming with confidence.

The game was a tad pedestrian and despite visiting striker George Lawrence having a hat-trick of good chances Southampton offered little to worry Spurs.

It was two headers that won the game for Spurs. After only nine minutes, Richard Gough rose majestically above Mark Wright to head home Hoddle's delicious free kick past a hapless Shilton.

We had seen this a few times already where Hoddle finds Gough at set-pieces and this was Gough's second goal of the season. Last assist was Hoddle, of course.

The home fans had to wait until the second half to see Spurs double their lead. Since Hoddle had announced he was leaving

Spurs he had been in sublime form. He grabbed his second assist of the day when he guided a wonderful cross from Spurs' right side of midfield to Steve Hodge sneaking around the back post to dive in and head past Shilton.

The range and angles and diversity of Spurs' goals over the last few months were astounding. The delivery from Waddle, Hoddle, Paul Allen, Hodge and Ardiles was an absolute pleasure to watch.

Spurs had lost 2-0 at The Dell back at the start of the season. Revenge had been gained and Spurs were going places.

Result: Tottenham Hotspur 2-0 Southampton
(Gough, Hodge)

Ossie Ardiles had been replaced by Nico Claesen on 63 minutes. Ardiles had featured in 21 of the 31 games played. Back in May 1986, Ardiles had undergone knee surgery and there were doubts he'd come back at all. But since pre-season training began, he hadn't missed a single day's training.

Speaking to Christopher Davies in *The Daily Telegraph*, Ardiles said, "I am as fit now as I have been in years, I would love to play on to next season and I did not think it was a possibility after my operation last May". He continued, "In terms of strength in depth, this is the best Spurs squad we have had since I have been here. Maybe if we win something Glenn will stay. We have a lot of quality here, but Glenn is special. Only Maradona is better because of his extra pace".

Wow. An Argentinian World Cup winner saying Glenn is on a similar level to Maradona highlights how good Glenn Hoddle was. Would Glenn stay if silverware was attained, possibly not, but it was good to give fans hope.

* * * *

A few days after the Southampton win. Hoddle, Waddle, Mabbutt and Steve Hodge all travelled to Madrid for England's friendly against Spain. No Clive Allen this time for Bobby Robson despite his 34 goals this season. Robson stuck with Lineker and Beardsley, but Clive was still included in the squad.

Where the last England international fielded a midfield four made up purely of spurs players, this time skipper Bryan Robson was back, which meant Gary Mabbutt was on the bench along with Mark Hateley and John Barnes.

With Hoddle, Hodge, Waddle, Viv Anderson and Kenny Sansom it took on a real North London vibe. Added into that was a debut for Arsenal centre-back Tony Adams who would line up alongside Terry Butcher.

The following 90 minutes would not only justify Robson's decision to stick with Lineker over Clive Allen but would be one of the most brilliant away performances in Bobby Robson's England reign.

I asked Steve of his memory of that game along with how the players saw Bobby Robson.

Hodge said, "Playing in the Bernabeu was a career highlight for me, it was a great team performance on the night and that game Tony Adams made his debut too if I remember correctly. All the squad loved Bobby, he was obsessed with football, he loved his players, and he was a lovely man. Great memories".

One of the reasons it was a memorable night for Hodge and co. was because England beat Spain 4-2 and Gary Lineker had grabbed all four goals.

Waddle and Hodge did not play the full 90 minutes, Hoddle however lasted the full game. And what a game he had. He was brilliant. The pitch was awful, but Glenn glided around like he was on another plain. Some of the Spanish midfielders were tough and brutish but Hoddle continually danced away from their hefty advances.

Hoddle's beautifully lofted cross set up Lineker's first goal and from a Hoddle free-kick, Viv Anderson knocked down for Lineker to score his second.

In the second half Hoddle, who apparently can't tackle, dispossessed an opposition midfielder to lay the ball into Beardsley who set up Lineker for his hat-trick.

In years to come, the esteemed French coach, Arsene Wenger, could not believe why England did not build a team around this generational talent. Pleat had seen that and had installed Hoddle in a free role behind Clive Allen during the last few months and we were witnessing some of Hoddle's best football because of it. Urgh, hindsight.

After the game, BBC's John Motson interviewed both Chris Waddle and Peter Beardsley as they were about to meet each other in a few days' time at White Hart Lane for the FA Cup fifth round tie.

Beardsley said, "We're the underdogs, there's not a lot of pressure on us and Spurs are expected to win".

Chris Waddle stood next to him smirking at Beardsley's attempt to play down Newcastle's chances. John Motson then asked Waddle his thoughts on what Beardsley had just said, Waddle replied with, "Yep, they are the underdogs but in cup football everything is thrown out of the window, it's a one-off game and we see cup upsets all the time".

Gough's Scotland were at home to Galvin's Republic of Ireland in an important Euro qualifier. Both players played the full 90 minutes, but it was a solitary goal by Liverpool's Mark Lawrenson that saw the Irish triumph 1-0 at Hampden Park.

* * * *

Saturday 21ˢᵗ February 1987 – White Hart Lane, London
(Att: 38,033)
Tottenham Hotspur v Newcastle United
(FA Cup 5ᵗʰ Round)

To showcase Spurs' recent excellent run of form, David Pleat was awarded Bells Manager of the Month for January and it was very well deserved too as Spurs' league and cup form had been excellent.

The team was picking itself by now. Pleat named an unchanged eleven, but this time Gary Stevens joined Nico Claesen on the bench as this was the season when two substitutes were allowed in cup competitions.

Stevens would come on a second half sub for Paul Allen. It was Stevens' second appearance from the bench since his injury against Wimbledon back in November. Frustrating for him of course, but you could not deny Danny Thomas of his starting place at right-back. This was Danny's 14th consecutive start and his game was improving match by match.

Thousands of Geordies had made the 280-mile trip south from the Northeast to cheer on their struggling heroes. Newcastle were bottom of the league but 12,000 fans came to White Hart Lane in hope for FA Cup success.

Manager Willie McFaul would rally his troops for a game that would surely be tight. Striker Paul Goddard was in excellent form and with Beardsley beside him you would expect Gough and Mabbutt to be slightly worried about their evidential threat.

Clive Allen would be up against his old QPR teammate and friend, Glenn Roeder. Roeder had a running style that looked awkward, but he was a mighty powerful defender. He was partnered with Peter Jackson too so Clive would expect his day to be quite physical.

Line up v Newcastle United: Clemence; D Thomas, Gough, Mabbutt, M Thomas; Waddle, P Allen, Ardiles, Hoddle, Hodge; C Allen. Sub: Claesen, Stevens.

It would be fair to say this was not a classic at all and not like the swashbuckling games Spurs had delivered in the last couple of months.

The game was won by Spurs and it was a single goal that was enough for Pleat's men. It came via the penalty spot and converted by Clive Allen. Richard Gough had been bundled over in the penalty area and the Newcastle players were not happy at all.

Gough said, "When Newcastle travelled down, they always brought great support. I remember the penalty incident, their centre-half, pulled me as I was reaching for a Chris Waddle free-kick". Clear as day Richard, clear as day.

Highlights of the game were on ITV that evening and commentator Brian Moore felt that Newcastle had no reason to complain as Peter Jackson clearly committed the offence despite the away team's protestations.

Clive's 35th of the season was enough to win the game and the remainder of the first half was quite stale.

The second half was no different. Apart from one lightening run from Waddle down the right wing saw him produce a lovely cross for Clive Allen who was just out of reach, this was a scrappy game.

Winning 1-0 meant yet another clean sheet and into the quarter final too.

Result: Tottenham Hotspur 1-0 Newcastle United (C Allen)

In *The Daily Telegraph*, Colin Gibson headlined his report with, 'SPURS ON COURSE FOR WEMBLEY'. His opening line had cause for concern though, with a little assumption thrown in by stating, "Tottenham, who already have one foot in the Littlewoods Cup Final, satisfied they also have an excellent chance of completing this alternative route to Wembley".

Yes, Spurs had done well in the League Cup first Leg against Arsenal but I'd assume Pleat would not want his men to be over confident.

Wednesday 25th February 1987 – White Hart Lane, London (Att: 16,038)
Tottenham Hotspur v Leicester City
(TODAY League Division 1)

Spurs were into the quarter final of the FA Cup, a semi-final second leg against Arsenal was next weekend but they were now back on the league trail as they hosted Leicester City at White Hart Lane.

A disappointing crown of 16,038 turned up for this and maybe it was the large number of games that some fans were struggling with and not the quality. The quality of the football was sublime from Pleat's men. Those who didn't turn up this evening would miss out, as the home team would put on another superlative footballing display.

A few players were rested and Gary Stevens was brought back in for first start since the bruising encounter with Wimbledon last November and he did not disappoint.

Everton were now the league leaders and Spurs were still in seventh place, ten points off the top. A win was a must.

Line up v Leicester City: Clemence; D Thomas, Gough, Mabbutt, M Thomas; Claesen, P Allen, Stevens, Hodge, Waddle; C Allen. Sub: Galvin.

Leicester were struggling this season at the lower end of the league table but both teams shared the chances and possession in the first 20-25 minutes before Spurs started to take hold of the game.

With 12 minutes to go before the break, Spurs went 1-0 ahead through Nico Claesen. This was Claesen's fifth league goal of the season, and he had Chris Waddle to thank for his assist. It was a sweeping move that saw Clive Allen let in Chris Waddle who turned and laid on a perfectly weighted ball for Nico to run on and strike with his first touch past away keeper, Ian Andrews.

The remainder of the first half was full of relentless attacking by Spurs, how it stayed 1-0 at half-time I'll never know.

Seven minutes into the second half, Clive Allen converted yet another penalty and this time it was won by Paul Allen, brought down after yet another buccaneering run.

Four minutes later it was 3-0 when Paul Allen scored after a wonderful through ball by Hodge. Spurs were rampant.

Then barely a minute later, Paul Allen cut through the Leicester midfield to lay a ball onto Claesen. Nico's swift cross found Clive Allen to toe-poke home for his second and Spurs' fourth of the game. Three goals in five minutes, Leicester didn't have a clue what was going on. 4-0 Spurs.

Spurs' final goal of the night was scored eight minutes later. Paul Allen was the architect once more as he slotted a path through to Claesen who shot from such a tight angle and into the back of the net. A brace for Nico, a brace for Clive and Paul Allen was involved in four of Spurs' five goals.

That night, Gary Stevens and Paul Allen absolutely bossed that central midfield area. It was a show of athletic strength and cunning vision as they covered for the resting of Glenn Hoddle and Ossie Ardiles.

Result: Tottenham Hotspur 5-0 Leicester City
(C Allen 2, Claesen 2, P Allen)

That result saw Spurs move into fourth position in the league table. Another five goals were scored making it 51 goals scored in the last 19 league and cup games. This was also Spurs' sixth consecutive clean sheet too. That was an amazing statistic considering how leaky that defence was back in the autumn.

The Daily Telegraph headlined, 'FIVE-GOAL TOTTENHAM DESTROY LEICESTER'. Christopher Davies wrote of Spurs' growing championship challenge and summarised a performance of sheer class and dominance.

Leicester boss Hamilton told Davies, "In that mood, Tottenham are surely playing the best football in the country".

On the same night, Liverpool had beaten Southampton in the second leg of their League Cup semi-final. This meant, the winner of Sunday's 2nd leg against Arsenal would face the mighty Liverpool at Wembley.

February's edition of *Spurs News* highlighted the plight of two reserve team players whose season at Spurs were to change. Shaun Close was out for the rest of the season having torn his knee ligaments in training and Richard Cooke, on the bench for Spurs in the UEFA Cup final first leg in 1984, was heading out of the club to Bournemouth having struggled to attain a first team place.

But what a month it had been for the club. Five games played, five games won, 14 goals scored and zero conceded. Exemplary stuff.

MARCH 1987

Sunday 1st March 1987 – White Hart Lane, London
(Att: 37,099)
Tottenham Hotspur v Arsenal
(Littlewoods Cup Semi-Final 2nd Leg)

Arsenal only had one win throughout February going into this game, so the form guide was firmly with Spurs and the home team were 1-0 up from the first leg too. What could go wrong for Pleat and his men?

Pleat's eleven was a case of the usual suspects but a cup-tied Hodge would be a huge loss as he'd been playing so well. Ardiles and Hoddle came back into the starting line-up and Stevens took his place on the bench.

Arsenal welcomed back Viv Anderson and David Rocastle who were missing from the first leg as George Grahams kept mainly the same players from last time out, but this time he brought in England U21 midfielder Michael Thomas to replace Steve Williams.

Line up v Arsenal: Clemence; D Thomas, Gough, Mabbutt, M Thomas; Claesen, P Allen, Ardiles, Hoddle, Waddle; C Allen. Sub: Stevens, Galvin.

The game was broadcast live on BBC1, and Barry Davies had the job of commentating what would be a tense afternoon of football.

Nico Claesen started but I often felt Nico went missing when there were tense, high tempo and physical battles to be won. Within the first minute he was played a simple pass by Paul Allen, and he completely fluffed it and lost possession with no-one really around him.

It was a sign that he was about to have an ineffective and innocuous game. For this game I felt Galvin should've started on the left with Waddle on the right in Nico's position.

Spurs did take the lead. Viv Anderson fouled Clive Allen just inside Arsenal's half. From the resulting free-kick, Richard Gough lofted a ball into the Arsenal box, Mabbutt challenged in the air with Lukic to see his header deflect down to Claesen. Nico completely missed the ball with his attempted left foot strike, but Clive Allen picked it up, switch it on to his left and smashed the ball home.

The crowd went crazy, White Hart Lane erupted as loudly as I had heard it all season. Spurs were 2-0 up and getting closer to Wembley.

The game went from box to box, both teams having the odd chance here and there but nothing concise. Just before half time a stretching Clive Allen effort was inches away from putting Spurs 3-0 up overall.

Half-time came and now comes a bizarre moment that, for some people, turned the tie on its head.

Spurs' match day 'voice of the stadium', Willie Morgan, announced how Spurs fans could get tickets for the Littlewoods Cup Final, despite their still being 45 minutes to go. I had read somewhere that Perry Groves was injured and, in the stands, watching the game. He heard this and made his way to the Arsenal dressing room to tell his colleagues.

Perry confirms and denies elements of this story. He said, "Yes, I was in the stands, I had an ankle ligament injury, so I was fully fit but was part of the squad. I would love to say yes about me going down to the dressing room and telling the lads but that was not the case. As I was walking down to the dressing room at half-time, I could hear that they started playing the *Ossie's on his way to Wembley* song".

Perry continued, "George Graham was in the middle of telling the guys that if we get a goal and we are easily back in it, then he stopped and asked if the players could hear the tannoy announcement about Spurs fans using your vouchers to get your Cup Final tickets. He told the lads that they were taking the piss out of you, these 'big-time charlies' think they're in the cup final already, what more motivation do you need".

So, this was that extra piece of motivation that Graham was looking for and when the second half began the rewards were real.

Clive Allen missed another golden opportunity early in the second half and two minutes later Arsenal equalised. From a long throw-in on Spurs' left-side Niall Quinn, unchallenged by Mabbutt, headed the ball on to the near post where Viv Anderson managed to scramble the ball in despite Gough's protests that he used his hand.

It was limp defending and poor goalkeeping to be fair, but Arsenal had been given the lifeline that Graham wanted.

For most of the game Spurs had in fact been a bit more defensive than usual and it didn't seem right. Further worry was embedded on 65 minutes when Arsenal went 2-1 up.

Clive Allen had missed two more brilliant chances before Chris Waddle saw his left foot drive saved by Lukic. Spurs were still the better side overall but from Lukic's save the ball travelled up the pitch and Paul Davis found David Rocastle unmarked who then put in a tantalising low cross across the six-yard box that was missed by everyone except Niall Quinn sliding in at the far post to put the away side ahead.

The Lane went quiet, the Arsenal fans drowning out that quietness with their delirium.

The rest of the second half was scrappy and Spurs were visibly shell-shocked. Chances were very rare as both teams headed for extra-time. This is where the mental resilience needs to show up and Arsenal looked a touch tougher than Spurs.

The game started in daylight and finished under floodlight. Arsenal were the happier of the two as they had forced a reply in three days' time.

Result: Tottenham Hotspur 1-2 Arsenal (C Allen)

Spurs were 45 minutes away from a Wembley appearance. Richard Gough recalls the disappointment of that game, "Arsenal played a high offside line against us, I remember Clive had three or four good chances and could have buried them quite easily. We gave them a chance to get back in and they took it. I can also remember that it then went to a third game".

The venue for the replay had not yet been decided on the toss of a coin.

It was reported that Pleat and Graham tossed a coin, but Gough remembers, "I tossed the coin, I am sure of it. I won it, the game was to be played at White Hart Lane and I remember Glenn Hoddle saying to me I'd made a mistake winning that as we had a good record at Highbury for the last few seasons".

In *The Independent* Barclay pointed out that Clive Allen's squandered chances were a huge factor in why Spurs were not at Wembley, but he did observe the obvious when writing, "This Arsenal side is comparatively short on stars but stacked with resilience". The mental toughness saw Arsenal succeed in two-legged affair that saw Tottenham have more than enough chances to win the tie.

Barclay wrote that Pleat refused to criticise his team and he agreed that, "Clive did well with the goal, but he missed a lot as well".

However, we go again. Wednesday, under the lights at the Lane.

Wednesday 4th March 1987 – White Hart Lane, London (Att: 41,005)
Tottenham Hotspur v Arsenal
(Littlewoods Cup Semi-Final 2nd Leg Replay)

The bad news for Spurs was that Glenn Hoddle would not be playing due to a stomach muscle complaint, he was replaced by Gary Stevens.

Mark Bowen took Steven's place on the bench and Claesen remained in the starting eleven too. I still felt Tony Galvin was a better shout for this contest as Arsenal remained unchanged from the last game.

Line up v Arsenal: Clemence; D Thomas, Gough, Mabbutt, M Thomas; Claesen, P Allen, Ardiles, Stevens, Waddle; C Allen. Sub: Bowen, Galvin.

The pitch on Sunday became very heavy and muddy. The White Hart Lane ground staff had worked wonders to get it back into a good state and it was actually a better playing surface than Sunday.

FANTASTIC DISAPPOINTMENT

Spurs, wearing white shirts and navy shorts, started at a quick pace with Claesen, Waddle and Allen all having good chances as Spurs started to dominate.

Niall Quinn was lucky to stay on the pitch when he clattered into Clem's face as the Spurs keeper lay on the ground having just made a save. It was so late, and Quinn's feet were nowhere near the ball, you wonder what made him do it. But he got away with it.

As expected, the first half was even as both teams attacked and defended equally as well but half time came and you could sense a touch of nerves in the crowd.

17 minutes into the second half Spurs made the breakthrough. For the third time in this epic trilogy of games, Spurs had gone 1-0 up and scored once again by Clive Allen.

Ardiles had won a free kick around the halfway line, Mabbutt and Gough went up as Ardiles lofted the ball deep into Arsenal territory. Richard Gough rose majestically above both Adams and O'Leary to head down to Clive Allen who, without breaking stride, volleyed home for yet another goal in a crazy season for him.

The fans went crazy. Finally, was this it? Can we think about Wembley now?

Spurs were very much worth their lead but then came a pivotal moment in the game. From the restart, Arsenal played the ball up front into Charlie Nicholas' feet. Nicholas fell to the ground having twisted awkwardly, he looked in pain.

Why this was pivotal is because Nicholas was having a shocker. He was non-existent throughout the game and that was due to the excellent defending by Gough and Mabbutt. With Nicholas off George Graham brought on Ian Allinson.

Now Allinson had been at Arsenal for a few seasons but only ever scored a handful of goals each year. With Niall Quinn's introduction this season Allinson played very few games as the Quinn-Nicholas dynamic was Graham's weapon of choice.

But today would be different. With Spurs looking good to hold on to their lead it all changed with eight minutes to go.

Davis had lofted up a speculative pass forward; Gough raised his arm calling for offside only to see Allinson collect the ball and scamper forwards. Gough got back brilliantly but Allinson swung around and hit an averagely struck ball through Gough's legs and inside Clem's near post for Arsenal's equaliser.

It's a save Clem should have made but just before Allinson shot Clem put his weight onto his other side which was enough to make him a millisecond behind getting down and saving it.

Spurs went on the back foot for the final few minutes hoping to get to extra time and in the 90th minute Arsenal had a free kick deep in their own half.

David O'Leary launched the ball forward as Quinn and Gough duelled in the air. The ball fell to Ian Allinson on the edge of the box who shot first time, it deflected off Danny Thomas' heel right into the path of David Rocastle. Rocastle's momentum carried him through as he struck a left foot shot low underneath Clemence for Arsenal's winner.

Some Spurs players fell to their knees, Arsenal were in a utopia and seconds after the restart the final whistle was blown by referee Joe Worrell that signalled the end of an epic encounter of three matches of high drama.

Result: Tottenham Hotspur 1-2 Arsenal (C Allen)

This was the third time in the last three months that Arsenal had been to White Hart Lane and won 2-1. They had also beaten Spurs 2-1 in the semi-final of the Guinness Soccer Six back in December. What the hell was going on?

Speaking with Richard Gough, John Sheridan, Clive Allen, Paul Allen, Danny Thomas and Gary Stevens, they all tell of how heart-breaking and sombre the dressing room was after that game.

Hero Ian Allinson has highlighted this as the best moment of his Arsenal career. He told me, "Towards the end of that third game was the only time we ever felt we were on top. Because Charlie came off with an ankle injury that gave me the opportunity to come on and score. As I turned Gough the ball bobbled ever so slightly and helped me get my shot in Clemence's near post". He continued, "Even for the winner, I don't know why I shot. It was just pure adrenalin, but the shot found its way to Rocky for the winner".

In Irving Scholar's 1992 book he talks about the devastation felt after that result. Scholar had champagne on ice in readiness for the team's celebration but instead he directs the champagne into the away dressing room for Arsenal.

Both Perry Groves and Ian Allinson confirmed that was a nice touch on such a memorable night for them, but one to forget for Spurs.

Paul Allen still remembers the heartache of that evening; "Even when I look back now, that result really hurts. It frustrates me as I think that over the three games we performed really well and if the result was different, it could have triggered something good. It may have even us the opportunity to build on something that was really good with that team".

Clive Allen also remembers, "I was given two huge bottles of champagne and congratulated as I had broken a league cup goalscoring record that had stood since 1967. I walked into that changing room and players were crying, laying on the floor and just didn't know what to do. It was devastating".

The newspapers all praised Arsenal's strength and mental resilience. *The Daily Mail's* sub-headline of the game read, 'Arsenal courage clinches Wembley reward as brittle Spurs concede injury time winner'.

The key word there is brittle. Liable to break easily.

For all the talent Spurs had you wished that some of the mental toughness that a Paul Miller, Steve Perryman or a Graham Roberts possessed was sprinkled across this group of players as it would have made them unstoppable.

Final perspective on this game comes from David Pleat. When speaking of that semi-final trilogy he said, "It was quite incredible really, it's a blur. The only thing I would say is the only time Arsenal led was in the last minute of the third game when Rocastle scored".

He continued, "I remember all the crowd just disappearing. It was such as such terrible anti-climax to those three games with Arsenal and I have to say, even though it is terrible, it was defensive mistakes in the last several minutes that led to those two goals".

Spurs had been defending so well in the last six weeks and a few errors had cost them a place in the League Cup Final, Spurs also had more than enough chances to win all three games. But once again, that's football for you!

Driving home with dad there was silence in the car. I must admit I had imagined going to Wembley but for the opportunity to have been pulled away at such a late stage in the game was galling. Typically, dad did not dig out any specific players, but I recall we discussed the lack of a 'bastard' in the middle of the field. Someone who would drag players through those high-pressured moments. We felt that Spurs were 'too nice' and although they were a group of brilliant footballers perhaps, we needed a Peter Reid type character to navigate moments like that. Unsurprisingly my dad would suggest that if former Spurs great Dave Mackay was playing then that would not have happened. He was right.

Saturday 7th March 1987 – White Hart Lane, London
(Att: 21,071)
Tottenham Hotspur v Queens Park Rangers
(*TODAY League Division 1*)

After the midweek disappointment Spurs were back in league action and hosting Queens Park Rangers.

QPR beat Spurs in the away fixture back in September, so Spurs were not just looking for revenge, they were also looking to re-assert a title challenge.

Steve Hodge was back in the fold after being cup-tied left him out of the last several days encounters with Arsenal and Ardiles would make way.

Hodge said, "It was frustrating to miss those games against Arsenal, we should have won that semi-final but Arsenal stole the tie near the end, the atmosphere in the players' lounge afterwards was very subdued obviously".

Going into this game Spurs had dropped to sixth and QPR were mid-table in eleventh.

Glenn Hoddle was side-lined for a second consecutive game but no matter, as Gary Stevens had played well in Glenn's absence and Tony Galvin was brought back in to balance the midfield with Nico reverting to the bench.

Ray Clemence was also in goal. Clem had a lot of negative press over the last several days, pointing the finger at him for a few of the Arsenal goals.

On the morning of this game, Pleat spoke to Brian Scovell in *The Daily Mail* and publicly gave Clem his vote of confidence. Pleat said Clemence had experienced criticism before during his career and highlighted that the people who are blaming him have clearly not been watching him the previous six games where he kept consecutive clean sheets.

This was also the thirteenth consecutive game that the Thomas, Gough, Mabbutt, Thomas quartet had played together and seen seven clean sheets during those matches.

Line up v QPR: Clemence; D Thomas, Gough, Mabbutt, M Thomas; Waddle, P Allen, Hodge, Stevens, Galvin; C Allen. Sub: Claesen.

Wearing all white, Spurs were expected to claim all three points. They would go on to win the game 1-0 and the goal came from a converted Clive Allen penalty, his 40th goal of the season. It was not a convincing win, but a win nonetheless.

Result: Tottenham Hotspur 1-0 Queens Park Rangers
(C Allen)

However, this game would be remembered for a completely different reason.

Twenty minutes into first half, the career of Danny Thomas would take a cruel turn. With the ball free to be won, both Thomas and Rangers defender Gavin Maguire, challenged. Maguire's challenge was all wrong and those close enough would have heard Danny's cries as he fell to the ground.

Speaking with Danny I was mindful to tread carefully as this turned out to be a scenario that changed his life. Danny recalls the encounter with Gavin Maguire being aware of him even before this game.

Danny said, "I remember seeing Maguire in a reserve team match and he was very similar in that match, his tackling was reckless. Now I don't think he went out to hurt people, but he may well have meant to let people know he was around, but I don't think he meant to hurt anybody. But this tackle seemed typical of him, and it was just reckless. In professional sport you need to have a level of control".

Danny's opening views were mature and well considered as he continued, "I recall the incident as the ball had spooned up in the air, players were looking around for it and I saw it, ran forward to pass the ball to Chris Waddle who was just in front of me. My right foot goes down to get into my running action and then boom, this guy hits me. I didn't see him coming at all as there was a melee of players looking around for the ball. He caught me in exactly the wrong place, above the knee on my standing leg. It was painful as hell".

Before Danny knew it, swiftly on the scene was physio, John Sheridan. Sheridan recalls this bleak moment and says, "As a physio you are always looking, always ready to run on. What I realised as soon as I ran on to see Danny was that it was a desperate injury. I had seen it happen therefore watched the mechanism of the challenge. Maguire had hit Danny on the inside of the knee and forced the whole lateral aspect of the knee to break open. It was a horrendous injury, and I was desperately concerned about nerve damage".

When recalling this moment, you could see that John was clearly emotional while telling his version of events. "I had to be so gentle when moving Danny, one wrong move and Danny could have lost the use of his leg forever. We put him on a spinal stretcher and got him into the changing room".

In the changing room, Danny remembers being given a pain killing injection straight away which immediately eased his excruciating pain.

Paul Allen has memories of seeing Danny at half-time, "I do remember that quite vividly. Danny was such a great lad, and he was playing so well at the time. I can't remember the challenge too much, but I can remember coming into the changing room and seeing Danny on the treatment table. It was so tragic when we found out the severity of the injury".

Another player who recalls that moment is Gary Stevens. Gary was not too far from the incident and Gary joined Spurs around the same time as Danny did back in 1984. They were friends, they are still friends to this day. Gary was the one who put me in touch with Danny when researching this book.

I asked Gary his memories of this incident and he was quite overwhelmed with emotion. We paused for a moment and then Stevens continued, "The emotion is all for Danny. Danny kept saying my knee is gone, it's all gone".

What made the moment even more poignant was two seasons later when Gary Stevens got injured in a home game against Wimbledon in near enough the exact same spot of the pitch. A challenge by Vinnie Jones that would see Stevens out of the game for some considerable time too.

Signs were rife even before the game. Maguire made his home debut a month before when QPR took on Luton Town in the FA Cup. The game's highlights were broadcast on BBC1 with John Motson on commentary.

The 19-year-old was playing at right back and ten minutes into the second half Rangers had just gone 2-0 up. Not long after the restart, Luton were moving forward and the ball was played out to their left wing, Luton striker Mike Newell chased the ball and was followed by Maguire. Newell failed to retrieve the ball which went out for a throw-in but in that moment Gavin Maguire came clattering into the back of him and leaving Newell spread out on the advertising boards. Newell leapt to his feet straight away and squared up to Maguire as he was clearly incensed with this 'reckless' late challenge.

As the referee separated the two and began giving Maguire a telling off, on commentary Motson's words were, "Gavin Maguire is an aggressive young man, he used to play rugby until he was 15 and has made rapid strides since, but the ref has told him any more of that and you are off".

Another sign that trouble may have been afoot was described by Clive Allen. Clive had mentioned this is his book *Up Front* and he recalled this moment in our conversation too. "In the tunnel before the game my cousin, Martin Allen (who played for QPR), was telling me to watch out for Maguire. He was playing mind games with me for sure, but he said beware as he's an absolute lunatic". Allen continued, "the tackle was awful, it was absolutely dreadful".

But the injury to Danny affected Stevens, Paul & Clive Allen and the rest of the squad and staff for some time. Career ending injuries at Spurs were not a common thing at all, but at the time it was reported that Thomas was out for the season and may return next. The reality would be different.

Later that evening Danny was in his hospital bed. "I was watching TV and there were images of the Zeebrugge disaster on the news. People at the port were not knowing if their family were alive or dead and watching that puts things into perspective. I am injured but I am alive. Having seen those images, I perked up and never felt sorry for myself again".

He was referring to the capsizing of the *Herald of Free Enterprise* ferry that sailed out of the Belgian port of Zeebrugge on the evening of Friday 6th March 1987 and killing 193 passengers. That tragedy gave him perspective and Danny remains an optimistic and philosophical individual.

Uncannily, in the QPR matchday programme, Danny Thomas was profiled, and he was asked a series of questions. One of the final questions were, 'Ambition outside of the Game', he replied, "to be happy and successful in my next career".

His football career ended this day and not long after he began a career in physiotherapy. To this day Danny practices physiotherapy, lives and works in Florida and it is safe to say that he is happy and successful in his 'next' career after football. A family man and one of the most positive people you will ever meet. An absolute gentleman and one of the finest full backs that has ever played for Tottenham.

Sunday 15th March 1987 – Plough Lane, London
(Att: 15,636)
Wimbledon v Tottenham Hotspur
(FA Cup 6th Round)

With the club still reeling from the horrific injury to Danny Thomas and the cruel semi-final exit to Arsenal, Spurs were back on the FA Cup trail with a visit to Plough Lane.

The game had been switched to the Sunday, as it would be televised live on ITV, and it would be a chance to see if resilience was an evidentiary trait within this team at all as a trip to Wimbledon was not for the feint hearted.

David Pleat's memories of this game remain strong as he recalls the lead up to this match, we briefly discussed some incidents of the game in November before Pleat said, "Talk of nemesis with Wimbledon and their horrible players. But I do have a good relationship with Dave Bassett nowadays. It was a difficult day as we'd stayed in Brighton overnight and I think we trained in Bognor as I took them away for a bit of sea air".

"Anyway, the bus got damaged, it was the Holsten bus so everyone could see it was Spurs, and we had to get a replacement. When we finally got to Wimbledon they tried the usual intimidation tactics, the loud music and tiny dressing rooms. No hot water, no soap and no towels but we went out and played very well. It was a great performance as it was such a difficult place to go because of the intimidating atmosphere".

Pleat had Hoddle and Ardiles return to the side in place of Gary Stevens and Tony Galvin. Stevens stayed in the team though as he reverted to his right-back role after Danny Thomas' forced exclusion.

Line up v Wimbledon: Clemence; Stevens, Gough, Mabbutt, M Thomas; Waddle, P Allen, Ardiles, Hoddle, Hodge; C Allen. Sub: Claesen, Ruddock.

The game would prove to be a defensive masterclass from Stevens, Gough, Mabbutt and Mitchell Thomas. The best defensive display of the season and the midfield battled hard too against the physicality the home side possessed.

Wimbledon's midfield included Vinnie Jones. Jones had joined the Dons in November from non-league Wealdstone. A marauder through the middle of midfield and if you thought Dennis Wise and Lawrie Sanchez were uncomfortable to play against, this guy was next level.

He was the disruptor extraordinaire. He would follow Hoddle around closely during the game and only one of them would come out on top today.

Watching the game back, it was impressive to see the restraint and control applied by the Spurs players throughout the game. Especially Gary Stevens.

Gary had a lengthy spell in the treatment room following Fashanu's challenge on his which broke his collar bone, but today, Stevens was a model of control and diligence as he challenged, defended and supported Chris Waddle brilliantly during his time on the pitch.

The game was goalless at half time, no one side stood out above the other, but you always knew some drama would ensue at some point.

During the first half, whenever Hoddle got the ball Wise, Sanchez and Jones would be on him like a shot. Glenn was picking up the free kicks, but no-one was punished as the treatment would continue. Jones produced the home side's best chance, and by far the save of the half too, when his volley was brilliantly tipped over the bar by Clemence. How is this guy nearing forty? Great stuff from Clem.

In the second half Wimbledon were starting to throw the ball forward more often, but Clemence was also having a great game, standing up to the high balls and crosses that would inevitably involve physical challenges, but wily-campaigner Clem knew what he was doing as he gobbled up any chances that came forward. It was also noticeable to see that Clem looked like her was nursing a swollen mouth or fat lip.

With twenty minutes to go Pleat gambled, he felt the game was there for winning and he made an attacking switch by brining Claesen on for Gary Stevens. Paul Allen went to right-back and on ITV, co-commentator Ron Atkinson didn't feel that was the right move by Pleat.

With six minutes to go and hugging the right touchline Claesen came in-field and laid the ball off to Waddle. The Spurs winger approached the box facing Winterburn. He checked back looking like he was going to curl the ball in with his left foot, but he dropped his shoulder and changed immediate direction which completely bamboozled Thorn and Winterburn. Then with two touches Waddle strikes the ball from such a tight angle and it creeps inside Beasant's near post to put Spurs 1-0 up.

Waddle sprints off with facial expressions of shock and awe, he falls to his knees to be embraced by Paul Allen and Steve Hodge as you can hear the Spurs fans celebrations echo around Plough Lane.

Pleat then brings on Neil Ruddock to help with the potential long ball onslaught that Wimbledon may now deploy. But it was Spurs who scored next and killed the game.

With two minutes to go, Waddle is on the ball again with another mazy run. This time he is hacked down and Spurs win a free-kick 30 yards out, quite central to Wimbledon's goal.

Up step Glenn Hoddle. He strikes the ball with such accuracy it flies into the top right-hand corner and past Beasant. It was sublime and ridiculous that someone would try from that distance, but Hoddle was Hoddle, he could do that, and Spurs were now into the FA Cup semi-final.

Result: Wimbledon 0-2 Tottenham Hotspur (Waddle, Hoddle)

The headline in *The Daily Telegraph* was apt. 'TOTTENHAM PROVE SKILL IS BETTER THAN SCUFFLE'. Brains won over brawn as the footballing connoisseurs from North London had swept aside the bully boys from south of the river.

A couple of minutes after Hoddle's goal, he skips past Fashanu in the midfield only for the Wimbledon striker to leave a sneaky foot into Hoddle's ankle when the ball had long gone. Fashanu was clearly not enjoying this defeat.

Hoddle and Waddle rightly got the plaudits for such brilliant goals, but the defending was superb, and the foundations laid by Clemence's superb keeping. After the game Pleat revealed what was wrong with Clem's facial appearance; "He had four teeth extracted on Thursday and his mouth was haemorrhaging on Friday. He has not eaten for two days but has battled through to another semi-final".

There was an emotional twist to this game, and it occurred in the post-match TV interview with Chris Waddle and Glenn Hoddle. Both were clearly delighted at the win, but Glenn had a special mention to someone who was not able to be there today. On his goal, Hoddle told Martin Tyler, "I was very pleased with that one and if Danny Thomas is watching, that one's for you Dan".

The weekend was made even sweeter as Spurs knew they would face Watford in the FA Cup Semi Final. The day before, Watford had beaten Arsenal 3-1 at Highbury in their quarter final match up. A surprising result, but most welcomed by Spurs and Watford fans alike.

Sunday 22nd March 1987 – White Hart Lane, London
(Att: 32,763)
Tottenham Hotspur v Liverpool
(TODAY League Division 1)

The following Sunday Spurs welcomed Liverpool to White Hart Lane.

Despite some of Liverpool's indifferent and inconsistent results during the autumn they had now clawed their way back to the top of the league. They were top on 67 points from 33 games. Spurs were 17 points behind, but they had five games in hand, yes five!

Tottenham's various cup exploits had seen them fall behind in their league fixtures and the pile up in April and May was looking a bit daunting.

Winning today would keep Spurs in the hunt without doubt, but it would not be easy.

Despite Clive Allen's huge tally of league and cup goals he was only one goal ahead of Ian Rush in the league goalscoring list. Allen on twenty-six and Rush on twenty-five.

Spurs had conceded only two goals less than the league leaders and this was due to Spurs' brilliant defensive record in the last couple of months. Spurs had only played six league games since New Years Day and five of them were clean sheets.

Pleat would field the same team that triumphed over Wimbledon last week, no need to change at all.

Line up v Liverpool: Clemence; Stevens, Gough, Mabbutt, M Thomas; Waddle, P Allen, Ardiles, Hoddle, Hodge; C Allen. Sub: Claesen.

Liverpool had stars across the pitch. Grobbelaar in goal. Venison, Lawrenson and Hansen at the back, Molby, Craig Johnston and Ronnie Whelan in midfield and future Spur Paul Walsh partnering Ian Rush up front. They could even afford to leave John Aldridge on the bench.

For the television audience there were two teams of superstar footballers on show. But, in all honesty it wasn't one of the most memorable matches of the season. Competitively fought by two footballing sides, it was a single goal that split the difference.

Chris Waddle had been in such good form since the turn of the year and followed up his wonder strike at Wimbledon with a 25-yard effort to win the game.

With six minutes to go until half-time, from an Ardiles quick free-kick Waddle picked the ball up on the right side of midfield, cuts inside past Ronnie Whelan and strikes the ball with pace. The ball skids and bumps on the wet, drizzly surface and beats Grobbelaar and into the back of the Liverpool net.

Waddle runs off and leaps into the air hand aloft.

Liverpool had the lion's share of possession in the second half, but this was a different Tottenham. They worked hard, defended as a unit, and dug deep to go on and win the game 1-0.

Result: Tottenham Hotspur 1-0 Liverpool (Waddle)

An excellent three points. A win over the league champions and league leaders. Another clean sheet that saw Spurs leap to fourth place and with games in hand.

Another amazing fact was that Spurs and completed the league double over Liverpool for the first time in what felt like all of human history! We rarely beat Liverpool, but we had notched up two 1-0 wins over them this season.

David Pleat spoke to *Spurs News* and said "We got the double over Liverpool, and I thought we did it in splendid fashion. We played very well at Anfield last October and our second half performance today was very good".

Wednesday 25th March 1987 – St James Park, Newcastle
(Att: 32,763)
Newcastle United v Tottenham Hotspur
(TODAY League Division 1)

A few days later, Tottenham travelled nearly 300 miles north to face one the re-arranged league fixtures against Newcastle.

Newcastle were bottom of the league but had already frustrated Spurs at home earlier in the season with a late equaliser in the 1-1 league encounter. Spurs had narrowly beat them in the FA Cup too, so the north-east strugglers seemed to do well against Spurs.

Pleat went with the same 11 for the third game in a row and only replaced Galvin on the bench instead of Claesen.

Line up v Newcastle: Clemence; Stevens, Gough, Mabbutt, M Thomas; Waddle, P Allen, Ardiles, Hoddle, Hodge; C Allen. Sub: Galvin.

Spurs started the game well and looked in control for most of the first half. Beardsley and Goddard up front were posing the odd threat but Spurs, in all pale blue, went 1-0 up after nine minutes through Glenn Hoddle.

Making his return for Newcastle after four months out with a pelvis injury was 19-year-old Paul Gascoinge. A talent that was making a name for himself was lucky not to be booked early on when clattering into Ossie Ardiles. Exuberance we were told.

It was from that free-kick that Ardiles put Gary Stevens through down the right wing, his deep cross was met by Clive Allen, but the ball fell to Hoddle who toe-poked home.

Hodge, Clive Allen and Chris Waddle all had good chances to double Spurs lead but it remained 1-0 at half time.

The second half progressed but Spurs did not look like having the same thrust as previous games. Newcastle were coming into the game more and Gascoinge was becoming a threat with his forward runs and passing.

Gazza, as he was affectionately known, would make a move to Spurs in around 18 months' time. A period of his career when he played some of the most amazing football an Englishman has ever delivered. But this evening, it was evident to see his desire to get on the ball and control the game. Whenever a Newcastle free-kick was won he demanded the ball but he was always ushered away by more senior Newcastle players.

Spurs failed to capitalise on the chances they made and it was to come back and bite them when Newcastle equalised in the final quarter of the game.

On 75 minutes a Newcastle cross into the box was poorly headed away by Gough into the feet of Beardsley. Beardsley who first time and it found Paul Goddard unmarked just outside the six-yard box to fire home.

That goal seemed to deflate Spurs more than it should have and the visitors did little in the final several minutes to claim a win that their performance deserved.

Result: Newcastle United 1-1 Tottenham Hotspur (Hoddle)

Newcastle did the same as their last league game with Spurs earlier in the season. A late equaliser. That was four points Spurs should have been better off by in their league points tally but it was not to be.

The Independent wrote, "Spurs comprehensively outplayed the First Division's lowest placed club and should have built an unassailable lead".

However, there was no rest and onto Kenilworth Road this Saturday to face Luton Town. A homecoming for David Pleat that would not be too tasteful though.

Saturday 28th March 1987 – Kenilworth Road, Luton
(Att: 13,447)
Luton Town v Tottenham Hotspur
(TODAY League Division 1)

For the away trip to Luton, Pleat had decided to give Ardiles a rest as he had played five of the last six games in March. Claesen came in and Ardiles dropped to the bench. Luton were having a good season were in the top Six.

FANTASTIC DISAPPOINTMENT

Due to Luton Town's ban on away supporters, there were no away fans to cheer Pleat's side on. The weather had turned too, and snow was falling.

To make matters even worse, Luton Town had an artificial pitch. These surfaces were hard and bouncy, not like the usual heavy pitches that most clubs had during this time of the year so adjusting may be difficult.

For the second game running Spurs would wear their all-pale blue away kit.

Line up v Luton Town: Clemence; Stevens, Gough, Mabbutt, M Thomas; Claesen, P Allen, Waddle, Hoddle, Hodge; C Allen. Sub: Ardiles.

Luton hadn't kept a clean sheet since the start of January, but they started well and went ahead with a Mick Harford goal on six minutes when he got ahead of Gary Stevens to strike a low shot under Clemence.

Spurs never really recovered from that, and the weather then went from blustery high winds to snow. Mitchell Thomas was booed every time he touched the ball - Luton fans still unhappy at his defection to Spurs last summer.

This was Luton's largest attendance of the season, clearly come to welcome the return of Pleat, Thomas, Hartley and John Sheridan!

It remained 1-0 at half time and nine minutes into the second half, an unmarked Mike Newall made it 2-0 to the home side. Mabbutt and Gough were struggling with the physicality of Newall and Harford and Stevens had been guilty of coming inside too often, perhaps hoping to sniff out any mistakes Gough and Mabbutt might have made.

Spurs offered little going forward but did get back into the game when Chris Waddle scored his third goal in four games when he nipped in ahead of an advancing Luton keeper Les Sealey to stroke the ball home.

The game was finally lost with five minutes to go when Darron McDonagh was found unmarked in the Spurs area to volley home for 3-1.

Result: Luton Town 3-1 Tottenham Hotspur (Waddle)

Bad for Spurs too as Hoddle hobbled off with a groin injury which meant he missed England's midweek game versus Northern Ireland.

Even though Spurs lost, the biggest disappointment was possibly the treatment of Pleat and Irving Scholar from their inhospitable hosts.

It was well reported of David Evans' dislike for Pleat to leave Luton and join Spurs last summer. But in Scholar's 1992 book, he opens the lid on some ugliness at boardroom level he was not expecting. He also labels this as the most 'intimidating and hostile' atmosphere he'd ever experienced.

Scholar remarked about seeing many placards in the crowd that read 'Judas' in reference to Pleat's departure to Tottenham, some Luton fans were positioned just above Spurs' dugout, so the media had a field day with these signs just above Pleat's face. In fairness Scholar did hear some Luton fans demand their supporters take them down.

But, towards the end of the game a fan came up to the Director's box and chanted "The Jews are on their way to Auschwitz, Hitler's going to gas them again". Scholar writes, "It was a highly provocative racist antisemitic song, which I had heard some years before at Maine Road. The antisemitic references aimed at Pleat and Tottenham was the final straw".

Scholar mentions that it clearly had nothing to do with the Luton board but as soon as the game finished, he registered his displeasure with the Luton Town Director, John Smith. He told Smith he felt that Evans had been responsible for the bad atmosphere at the ground and soon after Evans appeared to tell Scholar that if he had any complaints he should address them to him. He then accused him of not being able to take defeat!

Scholar was furious and left immediately with his Spurs colleagues.

Pleat recalls his first trip back to Luton for the same reasons too, he said "I remember it was a terrible situation with chants about Judas and Jews, Irving Scholar got a lot of stick that day and the Spurs Directors left the ground very quickly after that game. Mr Evans wasn't a good man".

The reality was, Pleat and Scholar could take defeat. They had been beaten by a Luton side that were clearly better on the day, that is not being denied at all. But there must be civility and respect, that day it wasn't necessarily felt by Tottenham's Chairman and Manager.

March had now ended and what a whirlwind month it had been for the club. The awesome February form was halted by the crushing semi-final defeat to Arsenal and then followed up with the awful injury to Danny Thomas. There were brilliant wins over Wimbledon in the cup and Liverpool in the league, but the month ended badly with only one point from the Newcastle and Luton fixtures.

Spurs needed a big start to April to even consider being a serious title challenger.

APRIL 1987

Saturday 4th April 1987 – White Hart Lane, London
(Att: 22,400)
Tottenham Hotspur v Norwich City
(TODAY League Division 1)

Spurs were in fifth place and 13 points off Liverpool who were top on 67 points. Spurs still had four games in hand over them as their chase continued.

Arsenal's league title challenge had dropped off but Everton were in a really good run of form.

Since the Luton defeat Chris Waddle had been on the scoresheet again, this time for his country. England had beaten Northern Ireland 2-0 in Belfast to continue their fine Euro'88 campaign trail. Hoddle was not playing due to the injury he picked up at Luton, but Hodge and Mabbutt also played which saw a second consecutive England game with three Spurs midfielders lining up alongside England captain Bryan Robson in midfield.

Captain Robson scored the first when a Mabbutt long throw found Terry Butcher who nodded on to Robson who powered through the host's defence with a power header.

Waddle got his goal from a sublime Beardsley cross field pass that he took in his stride, rode forward and cut back on his left foot to curl around the keeper from 20 yards out. A superb goal and a man in rich form.

With Hoddle still injured Ardiles came back in, Waddle would want to take on that creative role. Pleat also replaced Stevens with Chris Hughton and it was Hughton's first start since mid-November. He had finally come back from injury and Pleat felt this was the game for him.

Also in the team again was Nico Claesen. Midweek Claesen had smashed a hat-trick for Belgium in their Euro'88 qualifier against Scotland. And yes, sadly Richard Gough was subjected to Nico's brilliant form that night.

Gough remembers that evening in Anderlecht and laughs; "That was not a good night at all, Nico scored a hat-trick if I remember, he was a great player. We are still friends to this day".

Line up v Norwich: Clemence; Hughton, Gough, Mabbutt, M Thomas; Claesen, P Allen, Waddle, Ardiles, Hodge; C Allen. Sub: Galvin.

Spurs were desperate for a win. Norwich were on the same points total as Spurs but behind on goal difference. Ken Brown and his team had put in some excellent performances this season and former Spur Ian Crook was at the heart of most good things they did.

This was not a classic for Spurs at all. The result in the end looked impressive but for the first 70 minutes of this match Spurs looked second best until Pleat introduced Tony Galvin for Paul Allen and that tweak seemed to boost Spurs' attacking intent.

With fifteen minutes to go Spurs took the lead, against the odds and against the run of play. In truth, Clive Allen's performance had been poor up to this point but from an Ardiles pass he spun from his marker and shot low past a helpless Bryan Gunn.

Six minutes later he got his second of the game and this time assisted by club captain, Richard Gough. Once again, Gough rose above everyone else to head a Chris Waddle corner down into the path of Clive for his second.

Twelve minutes after his first goal, Clive Allen grabs a hat-trick goal that no-one had seen coming at all, especially on the evidence of his first 75 minutes this afternoon.

It was Galvin who orchestrated Allen's third goal of the game when Waddle's swiftness of thought took a quick free kick down Spurs' left wing which Galvin expertly centred for Allen to swoop home.

It was twelve minutes that crushed Norwich and in fairness, not a result that their performance deserved. For Spurs it was nice to win and win without playing well.

Result: Tottenham Hotspur 3-0 Norwich City (C Allen 3)

In *The Sunday Times*, Deryk Brown headlined Allen as 'SPURS' SOLO ARTIST'. It was Clive's 43rd goal of the season and he was now closing in on Club legend, Jimmy Greaves' record of 44 goals. Pleat told Brown, "Clive was not playing well and when I made the substitution I wondered if I'd taken off the wrong Allen"!

The weekend would end with Spurs joint-third in the table, but the big news was on the Sunday. Clive Allen was voted as the PFA Player of the Year, an award voted by his professional football peers. A wonderful award for a wonderful season he was having. He was a double award winner too as he also scooped the Football Writers Player of the Year.

Clive claimed his second hat-trick of that weekend when his third award was to be chosen as part of the 1987 PFA Team of the Year. Glenn Hoddle was the only other Spur included in the XI of the league's best players. A team that included Everton's Neville Southall and Kevin Sheedy, along with Arsenal quartet of Sansom, Anderson, Rocastle and Tony Adams. Hansen and Rush were the Liverpudlians also included, and Newcastle's Peter Beardsley was included despite his team languishing near the bottom of the league. In fairness, Beardsley had been quite brilliant for Club and Country this season.

Allen got the award but the player who was considered by his peers to be the second best in the league this season was Spurs' playmaker and visionary, Glenn Hoddle. Hoddle was thriving in the role Pleat had bestowed upon him, Spurs fans and the England fans were now finally seeing Glenn in the role he was meant to play.

Playing free behind Clive gave Glenn ultimate flexibility, there were countless games when Glenn was man-marked which was in some way considered a continental tactic to counter a continental role.

Tuesday 7th April 1987 – Hillsborough, Sheffield
(Att: 19,488)
Sheffield Wednesday v Tottenham Hotspur
(TODAY League Division 1)

48 hours after Clive scooped his well-deserved individual awards, he and his teammates were back in action and this time it was a re-arranged fixture away to Sheffield Wednesday.

Wednesday were mid-table and there last six results of three wins and three losses highlighted mid-table form.

Striker Lee Chapman was in good form as well as midfielder Gary Megson who was man of the match when Wednesday grabbed a draw at the Lane earlier this season. Winger Brian Marwood was apparently attracting the attention from the bigger clubs and ultimately of George Graham at Arsenal where he would join in the near future.

Pleat would bring Gary Stevens back to replace Chris Hughton and Nico came in for Ardiles.

He also rested Hoddle again, Galvin came in for him. Hoddle was unavailable with a stomach muscle complaint he'd had for some weeks now, but he was still turning up and performing.

On the bench was young defender Tim O'Shea. O'Shea had been at Spurs since 1983 and was an important part of the success the reserves who were top of the league in the Football Combination this season.

Pleat knew three points were a must, but he had to think about the next game in four days' time when Spurs would face Watford in the FA Cup Semi-Final.

Line up v Sheffield Wednesday: Clemence; Stevens, Gough, Mabbutt, M Thomas; Claesen, P Allen, Waddle, Hodge, Galvin; C Allen. Sub: O'Shea

Wearing all-white, Spurs were dominant for most of the first half. Waddle, playing in a central role, was at his creative best. He carved out 2-3 excellent opportunities for Clive, but nothing was paying off.

Half-time came, Spurs should have been ahead, but it was goalless.

Spurs finally got the breakthrough with twenty minutes to go. Some neat interplay between Mitchell Thomas and Tony Galvin saw the Irish winger play the ball centrally to Waddle. Waddle struck the ball with the outside of his left foot and brilliantly played in Steve Hodge who had made a wonderful run into the box. Hodge fired the ball across the six-yard box to find Clive Allen who thundered the ball home with his right foot.

A sparkling footballing goal and Spurs rightly ahead.

Pleat then made an immediate change and seemed like he was shutting up shop. Off came Claesen and on came defender O'Shea to make his senior Spurs debut. Waddle was pushed out to the right and O'Shea was placed in a holding midfield role.

Wednesday gave Spurs a scare late on when Hirst wasted a great cross provided by Marwood, but Spurs held on. Clive's tally was now 44 goals for the season.

Result: Sheffield Wednesday 0-1 Tottenham Hotspur
(C Allen)

Spurs' attacking football style was getting media attention, but something else was too this week.

Whether you listened to Capital Radio or Radio 1, there was a very catchy song doing the rounds and bizarrely it was being sung by Glenn Hoddle and Chris Waddle. The song was called 'Diamond Lights' and the Spurs duo were lead vocalists!

This bizarre circumstance came when, according to various interviews by Glenn and Chris, they were asked to attend an event in the Midlands after Spurs had a game nearby. Glenn recalls it was the Coventry game played at the end of 1986.

Hoddle, speaking to Steve Sidwell and Joe Cole on the Coral Podcast *All to Play For*, he recalls during the evening of that event they were both asked to go up on stage and sing with the band. A friend of theirs called Pat Mitchell then showered them with praise by telling them what good voices they had. From there it seemed to spiral and over the next few months they were badgered to sing this song which had been written for them.

That song 'Diamond Lights' was released in April 1987. Glenn sang most of the verses and Chris came in to sing on the chorus. It was 1980's pop gold! As a Spurs fan of course I bought a copy of it.

Lifelong Spurs fan and Radio DJ royalty Simon Mayo was quite keen on the song. He told me, "I played it first! I was deputising for Gary Davies and played it as a mystery track, asking listeners to guess who it was. No one had a clue obviously. Hmmm, I must dig it out for the Greatest Hits Radio Drivetime now".

Mayo had visited White Hart Lane earlier that season and was interviewed on the pitch. During that year he was unable to get to Spurs as often as he'd like as his *Radio 1* career had just taken off, but I had a recollection that he had been interviewed but wasn't entirely sure I had made it up.

Mayo confirmed, "No that happened. A mistake really as everyone, apart from club legends get booed. As did I, so I made some cheap Arsenal jibes to get some applause. I remember seeing Peter Cook do the halftime chat once at a Spurs-Arsenal match. He complained about the smell coming from the away end. He got away with it because he was Peter Cook, and it was the 70's."

As part of my research, I stumbled across a *Smash Hits* magazine article which reviewed newly released music. In this publication the magazine had asked *The Pogues* lead singer, Shane McGowan to review the week's single releases. There were some big hitters like Paul Simon, Level 42, The Cure and of course, Glenn & Chris.

McGowan said, "You're joking, are you joking? Hoddle and Waddle?". He then conceded, "It's not that bad really, I quite like it!"

I shared this Smash Hits/McGowan review with Simon Mayo, he confidently replied, "I agree with Shane McGowan".

So, Glenn and Chris, what more could you want but diverse approval from Simon Mayo and Shane McGowen!

Saturday 11th April 1987 – Villa Park, Birmingham
(Att: 46,151)
Tottenham Hotspur v Watford
(FA Cup Semi Final)

Anyway, music aside, it was back to football business as Spurs travelled to Villa Park to face Watford in their FA Cup Semi-Final encounter.

Pleat was able to choose between a near fully fit squad. Hoddle and Ardiles were available after their midweek rest and confidence was high.

Watford had been in good form and were mid-table in Division 1. Their journey to Villa Park had seen them beat Maidstone and Chelsea in rounds three and four only to face a trilogy of games against third division Walsall. Watford won the final game 1-0 after a 1-1 and 4-4 epic battle of games.

But their biggest scalp was their quarter final victory over Arsenal where a Luther Blissett brace and John Barnes strike was enough to record a famous 3-1 win at Highbury.

Yet to score in the FA Cup was Mark Falco. Falco left Spurs for Watford in the autumn and was their league top scorer on twelve goals. He had yet to score in the FA Cup this season and he had scored against Spurs back in December.

Villa Park was buzzing. I can still remember the apprehension amongst our supporters which I feel was mainly due to our exit to Arsenal in the League Cup last month. But on paper we should beat Watford.

The usual suspects were available for Watford, they had a very attacking group of players but at the back they were a tad suspect. The biggest news before the game was that Watford goalkeeper, Steve Sherwood, was carrying an injury he may not recover from in time and usual keeper Tony Coton was already out injured.

In short, it turned out Watford had a goalkeeping crisis and had to employ the services of a son of one of the club Directors - enter Gary Plumley.

Plumley had played for Newport County and Cardiff City between 1975 and 1985 but now he was facing Spurs in the last four of the FA Cup.

Line up v Watford: Clemence; Hughton, Gough, Mabbutt, M Thomas; Waddle, P Allen, Ardiles, Hoddle, Hodge; C Allen. Sub: Claesen, Stevens.

There was a delay to kick-off as Spurs and Watford fans flooded north to a Villa Park that was sparkling in sunshine and Spurs played sunshine football from the first minute. If this was a team still scarred from their semi-final defeat to Arsenal, then you'd struggle to see it.

The drive and attacking play in the first 35 minutes was quite stunning from Pleat's men. Poor old Gary Plumley stood no chance.

It turned into a rout when Steve Hodge put Spurs 1-0 up after 13 minutes when he was the first to react the Plumley failing to hold on to a blistering Clive Allen drive. Hodge had his first FA cup goal in Spurs colours.

Two minutes later it was pure elation for Spurs fans as Clive Allen struck the ball from 25 yards and the ball took a slight deflection of a Watford defender and Plumley was stranded. The noise being created by Spurs fans were drowning out the shell-shocked Watford support and things were about to get even worse for Watford after 35 minutes.

Hoddle and Ardiles took a short corner, Ardiles played the ball to Paul Allen in a central position ten yards outside Watford's box. With nowhere to go, Allen bursts into the Watford penalty area, bypassing defenders until he decided to strike the ball with his left foot from such a tight angle it rocketed into roof of the net.

He sprinted off, arms in the air, mouth wide open and his face covered in shock. Great finish and 3-0 to Spurs.

At half-time us fans were delirious, acutely aware there were 45 minutes left, but surely we couldn't mess this up?

Spurs coasted most of the second half, so much so, Pleat was allowed to replace Clive Allen with Nico. That moved paid off too when, after 73 minutes, Ardiles played the ball into Nico who was on the edge of Watford's box and back to goal, he lays a lovely ball on to Steve Hodge who strikes the ball first time into the bottom left-hand corner of Plumley's goal.

Once again, Plumley had no chance and now Spurs were 4-0 up.

Two minutes later, Watford did score a consolation goal when substitute Malcolm Allen, no relation to Paul and Clive, headed home having risen above Chris Hughton.

Gary Stevens came on as a last-minute sub for Paul Allen which saw Paul receive a brilliant and well-deserved ovation from the Spurs fans.

When the referee blew the final whistle, it was a mixture of euphoria and relief, we were finally back at Wembley. You could see the emotion among the players and they fully deserved their place in the final.

Result: Tottenham Hotspur 4-1 Watford
(Hodge 2, C Allen, P Allen)

Despite Plumley's 'fifteen minutes of fame', it was Spurs' stars that sparkled in a game dominated by the midfield mastery of Glenn Hoddle and Ossie Ardiles.

Paul Allen fondly remembers that day and admits they were not taking anything for granted, "I think we had a good feeling right from the outset going into that game as the team had been playing some consistent and open, attractive football plus scoring lots of goals. So, I think we were quietly confident, but we did very well in the end".

Paul Allen, Chris Waddle, Ossie Ardiles and Glenn Hoddle had all been brilliant, but arguably the player of the game was Steve Hodge. He was in a Wembley final and scoring a brace to help his team get there.

Hodge recalls, "The semi at Villa Park was another special day, we played really well and got a great start, it's always nice to score goals that take your team to a final. I can clearly remember the thousands of Spurs fans in their cars going back down the M1 after our victory. A great feeling".

For me, I recalled the quiet journey home after the Arsenal semi-final defeat but this journey back to London was euphoric. The excitement of reaching an FA Cup Final was like no other feeling to a football supporter as, back then, this was the pinnacle of Cup football in the British game. The way we were playing in the last couple of months made me want the game to be played immediately. Dismantling a very good Watford side was an impressive result and I can remember asking dad what it was like going to the 1981 and 1982 cup finals. I was lapping up any information I could to help visualise what a day like that would feel like. I had been to Wembley before to watch England internationals and England Schoolboy matches but never for a Cup Final. Oh man, we still had a month to go!

Wednesday 15th April 1987 – Maine Road, Manchester
(Att: 19,488)
Manchester City v Tottenham Hotspur
(TODAY League Division 1)

Tottenham were now in the 1987 FA Cup Final and they would face Coventry City who had overcome Leeds United in the other semi-final.

There were still nine league games to play and six of those nine games were away from home. This is when cracks started to show. Spurs had to play ten games in the next four weeks, with one of those weeks being an international break too. Pleat travelled to Maine Road without Ossie Ardiles and Chris Hughton.

City were still at the foot of the table and were in such a terrible run of form they looked favourites to go down. Three points would keep Spurs in the hunt, a loss would be devastating and a draw not great either. With Stevens and Claesen returning Spurs were still favourites.

City manager Jimmy Frizzell decided to counter Spurs' five-man midfield with a five man midfield of his own. He deployed one striker up front and that was their new signing from Blackpool, Paul Stewart.

As we all know, Stewart would go on to join Spurs and have significant success, but this was a new world for the former Blackpool man up against Richard Gough and Gary Mabbutt.

Line up v Manchester City: Clemence; Stevens, Gough, Mabbutt, M Thomas; Claesen, P Allen, Hoddle, Hodge, Waddle; C Allen. Sub: Bowen.

Spurs were pretty awful in that first 45 minutes. Just before half-time Peter Barnes was tripped by Gary Stevens and a penalty was awarded.

Neil McNab stepped up and scored past Ray Clemence. Clem was making a career record equalling appearance of 1,098 games. A record he now shared with former Spurs keeper, Pat Jennings.

Down by a goal at half-time Spurs lost Gary Stevens to a hamstring injury early in the second half. Patrick Barclay, in his *Independent* column, noticed the amusing scenario when Spurs brought on Mark Bowen to replace Stevens. Claesen, so used to being subbed, headed over to be replaced only to be shocked when he finds out that Stevens was coming off and not him!

Bowen played in an attacking central midfield role with Paul Allen going to full back once more. Claesen salvaged a point for Spurs when scoring via a glancing header from a Mitchell Thomas centre, and thatwas enough to see Spurs level and back in the game.

From that point on Spurs decided to play. Hoddle, Claesen and Clive Allen all had chances, but Spurs could not find the winning goal.

Clive did get the ball in the back of the net, but he was ruled slightly offside. The game finished 1-1 and two points were dropped.

Result: Manchester City 1-1 Tottenham Hotspur (Claesen)

With Everton now top of the league and moving further away from Liverpool, Spurs seemed the only candidates who could have kept up with their games in hand. Everton boss Howard Kendall would have been mighty pleased to see Spurs drop those points.

In *The Daily Telegraph*, Colin Gibson writes, "After that result, Tottenham almost certainly surrender their dreams of completing the double this season".

Keeping up was a tough task, it was now even tougher for Pleat and his men.

Saturday 18ᵗʰ April 1987 – White Hart Lane, London
(Att: 26,926)
Tottenham Hotspur v Charlton Athletic
(TODAY League Division 1)

Spurs were now nine points behind Everton and only one game in hand, but they still had to play Everton in two weeks' time.

Spurs' opponents today were Charlton. They were also in the drop zone and fighting for their division one status like Manchester City were midweek. Defensively they had improved since Paul Miller had joined them, but they still struggled to score.

Stevens' hamstring complaint meant Chris Hughton came back in. Ossie Ardiles returned, and he would take the place of Chris Waddle. Waddle had played 48 consecutive games up to this point so maybe Pleat felt it was time for him to rest.

Similarly, Gary Mabbutt was rested too after a run of 31 consecutive league games. He would be replaced by Neil Ruddock who would be making his first senior start in a Spurs shirt.

Line up v Charlton: Clemence; Hughton, Gough, Ruddock, M Thomas; Claesen, P Allen, Hoddle, Hodge, Waddle; C Allen. Sub: Galvin.

It was a lovely, bright spring day at White Hart Lane. Paul Miller got a rapturous reception on his return.

Spurs were in control for most of the first half without creating any clear-cut chances and the deadlock was broken on 22 minutes. Steve Hodge seemed to have settled in to Spurs so well since joining in December and he was the provider for Clive Allen's 46th goal of the season.

His darting run and low left foot cross was enough to serve up Clive's tap-in from a few yards out.

The lead at half-time was well deserved. The second half was a show of lethargy and zero spark.

There seemed a touch of apathy around the ground as Spurs lost control of this game but were very lucky not to concede on a couple of occasions.

Ardiles was replaced on the hour by Tony Galvin who tried to spark some life into the home teams attacks but alas that was not to be. It finished 1-0 to Spurs and all-round relief too.

Result: Tottenham Hotspur 1-0 Charlton Athletic (C Allen)

The newspapers all highlighted the tiredness displayed by Spurs. In the *Daily Telegraph*, Colin Gibson wrote, "If they are still dreaming of a league and cup double, they need to be a lot friskier at Upton Park on Monday night".

In 48 hours, Spurs would travel to Upton Park. 48 hours after that they would travel to Plough Lane to face Wimbledon and then 72 hours after that game, they would face Oxford at home. Four games in seven days!

The Charlton game was special for two other reasons too. One good and one not so good.

This match marked the 1,099th game in the career of Ray Clemence. This man had won the lot, apart from the World Cup of course, but domestically he was already a legend.

Of the 1987 team, Ray Clemence is the only member no longer with us, having passed away in November 2020. I was lucky and fortunate enough to spend some time with his son, Stephen.

Stephen Clemence has also played professional football for Tottenham along with spells at Birmingham City and Leicester City and has held Premier League coaching roles at Hull City and Newcastle United.

Stephen has some memories of that season, but when I asked how Ray was when it came to awards and accolades Stephen said, "He was very proud of everything he achieved and he still holds one or two records today, it's nice for the family. I think I remember him getting presented with that appearance award on the pitch with Pat Jennings. We had that picture at home of him holding a decanter set alongside Pat. He was very proud, but he didn't talk about them too much in public".

The second notable circumstance was the second half appearance of Tony Galvin. This turned out to be Tony's last home appearance for Spurs after a wonderful nine-year career with the club.

He would go on to play two more times for Spurs in the coming weeks, but it was a shame the crowd never got to appreciate he was going, and this was to be his last home appearance.

Monday 20th April 1987 – Upton Park, London
(Att: 23,972)
West Ham United v Tottenham Hotspur
(TODAY League Division 1)

Spurs travelled a few miles East to face West Ham in another re-arranged fixture. West Ham's season had been quite average in comparison to their 1985-86 campaign, they were in fourteenth place.

They had won only two of their last twelve league games. They had beaten Arsenal 3-1 two weeks ago which had also contributed to a wretched run of form Arsenal were in.

Arsenal were top of the league at the end of January and now found themselves twelve points behind Everton in fifth place. A significant dip in form, but Arsenal did have success to show for the season when they had beaten Liverpool 2-1 in the Littlewoods Cup Final earlier in the month.

Pleat brought Waddle back into the fold and rested Ardiles again while Charlton debutant Ruddock was replaced by his reserve team colleague John Polston. Tony Galvin started too in his penultimate game for the club.

West Ham had three old campaigners in their starting ranks that Spurs were hoping to exploit, in Phil Parkes, Liam Brady and Billy Bonds. McAvennie and Cottee would be a threat though.

Line up v West Ham: Clemence; Hughton, Gough, Polston, M Thomas; Waddle, P Allen, Hoddle, Hodge, Galvin; C Allen. Sub: Claesen.

Spurs, in all-pale blue for the fifth and final time this season, started the game well and were streaming forward in the opening 25 minutes.

Hoddle, Gough and Paul Allen had efforts on goal but there was no killer instinct. The service into Clive was not as it had been of late, so he struggled to get into the game.

Two minutes before half-time it was West Ham who took the lead. A long ball up to Frank McAvennie saw him bullishly turn away from his international colleague, Richard Gough, and fire home for 1-0 to the Hammers.

Not what the performance deserved but Spurs were still losing, nonetheless.

Fifteen minutes into the second half Spurs were level. Hoddle was lurking in the middle of the West Ham half. He picked up a poor Alvin Martin clearance and shaped up for a 30 yarder. He then chipped the ball into Clive Allen who had lost his marker to chest down and volley home.

Spurs were now back in it and rightly so too, they had been the better team over the course of the game.

But frustration crept in five minutes later when West Ham won a penalty. Stewart Robson received the ball on the edge of Spurs' area and he went down near Richard Gough. Arguably it was just outside the box but there was absolute minimal contact and Robson ran into Gough more than Gough bringing him down. Not a penalty in the 1980's but you even might struggle to find that as a penalty in the 2020's.

The ref was convinced and pointed to the spot quickly mind you. Cottee stepped up and scored his 21st goal of the season. 2-1 West Ham.

That decision and goal seemed to knock the life out of Spurs, and they offered little after that. If anything, Clem kept Spurs in the game with a couple of brilliant saves to deny Robson and McAvennie.

Result: West Ham United 2-1 Tottenham Hotspur (C Allen)

It seemed that Spurs' attempt to stay close to Everton at the top was now over. The odds were stacking anyway but they seemed ever higher now.

The Daily Telegraph's Colin Gibson wrote, "West Ham removed any lingering doubts fostered in Tottenham that the first division title would remain on Merseyside for the sixth consecutive season". Consolation for Spurs perhaps was Gibson's view on the penalty decision when he wrote, "Robson's theatrical dive over Gough's leg had been adjudged by referee Deakin to be merited a penalty". So, not really a penalty, was it?

Spurs were attacking and fluid in the first 30 minutes of this game, it was just a shame they couldn't capitalise on that good passage of play. To make things even worse, in under 48 hours Spurs had yet another game, and this time it was away at Wimbledon.

Wednesday 22nd April 1987 – Plough Lane, London
(Att: 15,636)
Wimbledon v Tottenham Hotspur
(TODAY League Division 1)

Spurs were still in third place and facing a Wimbledon team who were hungry for revenge from their FA Cup Quarter Final defeat to Spurs. Dave Bassett's men were in eighth place and having an excellent first season in top-flight football.

Wimbledon had not been getting many positive results of late but despite that poor recent form, you knew they would get themselves up for this London derby.

This would be Spurs' 13th London derby in the league this season of which Spurs had won only six but with the league challenge gradually dissipating Pleat started to possibly think about Wembley but also the five other games beforehand. Selection changes saw Polston move to right-back and Ruddock came into the side to partner Gough.

Ardiles returned in the midfield alongside Tim O'Shea who would be making his first senior start. Hodge, Waddle and Hoddle were rested again, and Clive Allen placed on the bench. Mark Bowen would come in for his first start of the league season too.

Line up v Wimbledon: Clemence; Polston, Gough, Ruddock, M Thomas; P Allen, Ardiles, O'Shea, Bowen, Galvin; Claesen. Sub: C Allen

This was to be a stormy affair in South London and Spurs took the lead when Claesen won a penalty in the 35th minute. He got up and converted for his ninth league goal this season. The first half was all Spurs and they were clearly the better team.

Yes, football is a game of two halves and this match proved that cliche.

Where Spurs had been a model of control and good football, Wimbledon decided to change the atmosphere of the game. Spurs went 2-0 up after 56 minutes and were in such good shape when Mark Bowen converted Mitchell Thomas's left sided cross for his first senior goal.

Bowen's goal came two minutes after home side centre back, Brian Gayle, was sent off for apparently striking Nico Claesen. Players erupted from both sides and even Dennis Wise was pleading with the referee it was him and not Gayle who caused

Nico to fall down. They were also unhappy as they felt Claesen went down very easily indeed.

TV replay shows that Gayle was simply talking to Claesen and Dennis Wise kicks the ball into Claesen's face causing him to go down. The ref thought it was Gayle.

Gayle got his marching orders. Spurs were 2-0 up and things were looking good for the visitors.

The game got very scrappy and it all started playing into Wimbledon's hands. Claesen, Ruddock and Gough were all booked, and the home team clawed one back with twenty minutes to go when Glyn Hodges scored a fantastic freekick from just outside the area into the top left-hand corner of Clem's goal. 1-2, game on.

With ten minutes to go Pleat must have been pulling his hair out. Up to that point, Mitchell Thomas had played supremely well but he clumsily fouled Alan Cork to give away a penalty.

From the resulting kick, Hodges stepped up and scored his second of the game. The game ended with Spurs hanging on for the point when, for 75% of the game they were worthy of claiming all three.

Result: Wimbledon 2-2 Tottenham Hotspur
(Claesen, Bowen)

In *The Daily Telegraph*, Donald Saunders was keener to point out this was Wimbledon's fifth sending off of the season and their conduct was of grave concern to the FA rather than footballing points of the game itself.

Claesen told Saunders that Gayle had spat at him too, but manager Dave Bassett said, "We do not want that continental falling about in our game". The problem was, Bassett proved yet again he could not control his players' behaviour and was always labelling them as the victims.

Just like at White Hart Lane when he failed to embrace the reality of the carnage Fashanu and Sanchez had caused by labelling them and his team as victims. This is an unaccountable behaviour and even though he made a slight concession in Sanchez's actions that day, he generally turned a blind eye to most things.

* * * *

It was Thursday 23rd April 1987 and we cast our eye over to Glenn & Chris' *Diamond Lights* – Back to Hoddle speaking on the *Coral Podcast*, he remembers a car coming to pick him and Waddle both up from Cheshunt after training. They were heading into London and to the Top of the Pops (TOTP) studios. They had recorded the music video a few months before and in that time had forgotten most of the words!

They were in the car, listening to their song on a cassette readying themselves for their live appearance on BBC1 that evening. Amazingly, there is TV footage of this car journey too. In the lead up to kick-off on FA Cup Final day, the BBC had a camera in the car capturing Hoddle and Waddle's journey from

Cheshunt to BBC Television Centre for TOTP. They were singing away in the car listening to their song. Brilliant stuff.

A few drinks were consumed to settle their nerves before going out and performing their song in front of millions of people. Just a reminder, around that time TOTP could command audiences in their millions as it was the No.1 music TV programme in Europe.

They were on stage following performances by The Smiths, then Kim Wilde and after their singing slot it was Terence Trent D'arby. These were TOTP pros and the Spurs duo were neatly nestled in between them having been introduced by Gary Davies.

Danny Thomas laughs as he recalls watching their appearance on TOTP. "Oh, they got some abuse for that alright. It still must be one of the funniest things I have ever seen on TV to see them both on Top of the Pops, and they were stood there like the stiffest people ever. Two terrific athletes but seeing them so stiff on stage was funny as hell. I don't think they drank enough".

The song had been released for sale a few days after the FA Cup victory over Watford and debuted in the charts at no.30. By the time they appeared on TOTP they were up to no.17. By mid-May they reached their highest chart position of no.12. Music and football always did have a connection, I guess!

Music and football would hit a peak in 1990 when Mancunian band New Order produced '*World in Motion*' for the England team who were about to embark on their Italian 1990 World

Cup assault. Amazingly, this song created some form of unity for England followers and spread across the country.

Before that music and football, or football culture, rarely worked in tandem. In 1987 music in the UK was going through a bit of a transitional phase. So far, the 1980's had seen musical diversity in The Clash, Wham, The Police, Duran Duran, and UB40 to name but a few. Overseas influences saw Michael Jackson, Prince and Madonna exert their brilliance across our charts, but things were changing slightly.

From a 'Pop Music' perspective, Charts would soon be dominated by the likes of Rick Astley, Bros and Kylie Minogue. The power producers of Stock, Aitken & Waterman would create acts that would lead the UK music industry over the next few years.

But underneath the bubble-gum pop that most people saw or heard, there was a movement starting. It was a shift that would change youth culture in the UK during the late 1980's and early 1990's. That music was House.

House music was originated in the USA. Chicago was one of the main areas to create music by smart, slick and innovative producers that would be a catalyst for one of the biggest music genres in modern history.

Hip-hop and rap was also on the rise. The 1970's and 80's had seen a similar boom in this genre of music that started to change youth and societal culture. The foundations built by DJ Kool Herc, Afrika Bambaataa, Grandmaster Flash and The Sugarhill

Gang had paved the way for the likes of RUN DMC, Eric B & Rakim and LL Cool J to take their music across America and beyond.

In the UK, hip-hop and rap were on the rise too. By adopting some of the US giants' music there was more of an appetite and desire for this type of music here in the UK. One of the UK rap revolutionaries was Derek B, a London based artist that had released his first major single called *'Get Down'*. On that track, he even name checks Norman Jay, the Spurs supporting founder of KISS FM.

With musical influences changing, the UK were about to be hit by the arrival of The Beastie Boys who would start a UK tour in May 1987. The New York rap group had just released their breakthrough album, *Licensed to Ill*, and it was a worldwide smash. But where the youngsters loved their music, the media and establishment feared the apparent loutish behaviour that went alongside it all.

Music of black origin was gaining traction, and this leads us back to Chicago. With the creation of house music, house tracks led to a change in the UK club scene.

Fast forward slightly to the summer of 1987 it has been well documented that UK House music was born when London DJ's Paul Oakenfold, Danny Rampling, Johnny Walker and Nicky Holloway went to Ibiza to celebrate Oakenfold's 24th birthday. This trip would be the catalyst of the UK Rave scene, as when they returned from their inspirational break they were to build foundations of a new UK club scene. That trip piqued their interest in the music they were hearing and wanting to take that feel-good vibe back home to the UK.

In fact, house music nights had been happening in England a few months before. A mecca for club goers was the Hacienda club in Manchester. The *Hacienda-FAC51 Nude Nights* presented 'Chicago House Party' on Monday 9th March 1987. It would feature the likes of Marshall Jefferson and Frankie Knuckles who would go on to be considered as House Music royalty and 24 hours before that, on Sunday 8th March 1987, Rock City in Nottingham had put on a 'House All-Dayer' which featured the same House artists.

One track that was released in 1987 was '*Someday*' by CeCe Rogers and was produced by Marshall Jefferson. Now this is not just a classic, it is an anthem and one of the originators in what made house music so powerful. The music, along with the vocals, provided deep and meaningful messaging that attempted to create unity. The piano and bass that was deployed in this track inspires pure emotion. I dare you to not like this track.

The track was a call to unify and would be an anthem across the Acid House music explosion that was about to take place.

One of the original superstar DJs was Londoner, Carl Cox. In 2016 Space, the Ibiza Superclub, closed its doors. Cox's closing set was a nine-hour marathon that saw him conclude his performance, and his association with the club, with *Someday* by CeCe Rogers. Emotion personified in his track choice.

The Acid House movement would, in a weird way, have an impact on the hooliganism culture that infected British football. In time, the music would rise and alongside that was a recreational drug known as Ecstasy. The music and drug went hand-in-hand and created an environment not often seen.

UK pub culture was sometimes brutal. When it came down to the team you followed it could end up in a brawl because of the tribal world that fans had created and lived within.

However, barriers started to get broken down slightly. In the club and rave environments, you would hear of numerous stories where fans of different football teams did unite and get along. That was the power of the music, the movement and, yes, the drug too.

At a club or rave, a common set of questions would be, 'What's your name? Where you from? What you on?" It would now include "Who do you support?". By answering that you would not necessarily end up in a fight, you'd more likely embrace each other and end up dancing for hours on end.

Between 1987 and 1992 this music scene and cultural change was possibly the biggest youth movement since the first Summers of Love in the 1960s.

And during this period, football would dramatically change too. We had already seen some of the commercial changes in the game, some led by Scholar and Spurs, but by 1992 the whole landscape of British, European and World football would start to change with the launch of the English Premier League,

European Club Competition and even World Cups would take on a completely different feel to that of the last 20 years leading up to Mexico 1986 as FIFA began exploiting commercial gains.

This is all part of change and evolution in society and culture. There were times when it was a real pleasure to experience some of this.

Back to the music and Top of the Pops for now. Glenn and Chris had done well but that would not be the only time Spurs would appear in the music charts this season.

* * * *

Saturday 25th April 1987 – White Hart Lane, London (Att: 20,064) Tottenham Hotspur v Oxford United
(TODAY League Division 1)

The weather was like the Charlton game, sunny & bright. White Hart Lane always looked so good in the sunshine. Despite the title challenge all but gone, there was an FA Cup Final to look forward to.

FA Cup Final souvenirs and merchandise were on sale in the Spurs Shop and the party atmosphere was starting to build. On the front of the matchday programme Glenn Hoddle was pictured signing with Spurs fans and musicians, Chas N Dave.

The cockney music maestros had concocted another FA Cup Final gem for the club as they looked forward to Wembley in the middle of May. They had already produced FA Cup Final sings in 1981 and 1982 and we had already seen them perform live on the pitch at half-time during the Forest home game back in November.

This was the penultimate home game of the season and essentially the penultimate time fans will see Hoddle play for Spurs at White Hart Lane. His impending departure affected most Spurs people, he had been part of our club's fabric for so long it felt odd to think he'd be gone next season. Fans were hoping for some vintage Hoddle performances between now and then.

Pleat was in a bit of a quandary. Mabbutt had returned from a small injury but in the next few days Glenn Hoddle, Chris Waddle, Clive Allen, Gary Mabbutt and Steve Hodge would all meet up with the England squad for a Euro'88 qualifier with Turkey. I'd imagine Pleat would be worried about energy loss and injury more than anything.

Scotland had a friendly against Holland so Richard Gough was spared, Belgium would be facing Republic of Ireland which meant Claesen and Galvin would see another 90 minutes in their legs which they did not need.

That aside, Pleat went with possibly his strongest eleven. The youngsters who played so well at Wimbledon all departed and Pleat welcomed back his big guns.

Oxford were still flirting with the drop. One or two more positive results would see them safe so Spurs knew Oxford would be fighting hard for points today plus they had Ray Houghton and Dean Saunders who were both in excellent form regardless of their team's league position.

Line up v Oxford United: Clemence; Hughton, Gough, Mabbutt, M Thomas; Waddle, P Allen, Ardiles, Hoddle, Hodge; C Allen. Sub: Claesen.

It was a bubbly atmosphere at the Lane despite the last two league disappointments. Like most games since the turn of the year, Spurs started the game in swift fashion with slick passing, good running and a touch of class about their approach play.

Waddle looked in delicious form from the start. One attack, he ran the length of the pitch, passing players, dropping his shoulder before flying in a lovely cross for Clive to nearly put Spurs in the lead.

It didn't take long after that for the scoring to begin, when after ten minutes Waddle headed Spurs in front. Yes, a Waddle header.

Hoddle launched a ball forward to Clive Allen and the ball scrambled to Steve Hodge. Hodge burst forward and lofted in a cross to the far post and from nowhere Waddle sprinted in and headed below Oxford keeper Peter Hucker.

One nil to Spurs and quality football indeed. This was Hodge's seventh assist in a Spurs shirt since his December move from Villa. Along with his three league goals and his goals/assist in the FA Cup, Hodge's transfer was looking like a superb piece of business.

Four minutes later Spurs scored again, this time it wasn't Clive Allen but Paul. Clive was the provider though. Dean Saunders was expertly tackled by Gary Mabbutt and the ball found its way to Ardiles. Speedy one touch football from Ardiles to Hoddle to Paul Allen then saw Clive being released on the right side of his central role. He took on a defender and slung in a low cross where Paul, who had not stopped running, side footed home for a goal that his first fifteen minutes clearly deserved.

This was stunning football and Oxford couldn't cope, but Spurs being Spurs gave Oxford a lifeline.

Six minutes later Oxford scored when Clem fluffed his attempted catch from a corner and the ball fell at the feat of Dean Saunders who scrambled the ball home.

Several minutes later Hoddle was running with the ball towards the Oxford goal and when 25 yards out he saw keeper Hucker off his line. With his right foot, Glenn delightfully chipped the ball, and it seems like it's hanging in the air for ages before it clatters the crossbar and out for a goal kick. The crowd applaud this genius of a footballer, he makes it all look so easy.

2-1 at half time and such an entertaining game with Spurs deserving their lead.

Early in the second half, Clive Allen nearly scores from a free kick. Everyone is waiting for Hoddle or Waddle to strike the ball and Clive drives it hard only to see Hucker tip his effort over the bar.

Spurs were flying forward from all angles and Gough nearly scored from a flying header when he connected with Chris Hughton's cross but straight into Hucker's hands.

Hucker threw the ball out immediately to start an Oxford attack, but Waddle came out of nowhere again and this time intercepted the ball from a defensive position. He played a one-two with Hoddle and then it was Waddle's turn to rattle the crossbar. He did exactly the same thing Glenn did in the first half, by chipping Hucker from distance only to see it hit the crossbar and go out for a goal kick. Clive Allen attempted to follow up the rebound but ended up hanging on the crossbar to avoid falling on Hucker.

This was entertainment, this was champagne football and Hucker was indeed a busy bee in the Oxford goal.

The buzz and murmur in the crowd was palpable. Even to this day, you can watch highlights of that game and feel the crowd excitement at this display of attacking brilliance.

Several minutes later, Clive Allen fluffed a good opportunity whilst he was one-on-one with Hucker and then down the other end a minute later, Clemence makes an unbelievable save to deny Billy Whitehurst. Whitehurst volleys the ball and it's heading into the top left-hand corner. However, Clem leaps in a cat-like state and acrobatically tips the ball over the bar! The guy is in his late 30's, what a world class save that was.

This game had it all, such good entertainment but the drama and quality was still not over.

In the final minute of the game, Spurs were still 2-1 up. Oxford right back, Dave Langan, has the ball in an advanced position as he looks to cross into Billy Whitehurst. Gough leaps like a salmon and heads the ball away brilliantly and it lands to Hoddle in the middle of the Spurs half, the counter is on.

Hoddle runs with the ball as he enters the Oxford half. Three defenders approach him and Clive runs to his left off the ball, Hoddle then splits the defence with his own pass and runs toward goal. He still has 35 yards to go as the crowd's excitement generates. Hucker runs out to the edge of his area to confront Hoddle and with a shimmy of his body, Hoddle sends Hucker the wrong way as the visiting keepers falls flat on his butt for Hoddle to dance through and side foot home.

The crowd applaud at the sheer genius they have just witnessed as Glenn kisses his fingers and then salutes his Spurs faithful. You can see he wanted that just for the fans.

Commentating legend Brian Moore's words described Hoddle's superlative goal perfectly, Moore said, "A superb goal by Hoddle, he salutes the crowd, he gets applause from his manager and the bench and from the Tottenham fans as well. A moment of true mastery".

The final whistle went a minute later, players shook each other's hands and Glenn turned to his crowd and clapped.

Result: Tottenham Hotspur 3-1 Oxford United (Waddle, P Allen, Hoddle)

This turned out to be Hoddle's last goal at White Hart Lane. A superb moment for the 20,000 fans that managed to get to the game and a goal that I and most fans will never forget.

Leaving the ground, I remember dad telling me to savour that moment. It was a bit like when he told me to savour the moment of beating Arsenal 5-0 back in 1983, scenarios like that do not happen often.

For the record, I did try to get in contact with Peter Hucker to see if he'd be happy to talk about this moment. I heard nothing back.

Clive Allen recalls Glenn's final goal at the Lane too, "He sat Hucker down. Obviously, Peter Hucker was a former teammate of mine at QPR but that was a perfect send off for Glenn. That goal highlighted everything about his elegance, quality and you know, he made it look so simple. That was Glenn at his best".

In *The Sunday Times*, Brian Glanville headlined with, 'HODDLE WITH A MASTER TOUCH'. He wrote, "In the end, it was a game that one will remember for Glenn Hoddle's sublime, last minute goal. Speed of foot, rather than thought, has never been his forte, but it was through sheer anticipation and intelligence that he beat the offside trap to then go on and score".

Glanville did conclude with an excellent point though. Mabbutt was brilliant and had been brilliant all season, Glanville wanted to see Mabbutt and Tony Adams be the England central defensive partnership in Wednesday's Euro qualifier in Turkey rather than see Terry Butcher in the team. No offence to Butcher, but Glanville did have a very good point there.

* * * *

Probably to Pleat's dismay, five Spurs players were chosen to start for England in the Euro'88 qualifier in Turkey. Mabbutt was chosen to partner Tony Adams and Hodge, Waddle and Hoddle all joined Bryan Robson in midfield.

For scoring nearly fifty goals this season, Clive Allen was given a starting role alongside Gary Lineker. The game finished 0-0, which kept England top of qualifying group 4, but still no international goal for Clive.

Clive did get the ball in the back of the net though. In the second half, Chris Waddle floated a lovely cross into Allen who chest the ball down and volleyed home. Only to find out the offside flag had been raised as Gary Lineker was stood in an offside position. Grrrr, thanks Gary.

The match did finish with zero injuries, Pleat sighed with relief no doubt.

MAY 1987

Saturday 2nd May 1987 – City Ground, Nottingham
(Att: 19,837)
Nottingham Forest v Tottenham Hotspur
(TODAY League Division 1)

A trip to Forest was never easy and despite Forest drifting away from their excellent early season form they were still in eighth place but only had one win in their last six league games and seem them drop off.

With the FA Cup Final getting ever closer, players were probably thinking about their final place and wanted to avoid injury. These next four league games in nine days were going to be a tough ask on the already fatigued players.

Pleat decided to rest Hoddle, Mabbutt and Clive Allen. Ruddock, Galvin and Ardiles returned to the team and making his senior debut for the club was young midfielder, Vinny Samways.

Pleat had to consider Spurs' next game, in 48 hours, when Spurs would face Manchester United on Bank Holiday Monday, juggling his players had been the biggest part of his job in the last few weeks and it would continue until the FA Cup Final.

Brian Clough still had plenty of quality in his team in the likes of Des Walker, Stuart Pearce, Neil Webb, Johnny Metgod and his son, Nigel Clough. Spurs would need to be wary.

This game would also throw up an unusual focus in the match-up between Stuart Pearce and Mitchell Thomas. England's left-back was Arsenal's Kenny Sansom. Sansom was about to undergo surgery on a troublesome hernia so Thomas and Pearce, who had both been included in squads before, were auditioning for the part.

Line up v Nottingham Forest: Clemence; Hughton, Gough, Ruddock, M Thomas; Waddle, P Allen, Ardiles, Hodge, Galvin; Claesen. Sub: Samways.

In white shirts and navy shorts, Spurs were on the back foot from beginning to end. Clemence was forced into some good early saves, and it seemed that Pleat's men were second best to everything.

In the first half alone, Forest had around 6-7 good chances, but Spurs registered next to nothing going forward.

On 64 minutes, a Forest corner was delivered into the heart of the Spurs area only to see Steve Chettle jump, relatively unchallenged, to head the ball past a helpless Clemence. Paul

Allen was tracking Chettle but that was a mismatch considering Paul's 5ft 7inches was way off Chettle's 6ft 1inch frame. The Spurs players stood frozen, looking at each other while Richard Gough threw his arms up in despair.

Spurs were being opened up at all angles. Nigel Clough had two very good efforts go wide and Stuart Pearce seemed to be running amok down Forest's left side.

The game was finally up with 15 minutes to go. A free-kick five yards outside the Spurs box was being lined up by Forest's Dutch midfielder, Johnny Metgod. Now considering Metgod as best known for his absolute rocket of a free-kick the year before, it was amazing to see how he stroked this set-piece over the Spurs wall and into the top right-hand corner of Clem's goal for the home team's second goal.

Clem had no chance again; Spurs' heads went down, and they trudged off to try and regroup.

Vinny Samways came on in the second half and Vinny has since evolved into one of the great players for the club. Little did he know that he was replacing another club great when he came on for Galvin. This would be Galvin's last appearance for Spurs.

However, this was Vinny's debut, and he remembers, "The City ground was always one of my favourite grounds, growing up watching football and now being around the legend Brian Clough was brilliant for me. I was expecting to travel with the first team for the experience as they usually take a couple more players who won't even get on the bench just in case. Not expecting to be named on the bench and then getting on the bench was an amazing feeling".

Vinny continued, "All my family are Tottenham supporters and here I am, I am actually making my debut for a team I grew up supporting was it was a dream come true".

The game ended with Spurs losing 2-0. The result was disappointing, but Samways was overjoyed with his debut.

Result: Nottingham Forest 2-0 Tottenham Hotspur

Spurs were so lifeless up front, Claesen got nothing at all out of Chris Fairclough and Steve Chettle. Even the Forest full backs were playing like wingers today. Des Walker filled in at right-back and he was never known for his forward play at all, he was adventurous going forward and that shows how dominant Forest were.

Worst of all, this was the first game in 38 consecutive league and cup matches where Spurs did not score. The last time was the 2-0 loss at Loftus Road in October. Spurs had scored 83 goals during that time, but nothing at all today.

Despite the loss, club physio John Sheridan has fond memories of this game, he said, "I remember going on the field to collect the tracksuits just before the start of play and I got a big hug from behind. I didn't know who it was until I heard Cloughie's voice. He told me he was so pleased that I had got to Wembley and wished me luck. He used my name; I couldn't believe he knew my name. He really was a lovely man".

On the Thomas-Pearce left-back match up, it was Pearce who came out on top. Defensively solid and going forward he gave Chris Hughton a massive headache. On the other side, Mitchell was nowhere near the performance to be considered as England's left back.

This was Spurs 53rd game of the season and it was Forest's 47th. Spurs had also thrown in the Hamburg, Bermuda and Linfield mid-season friendlies too, plus having three-quarters of his starting eleven playing international football too it was closer to a sixty-game plus season already for most of Pleat's men. Hard work indeed, but it's not done yet.

Monday 4th May 1987 – White Hart Lane, London
(Att: 36,692)
Tottenham Hotspur v Manchester United
(TODAY League Division 1)

Spurs barely had time to lick their wounds from the Forest defeat when they were back at White Hart Lane for the final home match of the season.

Manchester United were the visitors and manager Alex Ferguson had steered United to mid-table after he had taken over from Ron Atkinson last Autumn when United were languishing near the relegation zone.

Ferguson would go on to become one of the greatest British Club managers of all time but today he would find it a difficult experience against Pleat's side. Where David Pleat lost at the hands of Brian Clough, he would have been determined to put things right today against another talented peer in Ferguson.

Pleat brought back his big guns in Mabbutt, Hoddle and Clive Allen. Spurs were hoping to consolidate third place and hopefully push for runners up spot. They were five points behind Liverpool and this was their game in hand.

David Pleat's matchday notes were filled with emotion and great memories as he recalled how the season had panned out since that brilliant opening day win at Villa Park. He highlighted the squad's excellence by pointing out the large number of international players he had in his ranks. He reserved a special mention for former international greats, Ray Clemence and Ossie Ardiles.

Spurs' aged duo had been brilliant this season, an Indian summer in their career as they had both performed consistently well and had been world class on many occasions.

He welcomed Ferguson and his team and stated that United always promised entertainment.

Today, it would be Spurs who were the entertainers. Just like the last home game when champagne football prevailed as Pleat's men played some sublime attacking football. On this day a footballing lesson would be taught one of the greatest managers of all time.

Strap in people, grab the popcorn and enjoy the show.

Line up v Manchester United: Clemence; Hughton, Gough, Mabbutt, M Thomas; Waddle, P Allen, Ardiles, Hoddle, Hodge; C Allen. Sub: Claesen.

You got the feeling that today's eleven would be Pleat's chosen FA Cup final line-up. Hughton was preferred to Gary Stevens at right back and all other positions seemed locked down.

On a wonderfully sunny bank holiday Monday, this performance probably made Pleat realise that this was his starting eleven of choice.

The games started at a quick pace for both teams. United had some outstanding talent on show in Bryan Robson, Gordon Strachan, Paul McGrath, Jesper Olson and Norman Whiteside and it was Whiteside that had two early efforts. One a close-range header and the second a 25-yard shot, which resulted in Clemence making two superb saves.

But it was Spurs who began to dominate proceedings midway through the first half.

Paul Allen struck the ball into the side netting having been put through brilliantly by Chris Hughton, but it was Hughton's full-back colleague, Mitchell Thomas who'd be the unlikely star of today's performance.

Over 36,000 fans had come to see Hoddle's final home appearance at the Lane. But it was Thomas who stole the show. On 30 minutes, Hoddle started a move that covered the field from left to right, the ball fell to Waddle who cut inside and hit a 25-yard shot which found its way to Thomas. Thomas had crept in around the United defence to control the ball and then fire home past United keeper Gary Walsh.

Thomas was delighted and ran off to celebrate with Steve Hodge. That was his third league goal of the season and 1-0 to Spurs.

Half-time came and Spurs were well worth their lead. The second half would go on to show why Spurs were title contenders for so long as well as the most entertaining team to watch this season in English football.

Two minutes into the second half, it was the unlikely ball winners of Hoddle and Waddle who combined well to pressure Paul McGrath in giving the ball away. Waddle immediately darted a superb cross-field pass to Hodge who then sped past his marker and burst into the box only to be pushed in the back by United defender John Sivebek and win the penalty.

Penalty to Spurs and up step Clive Allen. Clive sent the keeper the wrong way and took his amazing season goal tally to forty-eight goals.

A few minutes later Spurs were on the charge again. Hughton bombarding forward saw his pass find Clive Allen on the edge of the United area, he struck the ball first time and keeper Walsh managed to palm it away. Hoddle retrieved the ball several yards away and with an unbelievable piece of Zidane-esque skill he turned Sivebek inside out and chipped the ball delicately over

Gary Walsh only to see Paul McGrath head his effort off the line. Audacious flair from Hoddle and unlucky not to get a goal.

United's defending was panicky to say the least. They were struggling to hold this attacking juggernaut and, on the hour, they nearly caved in again.

In the midfield battle, Hoddle and Hodge carved out a pass to Clive Allen who sprayed the ball brilliantly wide to Chris Waddle. Waddle took the ball lazily, but you knew he was milliseconds away from bursting into life. With a drop of the shoulder United were di-orientated as Waddle played a superb reverse pass to Paul Allen who had burst into the right side of the Untied box. Paul's cheeky cross bypassed everyone in the middle and found Mitchell Thomas all alone at the far post. Thomas took one touch and struck the ball, surely it was 3-0 but Thomas hit the post! A glaring miss, Mitchell had his head in his hands.

Three minutes later though, Mitchell made amends.

Gough to Ardiles, Ardiles to Hoddle, Hoddle to Hodge and Hodge on to Waddle on the halfway line. Waddle had given the United left back, Colin Gibson, and absolutely torrid time already and he was about to do the same again.

Waddle set off at an electric pace, Gibson did well to keep up and when he thought he'd tackle Waddle, the Spurs winger cut back and left Gibson on his butt. Waddle looked up and floated a lovely cross to Clive Allen. Clive was beaten in the air by McGrath and the ball looped up high. The ball came down and no one had retrieved the bouncy second ball when out of nowhere, with his back to goal, Mitchell Thomas's bicycle kick connected with the ball, and it flew past Gary Walsh in the United goal. 3-0 to Spurs, a brace for Mitchell and what an amazing goal from the Spurs left back.

Bizarrely, minutes before he had hit the post, he was close to scoring a hat-trick today!

Tottenham were coasting, United were punch drunk. The fun did not stop there though.

Nine minutes later, Mitchell was like a man possessed. Clemence rolled the ball out to Thomas and with a drop of the shoulder here and swooping past a United midfielder there, Thomas had travelled nearly half the length of the pitch before threading through a fantastic pass to Clive Allen who raced clear. Allen tried to go around the United keeper only to see a fingertip save fall into the path of a Spurs midfielder who had raced the length of the pitch to support Clive. Yes, it was Paul Allen. Paul took one touch on to his left foot and stroked the ball home for Spurs' fourth of the game.

What an effort from Paul Allen, that moment summed up his excellent season so far.

Result: Tottenham Hotspur 4-0 Manchester United (M Thomas 2, C Allen, P Allen)

Paul Allen had another great game. I asked Paul if he remembered Mitchell's goals against United and Paul laughs,

"Yeah, I do remember that. You know Mitchell was a good athlete. I remember him scoring against Arsenal too, he got box-to-box and would be up and down that left side. Even though we had five men in midfield, Mitchell would often bypass them all and get into the oppositions 18-yard box when the ball was on our right-hand side. He was a really good acquisition and fitted really well in that team and formation".

This was Glenn's final appearance, but it was Chris Waddle who was his creative best and he overshadowed Hoddle's effort. Waddle was on such good form, it was hard to see anyone who could cope with him.

In Waddle's autobiography he mentioned giving Gus Caesar the run-around in the League Cup semi-final at Highbury, I felt the way he humiliated Colin Gibson today was ten times more powerful than what he put Caesar through. He was a model of pace, power, class, creativity, desire and energy.

In *The Independent*, Joe Lovejoy's report agreed. He wrote, "Hoddle had no more than a supporting role on his farewell performance at White Hart Lane as Spurs romped to a convincing win that left Alex Ferguson red-faced with anger and embarrassment".

Ferguson said, "I hope the players feel as embarrassed as I am.". Spurs had completely out played United and Ferguson continued waxing lyrical over Waddle, "We just couldn't handle him. He was magnificent".

* * * *

The bank holiday Monday was a great footballing day for Spurs and their supporters, but any slim or mathematical chance of winning the league disappeared with results elsewhere.

Liverpool had won 1-0 at home to Watford which ultimately assured runners up spot for the departing league champions. It was their Merseyside rivals that claimed the league championship with Everton beating Norwich 1-0 at Carrow Road.

Just like Mitchell Thomas was an unexpected goal-scoring hero for Spurs, Everton's winning goal was scored by and unexpected hero of their own, defender Pat Van Den Hauwe.

In time, Pat Van Den Hauwe would join Spurs and become a cult-hero during Terry Venables' tenure at White Hart Lane. Via a few intermediaries, I had the absolute pleasure of talking with Pat to ask his memories of that goal and winning the league with Everton that year.

He said, "Losing to Liverpool the year before was heart-breaking for us but we felt confident this season and it was tight among Spurs, Arsenal and Liverpool for most of the season. We knew success at Norwich would win it for us, it was a very hard game and Norwich were not a bad side at all".

Everton scored their only goal, and the winning goal after only 55 seconds into the game. It was Van Den Hauwe who came up for an early corner and ended up smashing the ball into the roof of the net and past Bryan Gunn.

Pat laughs, "Well, it was great for me as I don't usually score do I? I remember running away, celebrating, and then thinking it's so early in the game and we have a long way to go. After that I thought, the game was on again, it's another war! It was very tight, and it was back against the walls for most of the game, but what a relief at the end".

Van Den Hauwe praised the quality of his teammates that season and, although his playing time diminished in his final seasons at Everton before moving to Spurs in 1989, he felt that season they fully deserved their title success.

Pat did remember he felt lucky to miss the game against Spurs at White Hart Lane in September when Spurs won 2-0 and Waddle was on fire. He said, "Waddle was brilliant. What an exceptional player he was. Bloody hell! You know, you had your work cut out when you're up against him. His pace and dribbling were world class. It was a shame he moved from Spurs just before I joined and Lineker came in too".

With Everton as League Champions, Arsenal winning the League Cup, it felt the time was right for Spurs to end their great season with an FA Cup victory.

* * * *

Saturday 9th May 1987 – Vicarage Road, London
(Att: 20,024)
Watford v Tottenham Hotspur
(TODAY League Division 1)

With the final now a week away, Spurs had to contend with two league games away from home.

Watford were in tenth position with Falco, Blissett and Barnes all playing well and scoring goals. They'd be keen to gain some revenge for losing to Spurs in the FA Cup semi-final last month.

Pleat had no major injury concerns apart from Galvin. Pleat brought Stevens in to replace Hughton but other than that, it was the same team who embarrassed Manchester United 48 hours before.

This was Watford's last league game of the season, and they were hoping to go out with a win. It was also a celebration for John Barnes. Barnes had been brilliant during his time at Watford, his contract was about to expire and like Hoddle he announced he was off to pastures new. In time he would head north in a deal that took him to Liverpool.

As mentioned earlier, during my conversations with David Pleat, he was happy to dispute some of the claims made by Irving Scholar in his book, about Pleat declining to sign David Rocastle, Ian Wright and Andy Gray. However, Pleat did admit he had opportunity to sign John Barnes though.

Pleat said, "There was an opportunity to sign John Barnes yes. His agent at the time, Athole Still, offered Barnes to us. But I decided not to pursue it as we already had Waddle and it would be hard to facilitate Barnes too".

Possibly the wrong decision with Hoddle leaving but Barnes went on to be outstandingly good for Liverpool, but Pleat did have a point. Waddle had been outstanding and was hitting peak age of his career too so it would have been a tough call.

Yet with Spurs playing five in midfield, and Hoddle about the leave, Barnes, Waddle and Hodge could all play wide and centrally so arguably Pleat could've found a way to work it. But we will never know.

That revelation aside, Watford knew they were underdogs in this fixture but would have been silly not to realise that Spurs players may be pre-occupied with next weeks' Wembley appearance.

Line up v Watford: Clemence; Stevens, Gough, Mabbutt, M Thomas; Waddle, P Allen, Ardiles, Hoddle, Hodge; C Allen. Sub: Claesen.

Vicarage Road was baked in sunshine as Spurs began their 55th league and cup game of the season wearing white shirts and white shorts.

After the brilliant performance in the Oxford league game, Spurs followed it up with a tired showing at Forest. After the brilliance of the United performance two days ago, Spurs followed it up with another tired showing at Vicarage Road.

Watford were in control for most of the game, Spurs offered little, in fact, next to nothing.

The game was won by a single goal in the 57th minute and that goal was scored by Watford skipper, Kenny Jackett. Jacket converted a penalty won by departing Barnes. Barnes had scampered through into the Spurs box, only to be brought down by Ardiles.

The only other notable event in this game is an image of Richard Gough playing out the remainder of the game with a huge rip down the front of his shirt after a tussle with Falco. It looked like the plunging neckline of all plunging necklines, but Gough battled to the end despite his ripped attire.

Result: Watford 1-0 Tottenham Hotspur

Spurs didn't even deserve a point and the football correspondents reporting on the game tended to agree.

In *The Daily Mail*, reporter Alex Bannister wrote about Watford's fully deserved win but followed it with Pleat's views on their final league game against Everton in two days' time and so close to the Cup Final.

Pleat said, "It's not our fault that the Everton match has been re-arranged through congestion of fixtures. Everton are already champions, and we are third so nothing rests on the result".

At the time, the Football Association took a dim view on any team fielding a 'weakened' side. Spurs had been fined £7,500 after fielding a weakened side against Southampton days before the 1984 UEFA Cup Final.

Pleat followed it up with facts about the large number of quality footballers he had in the club away from the first team. He said, "Our reserves only need one point to win the Combination League and they may get an early reward. I just want to get 11 bright players to Everton".

It was Pleat's veiled statement that he was probably going to field a batch of reserves in the final league game to preserve the energy and fitness levels of the players he wanted to play at Wembley next week. Nothing wrong in that I say, but the FA would suggest otherwise.

Monday 11th May 1987 – Vicarage Road, London
(Att: 28,287)
Everton v Tottenham Hotspur
(TODAY League Division 1)

A Monday evening game at Goodison Park saw Pleat travel with many Spurs reserve team players. Everton were champions and they'd surely not have an issue with whatever team Spurs put out or would they.

As predicted, Pleat did rest his star names and fielded a team that was completely different to the one that would start at Wembley. Ten of the names Pleat would be expected to choose to start against Coventry were quite obvious, but one role was up for grabs - right-back.

Danny Thomas had made the no.2 shirt his own before his tragic injury fifteen games ago, but Stevens and Hughton were alternating in that role since Danny's injury. Amazingly, they had both appeared an equal seven times in that role over those fifteen games, with John Polston being the other.

Both Hughton and Stevens would start this evening along with Nico, and they were the only first team regulars.

The team included four league debutants. Firstly, defender Mark Stimson had racked up over 20 appearances in the reserves this season and slotted in at left-back. He was joined by the creative midfielder, John Moncur. Moncur would stay at Spurs for a few seasons before having successful spells at Swindon Town and West Ham.

Phillip Gray featured in an advanced midfield role too, Gray would also stay at Spurs for a few more seasons and even went on to represent Northern Ireland at international level.

The final debutant was Sparrow. As David Howells had earlier mentioned, Paul Moran's nickname was Sparrow due to this tiny, skinny legs. We knew him as a winger who probably had more pace than creativity, but he too was another success in this seasons' all conquering reserve team.

Stimson would go on to have success at Newcastle United and Portsmouth but the other three were also part of Venables squad in the 1990-91 season where Spurs went on to lift the FA Cup.

Tonight they lined up alongside Neil Ruddock, John Polston and Vinny Samways who had already featured in the first team this season.

And finally, Tony Parks came in to replace Clem. This was Parks' second start of the season after his brilliant clean sheet at Stamford Bridge in December.

Line up v Everton: Parks; Hughton, Polston, Ruddock, Stimson; Moran, Moncur, Stevens, Samways, Gray; Claesen. Sub: Close.

Having won the league, it was a bit of a party atmosphere for Everton and their fans. A game that offered little drama or excitement but for most of it Everton were in control. Not surprising really considering they had the likes of Neville Southall, Gary Stevens, Kevin Ratcliffe, Dave Watson, Van Den Hauwe, Peter Reid and Graeme Sharp all playing. Everton A v Tottenham Hotspur B it seemed.

In truth, the Spurs youngsters played well. Marshalled excellently by Gary Stevens in the middle of midfield, the young stars really held their own against the Division 1 champions.

Goalless at half-time was a successful opening and they managed to hold on until ten minutes from time when Everton sub, Derek Mountfield, came on to score the winning goal. The goal came from a long Gary Stevens throw (the Everton one) and Sharp leapt above Stimson to head the ball on and Mountfield nipped in just before Polston and Parks to scramble in the winner.

Result: Everton 1-0 Tottenham Hotspur

It was Spurs second consecutive 1-0 defeat and it finally concluded their league programme.

This game was remembered well by Vinny Samways, "This was a few days before the Cup Final. I remember it well as it was my full debut, and we were playing a colossal team in Everton who were now champions. It was lovely feeling as I came through the youth system with players like John Moncur, Phil Gray and Paul

Moran. We'd grown up together and even though we'd trained often with the first team it was an amazing feeling that night".

One player who was disappointed that evening was Gary Stevens, "I knew as soon as I was selected for this game I probably wouldn't be starting in the final. I had to back myself though, I'd played and scored in an FA Cup Final for Brighton against United. I'd played in the UEFA Cup Final against Anderlecht and had the balls to take a penalty too, so I truly believe big games were not a problem for me".

Stevens would still need to wait until Saturday to find out, but as Chris Hughton played too, he might have been feeling the same as Stevens did.

Another player overjoyed after this game was Everton defender Derek Mountfield. Mountfield told me, "I had quite a while out with a leg injury, and I remember Tony Parks played really well that night". He laughed, "Coming on for Adrian Heath and scoring the winning goal was not a common thing for me. But even though we had won the league at Norwich, we still wanted to win this game too, it's essential to keep that winning mentality".

In *The Daily Telegraph*, Dennis Lowe's headline did not talk about the brilliance of a victory for the new league champions or even the fact that a promising, young Spurs team played well. Sadly, it was, 'SPURS FACE INQUIRY OVER WEAK LINE-UP', Pleat had to come out fighting on this one.

Pleat told Lowe, "This was our strongest available side – we have played eight games in 22 days, and I have been protecting the

England players for the last six weeks". Pleat had claimed that injuries to key players were a factor in deploying this team and he confirmed he had notified that fact to the Football League.

A Football League spokesman, told Lowe; "We received a Telex from Tottenham stating that eight players were injured and three were being rested. There will obviously be an inquiry and the management committee will discuss the matter when they meet on May 20th".

Tottenham would end up being fined £10,000 for fielding a weakened team. Pleat recalls that scenario, "I took a team up to Everton. I liked Howard Kendall, but Everton were my nemesis, especially in cup games while I was at Luton Town. I was very popular with the Everton board, probably because they always beat me, but I liked Everton, they were an upstanding club".

Pleat continued, "I remember taking a batch of youngsters with us like Polston, Samways, Moran and they beat us 1-0, days before the Cup Final mind you. They got a full house, league champions and they complained to the FA that we had defrauded the public by not taking our first team there, bear in mind they won the game".

A few weeks later, Spurs were called by the FA to face a disciplinary committee, and this provided a chance to plead their case.

Pleat attended the hearing and said, "We went to a tribunal at the Great Western Hotel in Paddington. I went with one of our Directors, Douglas Alexiou. Peter Swales was leading the FA

Disciplinary Committee and they decided to fine us £10,000 for not fielding our strongest team. It wasn't as though we had won the game 1-0. On appeal, we did get it down to £5,000 but it was unbelievable".

* * * *

The league campaign had now concluded. Spurs had finished in third place. This was a position which was a huge improvement on the previous season. However, considering some of the breath-taking football that had been played, some of the players which had been brought in and some wonderful results, Pleat and his team were left wondering what could have been.

TODAY League Division 1 – Final Table – Top Six

		Pl.	W	D	L	GF	GA	GD	Pts
1	Everton	42	26	8	8	76	31	+45	86
2	Liverpool	42	23	8	11	72	42	+30	77
3	Spurs	42	21	8	13	68	43	+25	71
4	Arsenal	42	20	10	12	58	35	+23	70
5	Norwich	42	17	17	8	53	51	+2	68
6	Wimbledon	42	19	9	14	57	50	+7	66

If Spurs had gained some positive results in the recent losses to West Ham, Forest, Watford and Everton then runners up would have been fully deserved. For me, the league challenge fell away in the final week of March when Spurs drew at Newcastle and then three days later, losing at Kenilworth Road. The Luton loss made it very hard despite having some excellent results thereafter.

Arsenal had fallen away dramatically in the league; they were top in January but defensively the second half of their season was nowhere near as strong as the first half.

Norwich and Wimbledon were the season surprise packages though.

Bassett's Wimbledon had finished in the Top six in their first ever topflight season. Some may question elements of their footballing style and some of their psychological and physical tactics, but what a great season for the South London side.

Norwich on the other hand were a wonderful footballing team. They registered only eight defeats during the season, the same as champions Everton. Seventeen draws were quite a significant number of stalemates, if five of them had been converted into wins they'd be runners up. What a story that would have been.

Spurs record against the top six, including Luton in seventh as Spurs finished third, was 15 points from a possible 36. The two wins over Liverpool were superb but only one point against Arsenal, Wimbledon and Luton saw Spurs drop a possible 15 points from these teams.

Against the bottom six Spurs fared better by gaining 30 points from a possible 36. Doubles over Villa, Leicester, Charlton and Oxford were good. A win and a draw over Man City was not too bad, but the two draws against Newcastle were quite pivotal.

Three teams were relegated from Division 1. Leicester City, Manchester City and Aston Villa. A final day win for Charlton over QPR saw them leap above Leicester out of the relegation drop, but not safe entirely.

This season there was a new 'play-off' system introduced. Derby County and Portsmouth had finished in the automatic promotion places in Division 2 but the teams in 3rd, 4th and 5th would now compete in a play-off semi-final with Charlton Athletic.

Charlton could retain their first division status by winning this play-off process.

The second and third week of May saw Charlton beat Ipswich Town 2-1 over two legs. They would face FA Cup Semi-finalists, Leeds United, who beat Oldham Athletic over their two-legged contest.

Charlton now included ex Spurs players Garth Crooks and Paul Miller. Charlton beat Leeds 1-0 in the first leg and Leeds won 1-0 in the second leg. Charlton finally won this inaugural, epic encounter 2-1 after extra time in the replay to confirm their inclusion in Division 1 for the 1987-88 season.

In other news though, the day before Spurs' trip to Goodison Park the Italian league was stunned. Napoli had won their first ever Scudetto when they won Serie A by finishing three points ahead of last season's Serie A champions, Juventus.

Diego Maradona had done it again. Within the space of 12 months, he had secured Argentina's status as World Champions by winning in Mexico and had now steered Napoli to their first ever Serie A title. To go even one step further, Napoli went on to win the Coppa Italia a few weeks later to claim a stunning double. This guy was a force of nature.

Maradona also felt this was bigger than his Mexican triumph too, said, "I feel like a son of Naples, but we must now plan for the European Cup".

Spurs had faced AC Milan in the Camp Nou back in August. The Milan giants had finished in a disappointing fifth place and seven points behind Napoli, but they had recently announced a huge signing to boost their league chances next season. They had agreed to sign Ruud Gullitt from PSV Eindhoven for a huge fee of £5m and over the summer they would also capture Dutch striker Marco Van Basten from Ajax. These captures would prove decisive as next season AC Milan would go on to win Serie A, this time finishing 3 points ahead of Napoli.

Amazingly, Milan would win the title only conceding 14 goals in 30 league games. Franco Baresi, Alessandro Costacurta and Paolo Maldini would produce weekly masterclasses in the art of defending to secure their first title in nearly ten years.

The tournament in Barcelona last summer saw Pleat's men play Baresi's Milan and also Gullitt's PSV. PSV would become league champions this season in a fitting swansong for the Dutch national captain Gullitt before his AC Milan departure.

* * * *

It was a shame that English teams were banned from European football. The way that Everton, Liverpool and Spurs played would have been a delight to watch them among some of Europe's big hitters.

Ian Rush would now be heading off to Juventus and it would also be time soon for Glenn to be heading off on to the continent too. Reports were starting to flood in of various teams Hoddle might end up at. Most roads seemed to be heading towards France.

Two days before the FA Cup Final, Patrick Barclay reported on Hoddle's most likely destination in his *Independent* column. Paris St Germain (PSG) were the leading candidates and although Scholar had not admitted any negotiations were ongoing, the French newspaper *L'Equipe* reported that Scholar and PSG chairman had met, and a deal was imminent.

PSG had finished mid-table and were way off Champions Bordeaux's standards. Manager Gerard Houllier was now in his second season at the Parisian club and saw the Spurs playmaker as the perfect addition to his plans.

Hoddle would come close to joining PSG, but he would ultimately end up elsewhere in France. Houllier ended up signing Ray Wilkins from AC Milan but would see his team finish only a few places above the relegation zone in the 1987-88 season.

Barclay had spoken to Pleat during FA Cup week about the Hoddle speculation with various teams, Pleat told him, "It's the way the game is these days (speculation). I heard Terry Venables has got four different letters on his desk at Barcelona from four different agents all offering Hoddle – but each at a different price. At the end of the day, whoever wants him has got to deal with the club".

It is fair to say that this would be resolved in the days following the FA Cup Final but for now, let us immerse ourselves in cup final build-up.

* * * *

Take a deep breath and in your best cockney voice sing….

"Ray Clemence, Mitchell Thomas, Gary Stevens, Steve Hodge,
they're all gonna put on a show for you.
And don't forget Ossie – specially cos' he,
back in '81 he had his dream come true.
Nico Claesen, Hughton and Galvin,
don't forget Clive and Paul Allen too,
Richard Gough, Chrissy Waddle
Gary Mabbutt and Glenn Hoddle
And Danny all the goals are gonna be for you".

Well, they're *Hot-Shot Tottenham*, they are the Super Spurs, everybody knows we're the football connoisseurs.

Move over Lennon and McCartney and make way for Hodges and Peacock.

FA Cup Finals in the 1980's were a spectacle and part of that spectacle was the production of an FA Cup Final song. But the fact was, no-one could do an FA Cup Final song like Spurs.

Everton's 1985 effort was limp, and Brighton's 1983 offering was just as bland, but you could not produce the excellence of a Chas N Dave cup final production. The cockney music duo had superb success with *Ossie's Dream* in 1981 and *Tottenham Tottenham* in 1982, and this year they had produced another classic.

The single had been released in early May 1987 through Rainbow Records and Dave Peacock remembers when the lyrics were written, he said "Chas and I were on holiday together with our families on the Shetland Isles at the time of the semi-final victory against Watford. When we got the result, we wrote most of the song in the hotel bar that night. We'd noticed the 'David Pleat's Blue & White Army' chant from the shelf that season so wanted to incorporate that into the song. We also did an update of Ossie's Dream for the B Side which featured a solo vocal from Nico Claesen - which took about 100 takes to get right (he wasn't happy as all the other players were taking the p*ss out of him!)".

The song spent five weeks in the charts and peaked at no.18. The song would not appear on TOTP until a week after the FA Cup Final, but the first live performance was on the BBC1 TV show, Blue Peter.

Dave recalls that TV appearance, "For the most part, players get into the spirit of it. Especially the likes of Ossie and Gazza over the years, but other players not so much".

Chas and Dave were joined by sixteen members of the Spurs squad, even Chiedozie was back signing and clapping away. Blue

Peter presenter, Caron Keating, mentioned an eighteen-man squad, but Nico and Waddle were not there that day.

In the front row, and looking like he was having a ball, was Gary Stevens. Clapping furiously, a beaming face and body moving in time with the song. He remembers that day vividly.

Stevens said, "Truth is, when you end up as a footballer doing a cup final song on a kid's TV show, and if you are up there doing it half-hearted then you look stupid and you look more stupid than if you are actually trying to give it a go. So, I gave it a bit of a go! I had some media training before, and you had to apply enthusiasm. I still get a lot of people sending that clip to me but it's great fun in the lead up to a big game".

At the back of the group was captain Richard Gough. Now he doesn't look anywhere near as happy as Gary Stevens or even Paul and Clive Allen.

Gough joked, "I'm sure I wasn't singing; this wasn't my cup of tea to be honest. I was always told cup final songs were a disaster and we had to wear these shiny blue jumpers too. I've seen a clip and it didn't look great".

The Allen's were front and centre too, looking like they were enjoying the occasion, while Gough was deploying a strained smile.

Paul said, "I think it's a great bit of fun and it's kind of a distraction too away from the game itself. Taking in the context that it was in, I think that we all enjoyed it. It was a wonderful experience. It was a good atmosphere around the club and certainly within the dressing room as well, so we needed that".

Part of the group, at the back and next to Hoddle, was Danny Thomas. True to type, Danny was looking bright and enthusiastic and enjoying being part of the squad's fun despite his horrific knee injury.

Danny laughs while remembering his Blue Peter experience, "Yep, I was there. I remember that and it was still a good time you know. At the end of it, we expected to win that cup. We really did. We had a terrific bunch of players that should have been the culmination of a really good season for us. We had a lot of a fun and it's always good when you're preparing for a cup final. Despite not being able to play, it's my first. Gary Stevens had been there before preparing for a cup final, so we had spoken about it before and in a way, it was a nice bit of time off for the guys".

Danny was right, this was still during final preparations for the showpiece event at Wembley on the Saturday. Pleat had all his key players available, and training had gone well during the week despite the news and media spotlight at Cheshunt on a daily basis.

On the morning of the FA Cup Final, Colin Gibson's *Daily Telegraph* column detailed that Bayer Leverkusen had visited White Hart Lane to thrash out a deal for £1m to bring Hoddle to the Bundesliga next year. Transfer figures like that had apparently worried the likes of interested suitors such as PSG and even PSV Eindhoven.

It was Hoddle's final hurrah. He had 90 minutes left of a wonderful 15-year career at White Hart Lane. Make it special Glenn, make it special.

Saturday 16th May 1987 – Wembley Stadium, London
(Att: 98,000)
Coventry City v Tottenham Hotspur
(FA Cup Final)

The weather was glorious. I can remember heading off to Wembley feeling so excited and could not wait to experience seeing my beloved Spurs in action during the biggest footballing event of the season.

I didn't live that far from Wembley Stadium. Growing up around it did not necessarily lose the lustre of what a great arena it was. I did not live close enough that you could hear the crowds on Cup Final days but when Live Aid was performed in July 1985, we could hear the music in our garden. That evening, I have vivid memories of dusk falling and hearing Queen play '*We Will Rock You*' and '*We are the Champions*', maybe the wind was in the right direction as it sounded pretty clear. Queen more than anyone put in some iconic performances that day and I feel quite humbled that I got to experience it in my own little way.

I had a cousin who lived on Barn Hill in Wembley, so we parked there and walked for a while until we approached Wembley Park tube station. It was a sea of white and blue as both Spurs and Coventry both had similar colours.

There is a cup final buzz that differs from most games you attend. I always loved going to the first game of the season when there is so much hope and anticipation for the year ahead but today, it was the same feeling for one game and heightened with emotion and tension. This was last game of the season and a game that would be watched by millions around the world.

The build up to Cup Final's on television was always fantastic. Being at the game I didn't witness any of this but looking back on old BBC1 footage you can get a flavour of that apprehension as both teams are showcased accordingly.

The game would be broadcast live on BBC1 and ITV. Heavyweight commentators on both sides with John Motson weighing in for the BBC and Brian Moore opposing him for ITV. In our house, BBC would usually be our weapon of choice on Cup Final day.

Des Lynam was anchoring the BBC coverage. Now, if Motson and Moore are considered football broadcasting legends then Lynam must be one of the Dons. Lynam had such a unique way about his delivery. It was calm, assured, intelligent and sprinkled with a touch of cheeky comedy.

Lynam's introduction to BBC's coverage began with, "Of all the great events that Wembley plays host to, the FA Cup Final remains the most famous. Just short of 100,000 people will be here for the 106th final".

Lynam was right. 98,000 people would be in attendance with record gate receipts of just below £1.3m.

Spurs had a unique record going into this game. The club had appeared in seven FA Cup Finals and had won every time. Today was Coventry's first FA Cup Final appearance. During this game, records would be achieved and broken.

The players had been out on the Wembley turf having taken their coach rides up Wembley Way. Spurs had arrived a little late due to traffic, but no panic had set in.

Club physio John Sheridan will never forget this moment, he said, "It was brilliant, I can remember going up Wembley Way on the coach thinking I was dreaming. You know dreams come true because you don't get a feeling better than that. I always had a dream about running out at Wembley, that was a professional ambition of mine."

One person who remembers walking out on the Wembley pitch was Ray Clemence's son, Stephen. He was around nine years old at the time but has fond memories of going out on the pitch with his dad and teammates, he said, "I was a very lucky boy to be honest and I had never seen my dad play at Wembley as I was quite young throughout most of his career, and he had stopped playing for England a few years before too. Dad told me it might be the last time I play here so he wanted to get me on the pitch. I was friends with Ossie's sons, Freddie and Pablo, and there were a few other kids there too when they did the walkabout at 1.30pm. I saw the bus come in through Wembley tunnel and then my dad popping his head out and then I got pulled in and went on the pitch. It was such a lovely sunny day and I know my dad loved taking me out there and then shortly after that I can remember the game came around quickly".

BBC's Bob Wilson interviewed Ossie during that walkabout, and he had young Freddie holding his hand, Wilson asks Freddie if he wants to say anything. Dressed in a Spurs tracksuit he replies, "Hi mum!" Ossie smiled proudly at his son's cheeky response.

A young Clem is also caught on camera. Clemence senior is stooping down and speaking to Stephen as he points to a part of the stadium while his son listens intently and looks on keenly. Young Clem was wearing a cool Adidas outfit as he stuck close by his dad to then be greeted by Chris Waddle who comes over to see him. Stephen's face is a picture as he gazes up at Waddle.

The players were looking splendid in navy suits, white shirts, and navy ties. Brilliantly, Danny Thomas is also part of the walkaround too. There is a lovely moment when Coventry's Cyrille Regis comes over to Danny and shakes his hand, Danny looking so happy as one of football's most iconic players acknowledges him.

When interviewed on the pitch, both Gough and Stevens gave stock responses of hoping to enjoy the day and getting a good result for the fans.

Mabbutt also spoke to Bob Wilson and said, "Even though I have been here a few times before with England, but nothing compares with this". Even back then, FA Cup Finals had a grander feel than playing for England.

The players moved to the dressing rooms from their walk to start preparations. Wembley was packed and the kick off was still under an hour away.

The twin towers and the old stadium were intoxicating. Whenever I visit Wembley now, it just does not have that same gravitas.

When I was younger, me and some of my friends found a way of getting into Wembley during the evenings. We would sometimes head up there on Fridays while there was greyhound racing taking place in the stadium. We found a way of tweaking the mechanism of the turnstiles, allowing them to turn and we would creep in. Three quarters of the stadium was in darkness as most people were congregating around the dug-out areas where the betting totes would be for the racing. Several hundred people were there at most.

We would head up to the Olympic gallery on the far side and spend the evening drinking, having a laugh and, ahem, stuff. We would stay there for the evening, no one would ever see us, no one would ever come up and we were looking down on the greatest stadium in the world whilst having a good time.

At the time, living close to Wembley and doing things like that, I didn't really appreciate the power and wonder of that stadium.

I had similar experiences at Lords cricket ground too. The greatest cricket venue on earth, but that story is maybe for another time.

On this day, we were sat in the Spurs end around three or four blocks away from the dug-out area. Watching Pleat lead the team out was a great moment for any Spurs fan, and for Pleat it was one of the greatest moments of his career.

At 2.45pm, and just before the teams entered the fray, one of the most powerful and emotional moments of any FA Cup Final happens. *Abide with Me* is sung.

This 19th century hymn was written by Scottish Anglican, Henry Francis Lyte, and had been sung at FA Cup Finals since 1927. Wembley was enveloped with glorious sunshine as the crowd sings, it is a piece that tends to make your hairs stand on end as you await your team to enter the arena and compete for a trophy that has been a huge part of your youth and upbringing. Tears may well and a lump may form in your throat, but that emotional connection was always part of FA Cup Final day.

Little did most fans know, but Spurs would be wearing a different kit today. Hummel had produced a kit for this match that would then turn into 1987-88's strip. There would be an issue too.

The Spurs players trotted out wearing tracksuit tops so you couldn't see the shirt. The teams lined up to be introduced to the Duchess of Kent. *God Save the Queen* rang out before the guest of honour walked to begin shaking hands and saying the odd word to various players.

She seemed to stop and spend a bit more time speaking with Hoddle. Maybe she was keen to get the scoop on where he was heading next!

Line up v Coventry: Clemence; Hughton, Gough, Mabbutt, M Thomas; Waddle, P Allen, Ardiles, Hoddle, Hodge; C Allen. Sub: Stevens, Claesen.

As expected, Stevens and Claesen were on the bench. Coventry were not throwing up any shocks either. David Phillips would come in at right-back to replace Brian Burrows, but it was the usual suspects on both sides.

The players dispersed and battle was about to commence. Tracksuits started to be removed and, at the time, no-one really noticed anything odd.

It appeared however, that several of the Spurs players did not have *Holsten* written on their shirts. Some did, some didn't. John Sheridan started to notice as he gathered up the tracksuit tops but none of the TV commentators mentioned it at the time.

BBC1 commentator John Motson remembers the moment he realised several Spurs players kits were different. He said, "I had spotted five of them with sponsors but didn't really register. Brian Moore rang me the following morning to say he hadn't realised and thought he had made a big mistake in not noticing. He felt better when I told him I hadn't, but it was hard considering we were commentating so high up and far back".

However, nothing could be done about it now. Kick-off was here.

Spurs kicked off and they were defending the end where the Wembley tunnel was. As the whistle went, John Motson was poised and ready with his opening comment of, "The scene is colourful, the mood is optimistic, and the stage is set for the 106th FA Cup Final".

Within the opening exchanges it was obvious to see that Coventry had deployed Lloyd McGrath to man-mark Hoddle. So much so, it was a keen McGrath that fouled Hoddle after two minutes to see Spurs win the first free kick of the day.

Hoddle, Waddle and Ardiles stood over the ball on Spurs' right had side around twenty yards from the Coventry box. Hoddle floats the ball into Gough, but he is beaten in the air by Houchen. The ball loops up and Clive Allen shields the ball away from Trevor Peake only for Micky Gynn to swipe the ball away to the far side.

The ball lands at Waddle's feet on the right touchline, he approaches City left-back Greg Downs and shapes to cross it with his left foot but drops his shoulder and now onto his right, he curls in a lovely cross to find Clive Allen darting towards the near post and beating his marker to head Spurs in front with a brilliant glancing header.

Scenes of mayhem and euphoria ensue. What a move by Waddle, what a finish by Clive and what a start to this game. 1-0 to Spurs and two minutes gone.

FANTASTIC DISAPPOINTMENT

Three days before the FA Cup Final, Marco Van Basten played in one of his final games for Ajax. They beat Lokomotive Lipezig 1-0 in the final of the European Cup Winners Cup and the goal was scored by AC Milan's new striker.

However, I am not sure if Clive Allen was watching the game, but Van Baston's goal after 20 minutes and was a carbon copy of Allen's FA Cup Final goal at Wembley. A v'Ant Schip cross saw Van Basten get across his marker to head home at the near post. Waddle and Allen had just carried out the exact same move. Lovely stuff.

It is safe to say that adrenaline and excitement levels are sky high in me and the Spurs fans. I kind of wondered if this could be a rout! Surely, we can rip them apart with our skill and talent alone.

Spurs had faced these same Coventry players twice this season. A 1-0 win at home in November and a 4-3 loss away at the end of December. The December game was an absolute belter as it was Spurs' class versus Coventry's courage. It deserved to be a draw, but Coventry won it late with Regis powering Coventry home to gain three points.

That would be a key factor today. Coventry had played 54 games this season and most Spurs players had played 60 plus games and that extra fatigue on some of those Spurs players could play into Coventry's hands.

Clive had scored his 49th goal of the season. He was injured in the second minute of his last FA Cup Final appearance in 1982 while playing for QPR so this was completely different.

If it was supposed to unnerve Coventry it didn't really work. After nine minutes Coventry were level. Gough had been pulled out wide by Regis while Downs floated a ball into the Spurs area where Houchen rose to head the ball with Hughton.

Houchen flicked the ball on and with Mabbutt and Thomas both slightly out of position, Dave Bennett nipped in to round Clemence and score. Hodge had seen the run, but he was a touch too late. 1-1 and game on.

There were no real strong chances for Spurs after that and you could get a sense that Spurs seemed a bit leggy as the half went on. Regis and Houchen were starting to exert themselves too as Houchen came close with a long-range effort tipped away by Clemence.

Minutes later Coventry had the ball in the back of the net. It was a long throw from Coventry's right-hand side which saw Houchen beat Thomas in the air and head on to Regis who nodded the flick on past Clemence and beating Gough in the air. Relief for Spurs fans though, referee Neil Midgely had already whistled for a foul on Mitchell Thomas by Houchen. On replay, it looks ok to me, so Spurs were lucky there.

With five minutes to go to half-time, the sun had drifted behind the clouds and Spurs had won a free kick on their right-hand side and close to where Hoddle floated in for Allen's opener.

Hoddle curled the ball into the heart of the Coventry area to see Mabbutt beat Trevor Peake and scramble the ball home. 2-1 Spurs and not necessarily deserved.

For the neutral it was a great game so far. Spurs were playing some great football and Coventry were at their combative best and as half-time came it had been a great spectacle so far.

The second half began, and one thing was quite evident. Mitchell was being given a bit of a run-around by Bennett. Even going forward Mitchell was a bit lifeless, and he'd occasionally be dispossessed by Bennett himself. On the other side, Hughton was having a solid game, but every time Regis or Houchen were up against him, he would seem to struggle.

Gough and Mabbutt seemed to be having mixed fortunes with the Houchen/Regis dynamic too. They'd both win and lose some aerial duels and ultimately Spurs did not look hugely solid at the back.

Coventry were strong in near enough every tackle and Spurs' free flowing attacks started to diminish. Mitchell Thomas was lacking his usual dynamism and thrust plus some of his passing would often go astray. Ardiles was still busy and keeping things flowing but Clive was not getting too much service from Hoddle, Waddle, and Hodge.

On the hour, a frustrated Clive Allen started to come deeper more to collect the ball. He received the ball just inside the Coventry half and turned Peake well but Peake shut him down straight away and Allen somehow ended up on his back being held by Peake. It was an amusing moment, but this instance was a sign that Spurs' midfield was waning as Allen was coming so deep again.

The game really turned on 63 minutes. Coventry were to score one of the most iconic FA Cup Final goals of all time.

City keeper Steve Ogrizovic launched a long kick up-field. Regis edged out Mabbutt to mod the ball onto Houchen who was quicker to react than Gough. He played the ball wide right to Bennett.

Mitchell was quite a distance away from Bennett and as he tried to close him down, Bennett floated in a lovely cross to see Keith Houchen leaping in the air, ahead of Hughton, to head the ball past Clemence for Coventry's equaliser. It was a fantastic goal and Coventry were ecstatic.

Houchen will never forget this moment. He said, "When you get in the box, you're just trying to get on the end of a ball anyway you can. I could see it in plenty of time and I knew I was going to get there but once I did get there, I had to make sure I got it on target".

Houchen is humble man, he knows the goal was some time ago and he that was his job as far as he was concerned, he said: "Once that match had started it was like, lets go to work. When I scored, I have never celebrated like that before. I was more of a handshake and maybe a hug type of guy but this time I was off jumping over the boards. None of the guys kept up with me so some of lads came up to me during the game to congratulate me as they were conserving energy and not chasing me".

For the record. I genuinely loved chatting with Keith Houchen. I wanted to hate him, and I told him so, but we had a wonderful conversation and he was a great guy. I just wished he'd never scored that goal!

In the final stages of the game, Gary Mabbutt burst forward and was about to swan past Brian Kilcline, in the middle of Coventry's half, but the Coventry skipper took Mabbutt out completely. The ball had gone past Kilcline as he clattered into the Spurs man to see him propel into the air and his legs flailing like a windmill. It was an awful challenge. Mabbutt stayed down, so did Kilcline.

Mabbutt slowly rose but Kilcline stayed down. Not sure why, as Mabbutt was the one who got clattered quite badly. Kilcline took his time to get up and the referee wanted to speak with him. There was no red card, there was not even a yellow. Just a telling off. Kilcline turned and trotted off as he smirked at Chris Waddle.

Two years before Manchester United's Kevin Moran got sent off in the final for upending Everton's Peter Reid. This challenge was similar, yet obviously worse too.

Houchen does remember the Kilcline challenge and said, "That tackle, well it wasn't malicious but he completely mis-timed it. I remember seeing Mabbutt's legs flying in the air. Nowadays he'd be sent off for that".

Pleat is still perturbed by that challenge to this day and feels Kilcline should have been punished. Pleat also pointed out that Kilcline was later substituted, and his replacement would play a pivotal part in the next goal.

Clive Allen did have a good chance with two minutes to go when he shot low into Ogrizovic's legs but the 90 minutes were up and the game was poised at 2-2.

Graham Rodger had replaced Kilcline and Pleat brought on Gary Stevens to replace Ardiles., John Motson mentioned that 34-year-old Ardiles had done well to complete 90 minutes of such 'sustained pace' in this hugely entertaining match.

Both sides were clearly working hard. Gaps were starting to open and the box-to-box stuff that had been riveting viewers at home continued.

But six minutes into the first period of extra time the game changed once more. Coventry, always behind, were now about to take the lead.

Coventry sub, Rodger dispossessed Paul Allen inside his own half and then passed the ball out to Coventry's right wing. This time it wasn't Bennett out there but Lloyd McGrath. McGrath had finally left his man-marking job on Hoddle to receive the ball and steam forward. Thomas was playing catch up and was looking exhausted but as McGrath approached Spurs box he put in a cross heading towards Houchen.

FANTASTIC DISAPPOINTMENT

The ball deflected off Gary Mabbutt's outstretched leg and looped over a helpless ray Clemence who flung himself trying to stop the ball looping into the net.

Clem couldn't stop it and Coventry went berserk. Mabbutt slumped down in despair, he looked drained and his efforts to stop the cross has ended in such bad luck for the brilliant Spurs defender.

Pleat immediately brought on Nico Claesen for Chris Hughton. Stevens moved to right-back as Spurs would now attempt to pile forward in search of an equaliser.

The pace in the second period of extra time was still relentless and you couldn't fathom how the players were still standing.

Spurs created very little and Clem made an outstanding late save to keep Spurs in it.

Hoddle was trying to orchestrate a final assault with Claesen now playing up alongside Clive but it was not to be.

Referee Neil Midgely blew his whistle.

Players from both teams slumped to the ground. Spurs players broken and Coventry players delighted.

It had been one of the best FA Cup Finals of all time, a sentiment shared by commentator John Motson.

Motson told me, "It was a pleasure to commentate on that Cup Final. That ranks as possibly the best and was right up there with

Spurs beating Manchester City in 1981 and Wimbledon beating Liverpool the following year in 1988. 80's Cup Finals were very memorable".

Result: Coventry City 3-2 Tottenham Hotspur
(C Allen, Mabbutt)

Motson was not wrong at all. It was a brilliant game but an awful result for Spurs fans.

I cried at that game. It is the only time I have cried watching Tottenham Hotspur. I can remember my dad trying to comfort me with realisms of: 'It wasn't meant to be' and 'the best team on the day won' blah blah blah. For such a talented football team not to win something after a season of footballing brilliance, that's what I found hard to swallow.

Maybe that hardened me, as over the last 30-odd years I do not feel anywhere near the same when Spurs lose in finals. I feel more hurt now over the Coventry defeat than I do for the Champions League final loss to Liverpool in 2019.

This was the underdog story of all underdog stories and the newspapers delighted in Coventry's success.

Pleat, candid as always, told me, "On reflection, if I could go back to that final, I would have sat higher up in the first half to get a better view of the game. I'd get a better picture. The emotion of the game and being on the bench is so great that you are not seeing it as clearly as you'd like to see".

Pleat's reflections continued, "I didn't realise, until it was probably too late, but looking back at the ascendancy which Bennett had over Mitchell Thomas. I always had a thing that pace would go up against pace, I felt Mitchell respected him too much, he didn't nail him early in the game and he ended up putting too many crosses in, and as a consequence of that, Cyrille did very well against Richard Gough. Keith Houchen did too".

Pleat could also see the toll that the game and season had taken on Gough and Mabbutt who had both played nearly 60 games this season.

He said, "Regis had a bit of a run on him in that final and Gough was struggling in extra time. So was Mabbutt too with his diabetes. It was a tough game".

On Gough, Pleat said, "Richard was brilliant for us. But he had so much energy and sometimes he'd be like a wild card. I'd often try to get him to just sit. Like Mike England would do or even Paul Miller. Occasionally I'd say just defend, don't keep coming out and sometimes getting caught out of position, just defend".

Paul Allen still finds it difficult to pinpoint how that team lost a game they were more than capable of winning. He said, "You only enjoy days like that if you are on the winning team. We played well in periods of the game and had a great start, but we didn't play as well as Coventry, simple as that. We had such a good group of players, and it was a great team to be part of. I often wonder, if we won that, what could we have gone on to achieve. After a result like that, you feel so low and sad for yourself and sad for the fans. When you have a bad result during the season you can make amends in the next game. With an FA Cup loss that's it. You have the whole summer to stew over it and wonder how we've ended up with nothing".

John Sheridan mentions the feeling in the dressing room, "It was an awful atmosphere. Players were so low and drained. Clive Allen was laying on the floor looking completely shot".

The Spurs players still had to attend a post-match function. Chas n Dave were performing and Dave Peacock can still remember the bleak atmosphere. He said, "We did go the match, and it was obviously a big disappointment. Something wasn't right from the off when we noticed half the players didn't have the sponsors name on their shirts! But otherwise, we all thought we had the match won after Clive scored the early goal - unfortunately the players might've thought the same. We still had to play at the after-match party, and I remember Pleaty coming in in tears".

A thought though for Gary Mabbutt. Mabbsy had played in England's midfield that year and was possibly one of the best central defenders across the country.

Despite his brilliance he felt the pain of scoring an own goal during that defeat. Even the following day the team bizarrely had an open-top bus arranged.

Mabbutt spoke back in September 2020, on Mark Godfrey's excellent *What Happened to You* podcast, and mentioned that an open-top bus route victory parade was booked, the roads were closed and they had to make their way to Haringey town hall. A victory parade with nothing to be victorious about.

Richard Gough is open to say that this result still remains possibly the biggest disappointment of his career. Dave Bennett had a superb game and Richard felt his impact might be quite telling. "The morning of the game there was a newspaper article and Bennett said that every time he plays against Mitchell, he rips him to shreds, a good record against him. I told Mitchell, first time he gets the ball put him into row Z. When the game began, Mitchell stood off him and Bennett put in a great cross".

Gough continued and jokingly said, "That's when I knew it was going to be a long day".

The Spurs captain did concede that Coventry played better than Spurs on the day, he added, "I went on to win a lot of trophies, but that one hurt the most".

Gough also added, "I think if we'd have taken them to a reply then we would have won, I'm sure of that". And, on the subject of a 'replay'.

Whilst researching this book I was put in contact with a lifelong Spurs fan called Lee Hermitage. I had been told that Lee had acquired a ticket for the 1987 FA Cup Final replay. That's odd, I'm sure Coventry won on the day.

Speaking with Lee, he tells me that it was not long after the FA Cup Final defeat to Coventry and he was visiting Wembley market. For those of you who don't know, Wembley market would operate in the surroundings of the stadium every Sunday.

On this particular visit, he is walking around the market stalls and he sees a large rubbish bag with a batch of tickets sticking out. On closer inspection he found they were discarded FA Cup Final replay tickets. Lee grabs one and toddles off.

The replay ticket date was Thursday 21st May 1987, kick off at 7.30pm, a mere £15 too. We can but dream of going to a replay now, but Lee says he still gets Coventry fans, from the UK and overseas, who have offered significant sums of money to buy this ticket from him. A piece of bizarre memorabilia sought by Coventry fans keen to keep alive every single moment of the greatest event in the history of Coventry City FC. A great story.

The newspapers were also reporting on the unhappiness of Holsten, considering only a handful of players wearing shirts displaying the company name. *The Daily Telegraph* even reported that it could threaten Spurs' £1m deal with the German lager company.

An emergency board meeting was called by Scholar. In his book he writes, "Myself, David Pleat, Peter Day and Mike Rollo met Holsten. We feared the worst, but Holsten were very understanding and there was no question of them withdrawing their sponsorship".

It did appear there would be some internal casualties for this mess though. Peter Day departed, and Johnny Wallis was demoted to reserve team kit duty.

According to an account in *The Spurs Shirt* by Darren Burney and Neville Evans. Peter Day was in discussions with the FA around the global audience apparently seeing an alcohol sponsor on a football kit for the first time. Hummel had sent a few sets of kits over and some were meant for the Youth team. They sat in Day's office and when the FA gave Spurs the go ahead to use Holsten, kitman Johnny Wallis grabbed two sets of kits and only checked the numbers on the back.

Yes, it was a mistake, but you'd expect every detail in a Cup Final to be considered. Why Peter Day lost his job when Holsten didn't have an issue, I don't know. Maybe something else was at play.

* * * *

As Paul Allen mentioned, after a result like that you would be desperate to get away and spend some time with your family. Sadly, not for these guys.

There was one final game to play before the players could enjoy a well-deserved summer break and it was to see the team travel to Miami to face Colombian opposition.

Spurs were invited to play in the Miami Classic at the Orange Bowl. They would face Colombian side Millonarios FC. Maybe it was a final getaway for the team or perhaps another commercial opportunity that Scholar felt was pertinent.

Millonarios had been invited to play the Marlboro Cup of Champions back in March 1987 and ended up winning the invitational four-team tournament.

They topped that group beating the United States national team into a runner up spot. The Brazilian giants Sao Paolo were third and fourth were Columbian side Deportivo Cali who included the 1987 South American Player of the Year, midfielder Carlos Valderrama.

Millonarios were based in Bogota and had been Primera A champions for the last two seasons. Incidentally, they were also the club who gave crazy Colombian goalkeeper, Rene Higuita, his professional debut back in 1985.

The game in Miami was on Thursday 28th May 1987 and took place twelve days after the Coventry defeat. Miami weather at that time of year peaks at around 30 degrees so an 8pm kick off was most welcome by the Spurs players. Temperatures in Bogota at that time of year was around 18-20 degrees so it was not very different to the beautiful and warm sunny day the Cup Final was held on.

David Pleat did not travel with the group and Trevor Hartley took charge. He spoke to the Florida based newspaper, *Sun Sentinel*, and said, "We understand that is important to project the game well in America. We'll look at how things go in the first half, and if need be, we'll make changes. But we will stick with our attacking style, because we do want an exciting performance".

The Sun Sentinel highlighted that Spurs had been playing a revolutionary five-man midfield which had confused English defences this season, but Colombian sides would be used to this style as was quite common in South American football.

The newspaper also spoke to Clive Allen who said, "We've come back together (after thr FA Cup defeat) but we haven't forgotten about that game, but we've put in the back of our minds. I'm sure we'll bounce back".

It was an evening that remained swelteringly hot and Millonarios won the game 1-0. The goal scored by Gabriel "Barrabás" Gómez, a central midfielder who would go on to gain 49 caps for Colombia and represented his national team in all four of their games at the 1990 World Cup in Italy.

Finding information on this game was possibly the most difficult throughout this whole process. Some players I had spoken to did not recall the trip, a few did though.

David Howells has fond memories of that trip, he said, "It was an incredible trip. Ten days in Miami and pretty much the whole squad went. Glenn didn't come but pretty much everyone else was there".

Howells joked, "It was very social! We flew on Virgin first class and stayed in a wonderful hotel that I believe a Bond film was once set. An immense trip, unfortunately we had to play a game too. It was sweltering heat and we lost 1-0. It wasn't much of a game, but I've got lots of funny memories from that trip".

Howells seemed tight-lipped on what else happened, but I guess, what happens on tour, stays on tour!

CHANGING TIMES II

May had now disappeared as quickly as it came. What a month it had been, but now the season had concluded. Things were about to change at Spurs over the next few months as the club headed into the 1987-88 season.

The rumour mill was still rife when it came to Glenn Hoddle but there were also squeaks of interest for another player who appeared to be getting a number of mentions in newspaper columns. That was Gary Mabbutt.

Two days after the final defeat, Mabbutt withdrew from the England squad to face Brazil. It was reported by Patrick Barclay in *The Independent* that he was likely to have surgery to cure a circulation problem in his leg. It also mentioned discussions had not yet taken place around contract renewal. Mabbutt's performances though had been attracting the attention of other clubs especially in light of his contract expiration.

Gough's partnership that season had been immense with Gary Mabbutt and on the 12th of June, Michael Dennis wrote in *The Daily Telegraph* that along with Hoddle's proposed move to PSG which was now mighty close, but Mabbutt's contract was now up and various clubs had been in for him. He mentioned that Spurs were keen to keep him, and talks were on-going.

Speaking on the *Hometown Glory* podcast in November 2021, Mabbutt mentions the day after the Coventry defeat offers started to flood in as he was at the end of his five-year contract.

He recalls, "I got phone calls from Kenny Dalglish at Liverpool, Alex Ferguson at Manchester United, George Graham at Arsenal, Athletico Madrid in Spain and Lyon in France. At that stage Liverpool were dominating most seasons and I had long discussions with Kenny Dalglish. He said that he wanted me to play alongside Alan Hansen and bring in three players who were me, John Barnes and Peter Beardsley. I was looking at the whole perspective of my life and it was tempting. But I had been at Spurs for five years. I was loving my football, I loved living in London, I had a great rapport with the supporters, and we had just had a fantastic season we can really build on to maybe challenge for the title in the next few years".

Signing for Spurs was always on Mabbutt's mind.

For Glenn Hoddle, the time to move on had now come. For some time, he had been linked with an apparent £800,000 move to Paris St Germain being offered £600,000 over a 3-year deal, personal terms had been agreed. Things were to change when that deal was sabotaged by another French club.

Frenchman Arsene Wenger had begun his managerial career a few years before with Nancy FC who were based in the North-western part of France. Going into the 1986-87 season Monaco, a team based in its own principality in the South of France, wanted Wenger as their coach but Nancy were reluctant to release him.

Monaco recruited the services of the great Stefan Kovacs. Kovacs was a Romanian coach, but he was revered in Holland, more specifically in Amsterdam. Kovacs led Ajax to European Cup success in 1972 and 1973 so his pedigree was strong. Monaco had finished in ninth place during 1985-86 and this season Kovacs had guided them to a fifth placed finish.

But the interim Kovacs was out and the revolutionary thinker Arsene Wenger was in. Wenger has spoken in the past of visiting England during France's mid-season break in early 1987 to watch English football and more specifically Tottenham and Hoddle.

Hoddle and Wenger were made for each other. Wenger had just brought in Mark Hateley from AC Milan but Hoddle was the one he wanted. PSG were possibly not too happy, and *The Daily Telegraph* reported that PSG vice-president, Charles Taylor, said, "The negotiations I have had with Mr Scholar have been the most difficult in my life". Roll forward 30 years, maybe Spurs Chairman Daniel Levy went to the same negotiating school as Scholar!

In the same article, the fire had been fuelled on a Monaco move when Hoddle had been sighted in a Monaco café with Mark Hateley and bizarrely a few seats away was the UK wrestling legend, Big Daddy.

Glenn Hoddle would sign for Monaco for £750,000 on a three-year deal. Nowadays Hoddle talks about his role at Monaco being the first time he was given free rein in an advanced midfield role. I slightly disagree as Pleat had done this during the last two thirds of the 86-87 season with him playing free just behind Clive Allen. But, in Ligue 1 he was in his element.

A recent addition to Ligue 1 that 86-87 season was Racing Paris signing Uruguyan playmaker Enzo 'The Prince' Francescoli from River Plate after the World Cup. 'The Prince' had scored 14 goals that season from an advanced midfield role, the role that Wenger wanted Hoddle to play in.

Speaking with Pleat now, he either refutes or cannot recall some of the deals that Scholar claims in his book, but he did reveal that Scholar did speak to him about Enzo Francescoli.

Just after the Mexico World Cup 'The Prince' was available and Spurs had the chance to sign him. Pleat felt that, with Glenn Hoddle, he would not be able to accommodate Francescoli but Scholar felt this was a deal too big to miss out on. Pleat had agreed with Hoddle for one final season and the Uruguayan may have added more headaches than not.

Francescoli joined Racing Paris alongside West German winger Pierre Littbarski and French midfielder Luis Fernandez and finished in 13th place. Two places above Sporting Club Toulon.

Toulon SC were a small team based in the South of France but they had a precocious talent in the 19 year old David Ginola. He was starting to make a name for himself with his swashbuckling wing-play and he played a handful of games in the 85-86 season but this past season he had played nearly every game.

During the 1987-88 season he would start adding goals to his game and then earned a move to Racing Paris and play alongside Francescoli. Ginola would go on to represent France at national level, he was voted Player of the Year in 1993 whilst at PSG and a couple of years later he joined Newcastle United. A few successful years on Tyneside saw him then move to Spurs in 1997.

For Tottenham, Ginola was superlative. I feel that the best football of his career was during that period. Spurs went through many torrid times in the mid-1990's but he was pivotal to Spurs winning the 1999 League Cup. This was season when Manchester United won an unprecedented Treble with the League Cup being the only trophy they didn't claim that season having being ripped apart by Ginola in the League Cup quarter final.

Ginola was voted the PFA Player of the Year in 1999 despite Manchester United's pure dominance. What a player, and if anyone can remember the day he signed, you will probably recall how terribly attractive he was too…grrrr!

Hoddle would go on to win Ligue 1 in his first season at Monaco under Wenger. Title recognition at last for one of the greatest players in the world in the last decade, well deserved too.

In the same *The Daily Telegraph* article that highlighted the café moment of Hoddle, Hateley and Big Daddy was a piece on

Diego Maradona. Maradona still heady from his recent Serie A success with Napoli had told the media that he expected to retire in two seasons time.

He said he wanted to leave football and spend more time with his family. A few weeks before this article, England had played Brazil in a friendly at Wembley. This was a couple of days after the FA Cup Final and a game that ended in a 1-1 draw.

The game was televised on ITV and at half-time David Pleat was on hand to give expert advice. Pleat summarised the first half action and then host, Nick Owen, introduced "The World's greatest footballer, Diego Maradona".

The camera pans to Pleat's right and Maradona is sat there with a cheeky grin.

Maradona was joined by Ossie Ardiles, his friend and translator. Owen started off with congratulations for winning Serie A and then asked him about his goal in Mexico against England. Maradona cheekily looks at Owen and said, "You mean the second one?". Owen asked if he would admit it was handball and, via Ardiles, he replies, "No, never".

Whilst answering the question he can see a replay of his 'hand of god' goal, but he smirks as Owen leads into his next question. He is asked if he would like to play in England and he replied, "I would like to play in England, for the kind of football and the respect they have for the game".

Owen then leaps in with one final, quick question. "Would you fancy coming to England joining Spurs? We've got the manager here tonight!" pointing to Pleat and Ardiles smiles with Maradona's reply, "The only team he'd want to".

Ah, once again. We could only dream of Maradona.

* * * *

One player who departed Spurs that summer was Tony Galvin. Galvin joined Sheffield Wednesday having spent nine years at White Hart Lane playing over 200 times and scoring 20 goals. This season he had a few injuries and still managed to play on 27 occasions in league and cup matches scoring two goals and providing three assists.

Pleat always spoke highly of Galvin and very much liked and trusted his wide left-wing play. But with Hodge's arrival it was fair to say Galvin may not have featured so much in the coming season.

Galvin's tenure was not forgotten though, as he was awarded a testimonial match which was played in the Autumn of 1987. Thousands of fans turned out to see Spurs draw 2-2 with West Ham and to remember the superb service Galvin had given to Spurs whilst winning two FA Cups and a UEFA Cup. Even Steve Archibald returned for that game and scored Spurs' second goal.

But with Galvin gone it was still clear that Hoddle needed to be replaced and Pleat headed to the Midlands to hopefully try and fill the gap.

Pleat would go on to sign Dutchman Johnny Metgod who had scored a wonderful free-kick against Spurs two weeks before the FA Cup Final when Nottingham Forest beat Spurs 2-0 at the City Ground on a day when Vinny Samways made his Spurs debut.

Metgod would be joined at Spurs by another Forest player, central defender Chris Fairclough. Fairclough had played in both league wins over Spurs last season and scored at White Hart Lane. He would provide excellent cover for Gough and Mabbutt as a pacey, agile and calm centre back who had played over 100 games for Forest since joining them in 1981.

Hoddle could never be replaced, and Metgod was never going to be the man to replace him, but we needed to remember that Chris Waddle was still at the club and would be even more pivotal in playing a central role as Spurs' creator supreme.

Waddle had lit up the FA Cup Final early on but fizzled out. He was dejected like most players at the final whistle, but it cannot be forgotten what an amazing season he'd had.

Richard Gough on Waddle. "Waddle and Hoddle were two of the best players I have ever played with and in my best all-time eleven. Waddle was lightning over five yards and he was similar to Brian Laudrup who was the same when he got possession of the ball".

* * * *

When the players returned from their summer break and into pre-season training, Pleat's men were led into their first friendly of the summer. Spurs travelled to Exeter City and won the game 1-0 thanks to a Metgod strike. A good start for Spurs' new midfield man.

Around that time Spurs also captured a talented young winger called Mark Robson from Exeter. Robson would not go on and have a successful Spurs career as he was loaned out over the next few seasons before enjoying spells at West Ham and Charlton Athletic.

Two days after the Exeter win, Spurs drew 4-4 in a friendly with Bournemouth. Clive Allen grabbed a brace with Waddle and Hodge getting the others. Four goals conceded though, yikes.

Spurs then headed to Scandinavia for a seven-day tour consisting of five matches. They lost two and won three. Clive Allen and Nico Claesen grabbed a few goals over those games and looked in good form, even Shaun Close scored four in one game.

Their final friendly that summer was a week before the season opener. The first league game of the season would see Spurs visit Highfield Road to face Coventry City, the team who they played in their last competitive game. But this friendly was against Arsenal.

This was Chris Hughton's testimonial match and just under 18,000 fans were in attendance.

There was even a chance Maradona would be back at Spurs and playing in this game. Hughton told *The Independent*, "If Maradona comes over for the Football League Centenary match, we will ask him to play in my game. A lot will depend on what Ossie Ardiles can do".

Galvin returned to play alongside his Republic of Ireland teammate and Spurs dominated George Grahams men's winning 3-1. Hughton had played over 250 games for Spurs in his ten years at the club, but he was sadly injured so he was unable to play, but on the night, Chris Waddle ran riot and was outstanding all evening. A touch of revenge for last season's semi-final disappointment.

Sadly, Maradona did not get to play in Hughton's testimonial but a few days before Gough, Ardiles, Waddle and Clive Allen joined the likes of Bryan Robson, Paul McGrath, Peter Beardsley and Liam Brady in representing the Football League in a game against a Rest of the World team. The Football League were celebrating 100 years of existence.

The Rest of the World team saw Barcelona's Gary Lineker line up alongside Diego Maradona and Michel Platini. The Football League won the game 3-0 with a brace from Bryan Robson and the other from Manchester United's Norman Whiteside who came on to replace Clive Allen.

* * * *

Spurs trip up to Highfield Road for the season opener ended in defeat. Greg Downs and record Coventry signing, David

Speedie, put Coventry 2-0 up at half time and looked in control. Mabbutt had been deployed in midfield pulled one back with 18 minutes to go but it was a disappointing start for Pleats men.

Spurs then won three of their next four games and things started to look more positive. But as September moved into October there were some troubling circumstances that would see the team and the club go through some very tough times.

Towards the end of September there were rumours circulating in the media that Gough was unhappy and was looking for a route back to Scotland. Souness had been an admirer since the 1986 World Cup and Rangers had spoken to Spurs.

Pleat said, "I feel Richard let me down a little bit because he was due to have an operation, but he went back to South Africa instead. And then, of course, Richard decides to move, and he's been tapped up by Glasgow Rangers, 100% tapped up by Graham Souness. He told us he needed to go back to Scotland and If not, I'll get a divorce. We initially said to David Murray, the Rangers chairman, we're not going to sell Gough at any price!"

Pleat continued, "Murray said there must be a price somewhere along the line. I said to him, rather silly of me, that the chairman Scholar, said it would take at least one and a half million to get him. Within days, they came back and offered £1.5m, Gough said he knew they had made the offer too. We doubled our money in a year. He wanted to go back, said it was he was going to get a divorce. Eventually he did get a divorce anyway. But Richard was a fine man. Great athlete. Super player".

John Motson also recalls the moment Gough left Spurs.

Motson said, "I was called in a panic by Mike Rollo, Spurs' commercial guy, and he asked me to get down to the training ground straight away and record a message for the Spursline clubcall telephone service to announce to supporters that Gough was leaving to move to Rangers. I remember there was such a huge feeling of disappointment in the club that he was leaving as he was such a great player".

Gough's departure hit fans and players alike. Mabbutt had a wonderful and long career at Spurs but still cites his partnership with Gough as truly memorable, he told me, "Goughy was my best partnership that I had at the back during my time at Spurs, we just hit it off as soon as he arrived and things just got better, it was such a shame that the team did not achieve what we deserved that season".

Mabbutt continued, "In all honesty I think that if he had stayed then we might have had a chance of challenging for the title in the following years, I am sure that deep down he regrets going back to Scotland so soon".

Gough moved to Spurs the summer before for £750,000 from Dundee United and he does have some regret at that move despite him winning a significant number of titles at Rangers. He said, "Rangers spoke to Scholar, and they asked him to give a figure. Spurs said let's double our money and Rangers said, ok then! Irving said I should have asked for £3m if that's how they felt. But Irving knew I was having a few problems domestically as well. I loved Scholar, he was great. He was a progressive Chairman and way ahead of the game".

Gough had a brilliant year at Spurs. So much of his game made him unique and was different to most defenders we have seen at Spurs over the years. Cyrille Regis did dominate him this season, but so too did Keith Houchen and Houchen would become a bit of a nemesis for Gough. As years would pass by, Houchen would move to Hibernian where he had an excellent scoring record against Gough and Rangers.

Houchen referred to Gough as a 'gentleman' but knew he had done well against him over the years. I asked Richard if he recalls those duels with Houchen. Gough laughed, "You know, people often say to me who is the best striker you have played against, and I say Marco Van Basten, the best striker ever. But Keith Houchen has scored more goals against me than any other striker I have played against. So, if you speak to him again tell him he was my jinx player! I have had Van Basten and Gullitt in my pocket, but I couldn't put him in my pocket".

That evening after speaking with Richard I sent Keith Houchen a text that read, "Richard Gough told me today that you gave him more problems than Marco Van Basten! So, I asked him straight….is Keith Houchen better than Marco Van Basten and he agreed!"

Houchen came back swiftly and said, "Well don't sound so surprised! We certainly had some great matches against each other. We seemed to follow each other around for a while. The respect is reciprocated".

A great moment between two great professional footballers.

I asked Richard for his final thoughts on such a wonderful season and he felt it was up there with some of the best things he has done in football. Gough concluded, "I look back on that season as my finest season of football ever played and I'm talking, we never won anything, but it was the best football that I ever played in as a centre back and I played with Dundee United, winning 18 trophies at Rangers but for one season of pure football ability it was that. I had so many unbelievable teammates in Hoddle, Waddle, Ardiles. You know Clive Allen, scoring 49 goals that season, so to go through the season and not win a trophy well, that was the most disappointing thing as a captain of Tottenham. That was the that was the biggest disappointment in it, but for pure football. I've never played a season of football like that in my life, yeah, it was the best".

Gough continued, "I'm talking one touch football, two touch football. You know the boys would do this so well. But it was just unbelievable football and the football that was played in front of me that year was pretty sensational. It was unbelievable for the crowd as well. Because the Tottenham crowd, loves good football and good football players too".

With Gough leaving for Scotland, another main player was about to leave the fold. This time it wasn't another transfer saga, but time had been called upon the career of Ray Clemence.

Clem was getting ever closer to 40 and in an away game at Carrow Road in October 1987 he injured his achilles tendon. It was an injury that would ultimately lead to retirement in early 1988.

Clem had been brilliant during his Spurs career. He had brought a winning mentality to the group and was part of the 1982 FA Cup and 1984 UEFA Cup winning teams. He had made well over 1,000 career appearances and notched up 61 England Cups to go alongside the numerous titles won during his time at Liverpool.

His place would be taken by Tony Parks, and it would be another few years before Ray was awarded a testimonial match at Spurs. In August 1990 Spurs would play West Ham in his testimonial game. Spurs would go on to win that game 4-1 with goals from Italia'90 heroes Gary Lineker and Paul Gascoigne.

Clem had returned to Spurs in a coaching role and a few years later he would be part of the England coaching group that successfully navigated England to the 1998 World Cup Finals in France. Clem is a true legend of English football, and I was glad to have had the pleasure of meeting him back in 1987 plus spending time with his son Stephen while researching this book. At time of publishing, he is the only remember of the 1986-87 playing squad no longer with us. RIP Clem, never forgotten and always revered.

The autumn of 1987 had seen the departures of Gough and Clemence to add to Hoddle's exit. These were key and significant players which left a few big holes in quality and experience.

But this period of football I wanted to cover ultimately concluded in the final week of October 1987.

Spurs were flying high in the league and a week after the Norwich defeat, where Clem got injured, Spurs hosted Arsenal at White Hart Lane. A second defeat in a row as Arsenal won 2-1 again! Spurs then travelled to Nottingham Forest and lost yet again, this time 3-0.

Pleat was under pressure but behind the scenes, Pleat was under considerable pressure.

It would be revealed that Pleat was subjected to media scrutiny of allegations concerning his personal life that had now involved the police. The press and media went to town on him, and the pressure built so much so that Pleat resigned from his role as manager of Tottenham Hotspur FC.

The Spurs board released a statement not long after the Forest defeat announcing his resignation and the papers were already speculating that Terry Venables would replace him.

Venables had signed a one-year contract extension with Barcelona that summer, but things were not going too well for Venables in Barcelona.

I was intent not to push Pleat too hard on what I knew to be a very tough time in his life. He did reveal the media had blown it so far out of proportion that it created too much pressure and anxiety for him to deal with.

He felt the board pushed him into resigning and he was asked to sign a letter resigning from his role at Spurs. In hindsight, Pleat feels he should now have had a solicitor present when he attended that meeting with Scholar and the board members.

I was keen to point out that I felt if that would not have happened then Spurs may have had some success in the year or two after 1986-87. So much so, he could well have been the next England Manager after Bobby Robson left that role in 1990.

Graham Taylor ended up taking on that job with a pretty disastrous set of results during his tenure. But Pleat's stock was just as high as one of the most progressive managers in English football at that time.

Pleat did reveal he had been considered in the future by the FA too. During his time at Sheffield Wednesday in the early 1990s, Graham Kelly of the FA wrote to his chairman seeking permission to speak to Pleat to discuss the role of Director of Football. Wednesday said no and Pleat mentioned he wouldn't have taken it anyway as he preferred to be out on the training ground more than upstairs. The role went to Howard Wilkinson who Pleat felt was a good fit.

But he admitted he was never approached about the England job despite others telling him he'd have done a good job.

Pleat recalls co-commentating with Barry Davies in 1998, "I remember Barry Davies saying to me one day, we were in Marseille during the 1998 World Cup, I think it was when Bergkamp got that wonderful goal against Argentina. And I remember Barry Davies saying to me, you know, David, we all reflect on things in our life. For example, he wanted the 1987 Cup Final that year, he didn't get it as Motson got it that year, it was a big rivalry. But I remember him saying to me. We all reflect on things in life, but you should have been England manager. I think I could have. I think I would have done it more in the Southgate statesman-like, diplomatic way then other managers have done it. But I don't know. Hindsight eh".

Pleat had a memorable 18 months at White Hart Lane but agreed the second season was nowhere near the same as his first.

On signing Metgod, Pleat said, "That team was so wonderful and if we'd had success players would have been happy to stay, except of course Glenn was leaving. I signed Johnny Metgod to replace him and retrospectively that was a mistake as there could be no number ten like Glenn Hoddle. Even though Metgod was a very skilful player it just didn't work for him, he didn't settle, and the crowd would draw comparisons. That taught me another lesson, if you have a star player like Hoddle you might have to adjust the system or the way you play rather than replicate the same system and get one player to come in for the player that you have just lost. Losing Glenn was a big thing".

Pleat concluded with, "I think Pochettino had a very good side in 2017. The best side was Bill Nicholson's 1961 team. They were wonderful and that made a massive impression on me, my life and everything. They were all wonderful and I thought at some point I want to manage Tottenham Hotspur. We had a great team in 1987 but it was the 1961 for me, the second-best team possibly was Pochettino's. Yeah, then that 1987 season and my team, my team I think was the third best".

Terry Venables would be the man to replace Pleat. As mentioned earlier in this book, Scholar coveted him back in the 1986 summer tournament in Barcelona where Pleat felt Scholar was fawning over him while they ate dinner one night.

Venables would go on to create wonderful and woeful memories during his time at Spurs. Some of the greatest games I have ever experienced were under Venables and the story of 1990-91 season is as powerful as it gets for Spurs fans. But those stories are maybe for another time.

We must highlight that only a few players stayed on for the success seen by Venables in 1991. Two of those players were Gary Mabbutt and Paul Allen.

Gary Mabbutt would go on to be chosen as the Supporters Player of the Year in 1987. What a player and what a guy he is. Mr Tottenham and our captain of all captains. He was a true leader and even when I watch the moment when he lifts the FA Cup in 1991, I still get goosebumps at seeing his face banish the disappointment of Wembley 1987.

Paul Allen though. Even though Hoddle was my hero, Paul was my choice for the Junior Spurs Player of the Year. He was immense and the moment he was moved into the middle of the midfield alongside Ardiles and Hoddle that autumn, was a day of reckoning in his Spurs career and that season.

That season Glenn Hoddle topped the Spurs assist charts with nineteen in league and cup games. Most would expect Chris Waddle would not be far behind him, but it was Paul Allen just behind Hoddle. Allen only scored four goals that season, but he notched up an amazing eighteen assists, one more than Chris Waddle.

The player who benefitted most was his cousin Clive. Of Clive's 49 goals that season, Paul assisted ten of them, two more than Waddle on eight assists and Hoddle on seven.

When I revealed that statistic to both Paul and Clive, they were both amazed but on reflection, Clive was not surprised. Clive said, "You know, that doesn't surprise me actually. Paul was very underrated and when you have Glenn, Chrissy Waddle and Ossie Ardiles plus Steve Hodge arriving too, but he was fantastic, his level of consistency was incredible".

In the September edition of *Spurs News*, there was an article about the future of Danny Thomas. Danny had recovered from knee surgery and was starting the slow road to rehabilitation. He had spent 13 weeks at an RAF rehab centre at Headley Court and he was hoping to start riding a bike soon.

Soon after, he was told that no matter how much rehabilitation and recovery he went through he would not be able to play professional football again. Something feared by club physio John Sheridan back in March, but until you start rehab you never truly know.

Danny was granted a benefit match which would take place in March 1988, a year on from when he sustained his injury in the home game against Queens Park Rangers. Speaking with Danny, I was under the impression that the club arranged this for him. He told me that most of the arrangements had to be done by himself, especially when it came to seeking an opposition.

Danny said, "Growing up as a kid, like most kids, I wanted to be a professional footballer and coming from a small town in Nottinghamshire I never expected this to happen. So when it does and then it's over all too quickly it was a very emotional time. But I have always tried to be positive, call it the end of one career and the beginning of another rather than putting it in terms of tragedy. I had a wonderful time, I met and played with some very talented players. I found the higher the standard you played; the less arrogant players were. Ossie Ardiles didn't have to tell everyone he was a great footballer, everybody knew that. That team were great players, and they were great people too."

He continued, "I have to say a big, big thank you to Sir Alex Ferguson. When arranging this Game, I spoke to a few clubs. I had spoken to George Graham, and like other managers, he said they were not too sure as it was mid-season and all the games they had to play, couldn't fit it in etcetera, etcetera".

"I approached Sir Alex Ferguson, and his response was instant. A whole different response and instantly recognising my situation, wanting to help out and then doing so. He brought his full team with him. Kudos to Sir Alex in doing that for me, he was fantastic. I even had the likes of John Barnes and Kenny Dalglish coming down to play. I spoke to John, and he said he'd get Kenny to come down with him and play".

At that point, Danny showed me the pennant on his wall of that game against Manchester United and said, "I had a great night, a great send off from my teammates and it was time to move on. But yes, an emotional night".

My time with Danny had ended and his final words to me were, "I have had a great time and you brought back some more great memories for me today. Even though it's such a long time ago but thank you very much". Many other players I spoke too said near enough the same.

For David Pleat this was a season of highs and lows. From the superb Cup wins over West Ham, Watford, Wimbledon and even Arsenal, to the stunning League performances against Liverpool, Manchester United, Aston Villa, West Ham (again) and eventual Champions Everton there was so many good things to remember.

David's final thoughts were, "Was it really 37 years ago. Sadly, our efforts failed at the final hurdle. We climbed to third position in the league, and denied European football, lost to last minute mistakes in the League Cup semi-final – and most painful of all was losing to an extra time own goal in the FA Cup Final".

Yes, nearly four decades had past but some things are never forgotten.

This whole process was to remind people of an entertaining season in the history of Tottenham Hotspur Football Club. Despite no silverware won, there were so many things that have been so memorable for me and other Spurs fans around the world. This period had some of the greatest players in the club's history playing and some of the football was simply exhilarating.

In my lifetime I have been lucky enough to see some truly world class players at Spurs. Harry Kane is the current king, a sublime footballer and supreme finisher. Luka Modric and Gareth Bale were brilliant at Spurs and both went on to embed their world-class status at Real Madrid.

David Ginola, Jurgen Klinsmann, Gary Lineker and Teddy Sheringham gave Spurs fans such joy during a decade when not much was worth cheering about.

Paul Gascoinge was a genius. His time at Spurs, especially around the end of the 1989-90 season, into Italia'90 and followed by the 1990-91 season, was easily the best football he produced in his whole a career and we were lucky to have him at Spurs to witness his audacious brilliance.

But the 1987 team contained, for me, the best Spurs player I have ever seen. Ray Clemence, Chris Waddle and Ossie Ardiles were all world class players. It cannot be understated enough the amazing feat of Clive Allen's 49 goals, but Glenn Hoddle was the one. The one I wanted to play like and the one that made me want to keep watching Tottenham Hotspur.

Seeing him in that role in 1987 made me, and many others wonder, what could have been for both Spurs and England if he was allowed to play in that floating role behind the strikers like Michel Platini enjoyed so much.

There will always be many 'what ifs'.

What if Spurs were still in European football with a team like that? Playing that style of football would have been a delight to see and successful, I am sure.

What if Terry Butcher had signed instead of Gough? Butcher probably would not have departed after one season and he and Mabbutt could've been just as strong together. Butcher had a winner's mentality too which some say Spurs lacked.

What if Graham Roberts and Paul Miller had stayed? Well, Steve Hodge might not have arrived, but they could've applied that steel and resilience that was lacking in the semi-final defeat to Arsenal.

What if Pleat, Hoddle, Hodge, Waddle, and Gough had stayed at Spurs? Well, we will never know, but we do know if they had stayed then Venables may not have arrived, thus Paul Gascoigne probably would have never landed at White Hart Lane either.

Following on from that, would Nayim still have scored from the halfway line for Real Zaragoza in 1995? It turned into a great story for Spurs physio John Sheridan as Nayim sent him the shirt he wore that night whilst lobbing David Seaman from such a distance!

That is what football is all about. The moments that did happen along with the moments that could have happened.

Around 1.8 million people attended the sixty-eight league, cup and friendly matches that involved Spurs over that season and each one of them will have a conscious or less-conscious memory tucked away of those experiences that will echo in some way, shape or form.

I hold an affinity and connection with those players of 1987 and until recently I had never met any of them at all. Well apart from a brief encounter with Clem in the spring of that year.

The football they played, and the feelings it resonated, are sometimes indescribable as a football fan. It was a snapshot in time that's allows me to connect with music, films and social changes that reminds me so well of that season and time in my life. That season was fantastic but so disappointing.

The game is about glory, this is Spurs' ethos.

Granted, no silverware was won that season, but some of the football was glorious to watch.

So yes, the game is still about glory. COYS.

ABOUT THE AUTHOR

Steve is a London born and Lincoln based business owner who specialises in developing *leadership learning* and *high-performance cultures* across various industries and sectors within the UK and overseas.

Steve's fascination in the psychological side of performance has been gained from a near 30-year career in Finance, Human Resources and Learning & Development. This has seen Steve become a TED Talker, facilitator, executive coach and Insights psychometric practitioner with a drive and passion for developing people, teams and organisations.

SOURCE NOTES

Official Tottenham Hotspur FC Matchday Programmes
Thames News
Spurs News (THFC periodical Newspaper)
ITV News
BBC TV
Thames TV
Daily Telegraph
The Times
Sunday Times
The Guardian
The Observer
British Library
Sunday Times
BBC Sport
The Guardian
Daily Mail
The Sun
Birmingham Evening Mail
BBC Radio
YouTube
France Football Magazine
BBC Sportsnight

www.englandfootballonline.com
Smash Hits Magazine
Scottish TV – 'The Rangers Revival (documentary of 86-87 season)'
'FIFA Uncovered' - Netflix
'Birth of Rave' - www.guardian.com
'Playmaker; Glenn Hoddle' - Glenn Hoddle & Jacob Steinberg
'Up Front' - Clive Allen & James Olley
'Behind Closed Doors' - Irving Scholar & Mihir Bose
'Chris Waddle – The Authorised Biography' - Mel Stein
'Diego Maradona' - Asif Kapadia
'HERO – Official FIFA Film of Mexico World Cup 1986' - FIFA
'Team Spirit; the elusive experience' – John Syer
'The Art of Captaincy' – Mike Brearley
PODCAST – Coral All to Play For; Hoddle & Diamond Lights – Cole & Sidwell
PODCAST – What Happened to You - Godfrey
PODCAST – Hometown Glory - Parrish
PODCAST – The Spurs Show Live – Myers & Leigh